booksonline

Read this book online today:

With SAP PRESS BooksOnline we offer you online access to knowledge from the leading SAP experts. Whether you use it as a beneficial supplement or as an alternative to the printed book, with SAP PRESS BooksOnline you can:

• Access your book anywhere, at any time. All you need is an Internet connection.
• Perform full text searches on your book and on the entire SAP PRESS library.
• Build your own personalized SAP library.

The SAP PRESS customer advantage:

Register this book today at *www.sap-press.com* and obtain exclusive free trial access to its online version. If you like it (and we think you will), you can choose to purchase permanent, unrestricted access to the online edition at a very special price!

Here's how to get started:

1. Visit *www.sap-press.com*.
2. Click on the link for SAP PRESS BooksOnline and login (or create an account).
3. Enter your free trial license key, shown below in the corner of the page.
4. Try out your online book with full, unrestricted access for a limited time!

Your personal free trial **license key**
for this online book is: tfqz-5gwh-x3m2-ydpj

Welcome to the Galileo Press *Discover SAP* series. This series was developed as part of our official SAP PRESS imprint to help you discover what SAP is all about and how you can use the wide array of applications and tools to make your organization much more efficient and cost effective.

Each book in the series is written in a friendly, easy-to-follow style that guides you through the intricacies of the software and its core components. With this series, you'll find a detailed overview of the core components of SAP, what they are, how they can benefit your company, and the technology requirements and costs of implementation. Once you have a foundational knowledge of SAP, you can explore the other books in the series covering CRM, Financials, HCM, BusinessObjects, and more. In these books you'll delve into the fundamental business concepts and principles behind the tool, discover why it's important for your business, and evaluate the technology and implementation costs for each.

Whether you are a decision maker who needs to determine if SAP is the right enterprise solution for your company, you are just starting to work in a firm that uses SAP, or you're already familiar with SAP but need to learn about a specific component, you are sure to find what you need in the *Discover SAP* series. Then when you're ready to implement SAP, you'll find what you need in the SAP PRESS series at *www.sap-press.com*.

Thanks to the expertise of JC Raveneau and Chris Dinkel, along with Thierry Audas, reading this book will put you in the best possible position to truly understand SAP BusinessObjects offerings and potential. Throughout the course of writing the manuscript, the authors continually impressed me with their knowledge of this subject and dedication to this work. You are now the recipient of this knowledge and dedication, and I'm confident that you'll benefit greatly from both.

Thank you for your interest in the series. We look forward to hearing how the series helps you get started with SAP. We encourage you to visit our website at *www.sap-press.com* and share your feedback.

Thank you for purchasing a book from SAP PRESS!

Meg Dunkerley
Editor, SAP PRESS
Galileo Press America

 **PRESS**

SAP PRESS is a joint initiative of SAP and Galileo Press. The know-how offered by SAP specialists combined with the expertise of the Galileo Press publishing house offers the reader expert books in the field. SAP PRESS features first-hand information and expert advice, and provides useful skills for professional decision-making.

SAP PRESS offers a variety of books on technical and business related topics for the SAP user. For further information, please visit our website: *www.sap-press.com.*

Nancy Muir and Ian Kimbell
Discover SAP
2010, 440 pp.
978-1-59229-320-9

Manish Patel
Discover SAP ERP Financials
2008, 544 pp.
978-1-59229-184-7

Martin Murray
Discover Logistics with SAP ERP
2009, 385 pp.
978-1-59229-230-1

Greg Newman
Discover SAP ERP HCM
2009, 438 pp.
978-1-59229-222-6

Shaun Snapp
Discover SAP SCM
2010, 384 pp.
978-1-59229-305-6

Chris Dinkel, JC Raveneau, and Thierry Audas

Discover SAP® BusinessObjects™

Galileo Press

Bonn • Boston

Galileo Press is named after the Italian physicist, mathematician and philosopher Galileo Galilei (1564–1642). He is known as one of the founders of modern science and an advocate of our contemporary, heliocentric worldview. His words *Eppur si muove* (And yet it moves) have become legendary. The Galileo Press logo depicts Jupiter orbited by the four Galilean moons, which were discovered by Galileo in 1610.

Editor Meg Dunkerley
Copyeditor Julie McNamee
Cover Design Graham Geary
Photo Credit iStockphoto.com / M-X-K
Layout Design Vera Brauner
Production Editor Kelly O'Callaghan
Assistant Production Editor Graham Geary
Typesetting Publishers' Design and Production Services, Inc.
Printed and bound in Canada

ISBN 978-1-59229-315-5

© 2011 by Galileo Press Inc., Boston (MA)
1st Edition 2011

Library of Congress Cataloging-in-Publication Data
Dinkel, Chris.
  Discover SAP businessobjects / Chris Dinkel, JC Raveneau, Thierry Audas. — 1st ed.
    p. cm.
  Includes index.
  ISBN-13: 978-1-59229-315-5
  ISBN-10: 1-59229-315-8
  1. BusinessObjects. 2. Business intelligence—Data processing. 3.
Management information systems. I. Raveneau, J.C. II. Audas, Thierry. III.
Title.
  HD38.7.A93 2011
  658.4'038028553—dc22
2010042026

Contents at a Glance

Contents

PART I   SAP and Business Objects

7 SAP BusinessObjects Enterprise Performance Management Solutions 183

8 SAP BusinessObjects Governance, Risk, and Compliance Solutions 227

9   Solutions for Small Businesses and Midsize Companies 263

PART III   SAP BusinessObjects Solutions for Non-SAP Customers

PART IV   The Future of SAP BusinessObjects Solutions

Acknowledgments

We would like to thank SAP PRESS for giving us the opportunity to write this book, supporting us, and sharing best practices throughout the process. We'd also like to thank all the colleagues who kindly spared some of their time answering questions, especially Thierry Audas for his major contribution. And last but not least, a huge Thank You to our families for gracefully coping with the late nights and vacation days spent writing this book. We love you all!

Preface

Global market surveys and industry analysts continue to report that business intelligence (BI) has been the top priority for the majority of CIOs for several years.

They also show how organizations across all industries struggle with the same key challenge: getting timely access to quality information needed to make informed decisions. The consequences are underperforming organizations run by a poorly informed workforce whose decisions are based largely on gut instincts instead of facts.

To help its customers face this challenge with information access and low business performance, SAP dramatically shook up the BI market in 2008 by acquiring Business Objects and its portfolio of best-of-breed BI technologies.

Two years after SAP acquired Business Objects, many SAP customers still want to better understand why SAP moved to Business Objects when SAP already had its own BI strategy before the acquisition. Part of the answer lies in the fact that SAP ultimately decided to standardize a number of its BI offerings on Business Objects technology, slowly phasing out corresponding legacy SAP BI technology.

P has publicly announced this strategy, so users naturally want
ore clarity on the rationale and reasoning behind this strategy and
quisition. After they have a better understanding of the business
lue of the new SAP BusinessObjects solutions and know that SAP
usinessObjects is now the new face of BI for SAP, their next logical
questions are how to move forward and what are the best strategies
for transitioning to the new solutions for enhanced premium BI capabilities.

These customers, who don't run their business processes on enterprise resource planning or other enterprise applications from SAP,
whether they have some BusinessObjects technology in-house already
or not, also want to better understand what this acquisition means to
them and to their past or future investments in BI technology. They
especially want to know how the new SAP BusinessObjects portfolio
of solutions will provide value to their business.

Discover SAP BusinessObjects addresses all of these needs. This book
first lays down the foundation for the acquisition and why SAP chose
Business Objects. Then it focuses on describing and positioning all of
the key solutions in the new SAP BusinessObjects portfolio, and how
they fit together and into existing typical SAP customer landscapes,
while adding value to all customer profiles.

Who Is This Book For

Let's look at the value readers will get depending on their profile:

> Business decision makers that consider business intelligence or
  performance management will become more familiar with the SAP
  BusinessObjects portfolio, the terminology, and the overall strategy.
> Consultants will find a complete overview of the portfolio and how
  it fits with existing SAP landscapes as well as non-SAP systems.
  You will also gain insight into the newer SAP BusinessObjects 4.0
  release.

> Managers on either the IT side or the business side will understand the technology their teams work with and get the overall picture to best leverage the portfolio.

> Those who know Business Objects but don't know SAP systems will learn about the key integration points between the systems and how the SAP BusinessObjects portfolio now brings all solutions under one umbrella.

> Those who know SAP systems but not the SAP BusinessObjects portfolio will discover the incredible value and competitive advantage they can get from their existing data.

Ultimately, this book helps SAP customers map out strategies for the transition to the new SAP BusinessObjects solutions and helps all customers plan for strategic BI deployments across the enterprise.

Navigational Tools for This Book

Throughout the book, we've provided several elements that will help you access useful information:

> Tips call out useful information about related ideas and provide practical suggestions for how to use a particular function.

> Notes provide other resources to explore, or special tools or services from SAP that will help you with the topic under discussion.

> Examples provide real-world scenarios and illustrations of how the tools are used.

> Warnings draw your attention to areas of concern or pieces of information that you should be aware of while evaluating specific functionality.

> Marginal text provides a useful way to scan the book to locate topics of interest for you. Each margin note appears to the side of a paragraph or section with related information.

This is a marginal note

Organization of This Book

The book is organized around four major sections that you may read in sequence or independently depending on your needs:

> **Part I: Why SAP and Business Objects**
> Part I covers the basics of business intelligence by exploring the Business Objects company history. It underlines the value of BI for helping organizations improve their performance and covers the overall SAP BusinessObjects product strategy.

> **Part II: SAP BusinessObjects Portfolio of Solutions**
> In Part II, we explore the SAP BusinessObjects portfolio of solutions with detailed descriptions of the respective capabilities and functions across all four pillars (BI, EIM, EPM, and GRC). You get a good understanding of the value propositions of the various solutions independently from each other and all together.

> **Part III: SAP BusinessObjects Solutions for Non-SAP Customers**
> All SAP BusinessObjects solutions remain available to non-SAP customers (i.e., those customers who run business processes on non-SAP solutions and technologies), so Part III reassures those customers with previous investment in SAP BusinessObjects that their investment is safe and invites other non-SAP customers to look into SAP BusinessObjects solutions.

> **Part IV: The Future of SAP BusinessObjects Solutions**
> This fourth and last part goes through all public information available in terms of product directions and planned innovations for the SAP BusinessObjects portfolio of solutions.

 Note

In addition, we will provide a downloadable chapter on SAP Business Suite Customers, where you can learn about SAP BusinessObjects BI Solutions Embedded into Business Processes and SAP BusinessObjects Business Content. This chapter will also include case studies and examples.

PART I
SAP and Business Objects

Why Business Intelligence Matters

According to industry analyst groups, business intelligence (BI) is the most highly recommended strategic investment a company can make. The industry analyst firm Gartner cites BI as the top strategic technology that has the potential to positively affect the business performance of your organization and dramatically improve your ability to accomplish your mission by helping you make smarter decisions at every level of the business [Gartner09].

Industry research indicates that BI is a sound strategic investment

Additionally, management consultant firm McKinsey & Company suggests that mining your data for insights may generate savings and revenues that exceed any cost-cutting measures [McKinsey08].

And industry analyst firm Forrester Research finds that the value of BI becomes even more apparent in tough economic climates when it is used as a corporate asset to continue to survive, compete, and thrive [Forrester09].

Did You Know?

Business intelligence (BI) has the potential to positively affect the business performance of your organization. High-performing companies use BI as a key strategy element five times more than low performers [Davenport07].

Through the acquisition of Business Objects and its portfolio of best-of-breed BI product and technologies in 2007, and in combination with already-existing enterprise information management (EIM), corporate performance management (CPM), and governance, risk, and compliance (GRC) technologies, SAP is now offering a complete portfolio of best-of-breed solutions aimed at helping its customers facing the challenge of poor information access for business users and its consequence on business performance.

SAP Business-Objects portfolio of solutions

This book gives you a solid foundation in this new SAP Business-Objects portfolio of solutions and a better understanding of the business value it offers. In this first chapter, you'll get an overview of the basics of BI and its value to organizations as a backdrop for the SAP acquisition of Business Objects.

The Business Intelligence Fact Gap

All corporate organizations worldwide, from all sizes and across all industries, continue to face demands to cut costs, improve business performance, streamline processes, and increase productivity. Most, if not all, of these organizations also face a mission-critical issue that challenges these efforts: the inability of the majority of business users to access and share timely, relevant, and trustworthy information that can lead to confident, strategic, fact-based informed decisions.

Did You Know?

> Surveys indicate that business users have limited confidence in the ability of their companies to perform at optimal levels.

Actually, business researchers keep highlighting two parallel trends — subpar access to an exponentially growing volume of information and greater pressure to make sound decisions — which have conspired to undermine the confidence that business users have in the ability of their companies to perform at optimal levels.

Growing volume of information and more decision-making pressure

Gartner refers to this disconnect between information and decisions as the BI fact gap (Figure 1.1).

BI fact gap

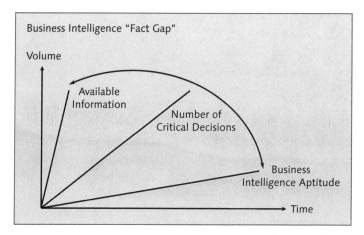

Figure 1.1   The Business Intelligence Fact Gap (Source: Gartner Research)

Typically, the majority of business users in any organization know of bad business decisions made within their organization because of insufficient information; nearly all recognize that inefficient information access significantly impacts productivity (Figure 1.2). The culprits behind this regrettable reality are the glut of incompatible applications and databases found within most global organizations.

25

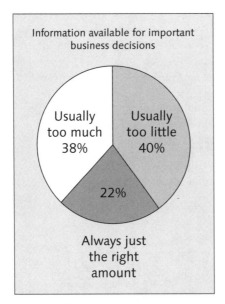

Figure 1.2 Information Available for Important Business Decisions
(Source: BusinessWeek Research Services)

Despite investments in data management systems, organizations worldwide continue to grapple with making these systems work together. As a result, a majority of business users make well over half of their decisions based not on empirical information but on simple gut feelings (Figures 1.3 and 1.4).

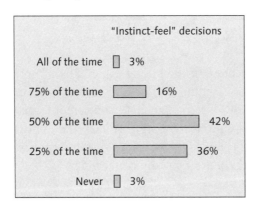

Figure 1.3 "Instinct-feel" Decisions (Source: BusinessWeek Research Services)

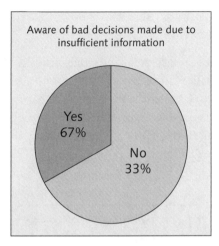

Figure 1.4 Aware of Bad Decisions Made Due to Insufficient Information
(Source: BusinessWeek Research Services)

A Business Intelligence Definition

There are different ways to define BI, and specific detailed definitions may evolve as they follow trends in the market and improvements in information technologies. A stable, high-level perspective views BI as a set of products, systems, and practices aimed at allowing all organizations, from all sizes and across all industries, to improve their business performance by enabling insightful decisions about significant changes and opportunities in their business and markets.

Insightful decisions

 BI Definition

> BI provides business users with the insight they need to make informed decisions.

BI products, systems, and practices provide corporate business users with the insight — derived from quantitative information — they need to make informed decisions. It's all about collecting, storing, managing, accessing, visualizing, analyzing, reporting, and sharing valuable business information in an attempt to understand it and

Business users

communicate its meaning to help business users decide on a strategic course and ultimately optimize the performance of the organization.

Traditional BI products and technology access quantitative historical data usually found in corporate data warehouses or data marts and present it in reports, Microsoft Excel spreadsheets, and dashboards. Analytical staff and decision makers use this information to track and understand how the business has performed and to analyze what will improve the performance going forward.

 Tip

BI differs from business process automation, which has been the core historic strength at SAP. BI focuses on the world of decision makers as opposed to task-oriented persons. In the decision maker's world, the following matters most:

> Information as opposed to transactions

> Ease of use as opposed to repeatability

> Intelligence as opposed to discipline

BI is traditionally used within the firewall environments ranging from departmental workgroups of a few users to enterprise-wide deployments of thousands. BI is also more and more often deployed outside the firewall across the enterprise network as Internet applications that allow organizations to deliver new services and build stronger relationships with an even wider business user base comprised of customers, partners, and suppliers.

 BI History in a Few Dates

The term and concepts of business intelligence first appeared in 1958 in a visionary article from IBM researcher Hans Peter Luhn. In the 1980s, BI concepts surfaced with technologies then known as Decision Support Systems (DSS) and Executive Information Systems (EIS). Later, in the 1990s, BI became more popular after industry analyst firm Gartner started to establish this term as it is typically used in the industry today.

How BI Can Help Your Organization

BI should be deployed within your organization across functional areas and business processes for a variety of compelling reasons. In this section, we'll focus on the key high-level points to clearly highlight why BI should be considered to optimize the business performance of your organization.

Better Transparency of the Organization

Executives and managers within an organization always strive to better understand how their business works. In reality, though, the view most executives and managers have of their business is simply through the balance sheet and income statement. Knowing the assets and liabilities on the balance sheet is one thing but to truly understand all of the drivers in a business — from sales figures to inventory levels to measurements of lead generation from various marketing programs — these members of the organization must have a technology that delivers greater visibility over all parts of the business.

Up and down the value chain, BI not only gives executives and managers better visibility into the performance of the organization but also enables them to gather this information quickly and provides a mechanism for analyzing their findings.

BI gives better visibility into the performance of the organization

Running the Organization by the Numbers

A term used often in the corporate world is *operational excellence*. What does this mean exactly, and is your company achieving this? Operational excellence is the ability of an organization to continuously optimize the ways it does business by continuously doing them better, faster, and cheaper.

Operational excellence

To achieve greater operational excellence, the first thing any organization needs is a means of tracking the different variables within it, such as specific products, customers, parts, suppliers, and so on. Secondly, there must be a means of reporting this data to the necessary users in the organization. Finally, the business users must be able to analyze this information to recommend optimization and plan for greater efficiencies in the future.

BI lets the numbers tell the story Systems and processes must be implemented in an organization to achieve these objectives. And the cornerstone for any system that allows you to track, report, analyze, and plan is business intelligence. BI enables your company to constantly see how it is performing by having the numbers tell the story.

Helping You Hold on to Your Customers

The benefits of BI are not just giving executives and managers better visibility of the organization's performance or allowing for operational excellence. Even more than that, certain corporations are taking this a step further and improving customer satisfaction thanks to BI. Being able to retain customers' loyalty is as important, if not more so, than gaining new ones.

 Did You Know?

> Those in business commonly accept that it is five times more expensive to attract a new customer than to keep an existing one.

BI can help retain customers' loyalty Knowing that, a company should therefore do everything possible to understand not just what products or services their customers purchase but also why they purchase them, to identify customers with the greatest profit potential, and to increase the likelihood that they will want more products or services.

A Solution with Immediate Impact

Economic cycles most often induce flattened IT budgets when there is a downturn. In such times, the challenge for most CIOs is to determine where they should spend this smaller allotment of money. "Do I continue to spend on the ERP upgrade project we began last year?" "What about the CRM initiative the executives were talking about six months ago?" These are the types of questions many CIOs may be facing.

Rather than focusing on the larger implementations that will not allow you to see results in the short term, the focus could be on what solution will have the most positive impact on the bottom line of the company in the shortest period of time. If you are asking yourself, where you can find the biggest bang for your buck, the answer is BI.

In the short term, a company cannot afford to sink money into a project that doesn't positively impact the operations of the company, mainly because you stand to lag behind your competitors, who are already focusing on the immediate benefits they might receive from their implementations. BI offers immediate benefits, provides fast return on investment (ROI), and will *still* be an integral part of the infrastructure you put in place later. BI will be the "frontend" of any successful ERP or CRM system down the road, for example, and there is nothing stopping you from rolling out BI now and completing your "larger" project later.

BI offers immediate benefits and fast ROI

Increasing the Value of Your Business Process Automation Systems

Although agility and speed of the deployment is an important quality of a BI solution for some, for others, it is the means by which they can leverage their preexisting investment in business process automation systems, such as ERP and CRM, which are essential to any modern organization from any size and in any vertical market.

By design, these systems generate massive amounts of data; however, many large automation systems aren't designed to allow you to extract and access information out of this data in a timely and easy fashion. BI allows you to harness the information you already have accumulated in these automation systems and put it to work for your company. With a BI solution, you can leverage your investment in these automation systems and extract information from the data they collect to effectively give business users the information they need now to make informed decisions.

BI leverages your investment in ERP and CRM applications

Key BI Functionality in the Market Today

BI industry experts tend to differ on how exactly to draw the lines between different types of BI functionality. Although many legitimately define BI with a narrow scope of functionality focused on suites of frontend tools aimed at reporting and analysis, keeping data warehousing and performance management (PM) applications separate, there is a broad agreement about the following high-level software categories as key ingredients of end-to-end corporate BI solutions (see Figure 1.5).

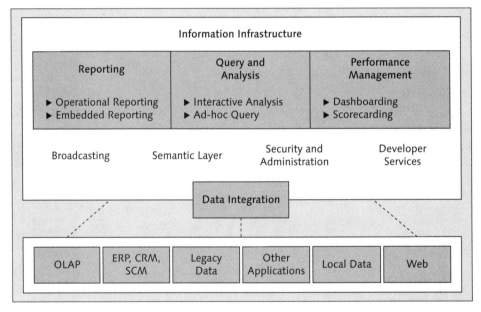

Figure 1.5 Key BI Functionality

Database Management Systems

Data warehouses and data marts

Database management systems (DBMSs) provide the functionality to store and manage information efficiently for end-user access. Data warehouses and data marts enabled thanks to DBMSs are sometimes considered separately from the rest of the BI product choice but are clearly a foundation of the overall BI system.

Did You Know?

At a glance, there are three different high-level technical architectures for mainstream DBMSs:

> Relational

> Online analytical processing (OLAP)

> Columnar

Database Integration and Data Quality Management

Data integration is the process of extracting data from broad disparate sources, transforming the data, and loading it into data warehouses and data marts serving BI purposes. Therefore, data integration software products are also known as extraction, transformation, and loading (ETL) software.

Extraction, transformation, and loading (ETL) software

The data quality management functionality allows you to profile, cleanse, match, and consolidate your data across multiple environments. It comes as an instrumental complement to data integration to complete a successful BI system foundation in conjunction with a DBMS.

 Warning

Business decisions are only as good as the data used to justify them. The most impressive dashboard is worth nothing if the underlying information is not reliable. End-user surveys show that the lack of trust in the information end users have access to is a major inhibitor to successful broad BI adoption across the organization. Strong data quality management is instrumental to address this risk.

Reporting

Reporting is generally the most visible piece of a BI system because it usually reaches the largest user population. Reporting is the process of retrieving, formatting, and delivering data as static information to potentially very large groups of end users inside the organization and

Retrieving, formatting, and delivering data

sharing it in a secured manner with customers, partners, and suppliers outside the organization.

Hundreds to thousands of users

A reporting solution is ideal in situations where questions are predefined and the structure of each answer is fairly well known in advance. In this case, the majority of users are information consumers who want snapshots of business activity. Developers and report designers author reports that answer the most regularly asked questions and distribute them to hundreds or thousands of users. A key attribute to successful reporting is the ability to print high-quality reports.

Management reporting

Management reporting focuses on providing executives and managers with formatted views of the historical information they need to make informed decisions. Examples of management reports include typical financial reports such as profit and loss (P&L) and balance sheet (BS) reports.

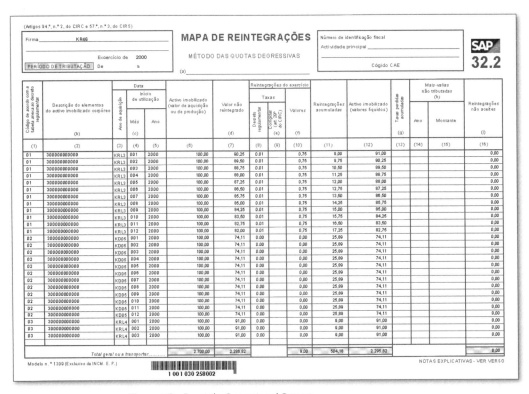

Figure 1.6 Example Operational Report

Operational reporting provides reports for the systems used to run the organization on a day-to-day basis. Operational reports are often embedded as a seamless part of the business process management applications. Examples of operational reports include bills of lading, invoices, and payroll slips (see Figure 1.6).

Operational reporting

Reporting is also a critical part of any legal and regulatory compliance management system aimed at ensuring that compliance is aligned with the company's business objectives and risk management strategies. Examples of legal and regulatory compliance reports include financial and accounting disclosure information according to the Sarbanes-Oxley Act (SOX), U.S. Generally Accepted Accounting Principles (GAAP), International Financial Reporting Standards (IFRS), and Basel II.

Legal and regulatory compliance reporting

Query and Analysis

Query and analysis tools are designed to give business users autonomous and interactive access to business information so that they are empowered to answer ad hoc business questions as they arise with minimal knowledge of the underlying data sources and structures.

Query and analysis functionality is ideal for data analysts and other business users who need self-service information access with moderate-to-high amounts of interactivity. End users are not limited to the subset of information available in a particular and predefined report or query result, so they can explore and analyze any of the information stored in the database, data warehouse, or data mart. Query and analysis tools support ad hoc query generation and basic report authoring integrated with analysis capabilities.

Autonomous and interactive access to business information

Managing a strong set of user-friendly business logic and business semantic definitions, also known as the metadata layer, is instrumental to end users successfully adopting the query and analysis functionality. The metadata layer shields end users from database complexity.

Metadata layer

35

Predictive Analysis

The predictive analysis functionality enables sophisticated, automated analysis of large amounts of data with many different variables. It helps users to mine past and present business scenarios to uncover trends and identify outliers to project future outcomes. Predictive analysis software products are also known as data mining software for this reason. Tuning and interpreting the results of these sophisticated systems typically requires specialized expertise in statistical modeling.

Dashboarding and Visualization

Dashboarding and visualization tools offer a compelling user experience designed to deliver user-specific information related to the performance of the business, typically modeled by key performance indicators (KPIs). Thanks to modern interactive visualization technologies that provide sophisticated visualization of multidimensional data using the color, size, and shape of an object, the user's attention is focused on important information, trends, changes, and outliers. Users can easily explore data by interacting with the visuals, for example, by clicking on a pie wedge in a pie chart.

EIS   Dashboards are direct descendants of the Executive Information System (EIS) that pioneered BI in the 1980s. Thanks to web-based information-delivery capabilities, dashboards are now reaching many more people in the organization, beyond the executive and senior management teams. You can see an example in Figure 1.7.

Dashboarding and visualization tools are essential for providing a common view of what's important to your organization or team in an intuitive way that encourages a culture of information appreciation and use.

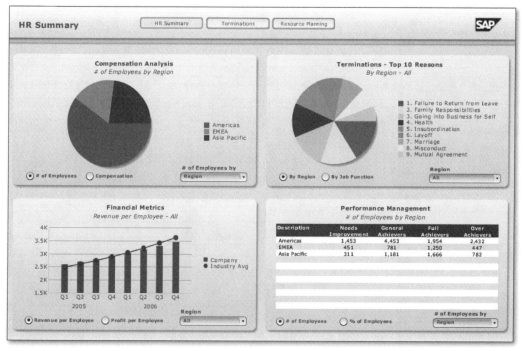

Figure 1.7   Example of a Dashboard for the HR Function

 Note

> Performance management (PM) applications, such as scorecards, can incorporate dashboards effectively to display and communicate information, but the dashboarding interface itself is not an application because it lacks the process support that is critical for business performance applications.

Performance Management Applications

Performance management (PM) applications, which are aimed at ensuring optimized performance from strategic decision making through planning and consolidation, modeling, and optimization, typically encompass a broad set of capabilities. This section focuses on key highlights.

› Scorecarding applications

Scorecarding

Typical scorecarding applications are cross-functional applications that improve your ability to align KPIs with strategic objectives using strategy maps and business performance management methodologies. They enable you to define, monitor, and analyze business strategies according to goals, initiatives, and KPIs assigned to accountable individuals, that is, to align people with corporate strategies. Scorecarding applications also manage causal relationships, supporting the closed-loop process of measuring and managing the execution of strategic goals across the organization.

 Did You Know?

The most famous approach to scorecarding is the Kaplan-Norton "balanced scorecard," which incorporates a business methodology for defining and relating financial and nonfinancial key indicators of performance.

› Budgeting and planning applications

Budgeting and planning

Budgeting and planning application provides accurate and timely financial and operational data so organizations can more effectively plan, budget, forecast, analyze, and report. With budgeting and planning applications, organizations can integrate corporate and departmental planning, intelligently model costs, and perform sensitivity analyses to determine operational budgets based on strategic plans and assumptions.

› Financial consolidation applications

Financial consolidation

Financial consolidation applications enable large organizations to consolidate and reconcile their finances in the increasingly complex, vast, and international realm of corporate finance. With financial consolidation applications, organizations can deliver consolidated financial management reports to fulfill requirements from shareholders to compliance and financial management officers.

› Analytical applications

Analytical applications provide prepackaged metrics, reports, and analytics covering customers, products and services, supply chains, human resources, and finance functions. These applications contain best practices for business analysis and are supported by a customizable framework that enables the company to adapt to the unique needs of each customer.

Examples of analytical applications include profitability and cost management applications, which allow organizations to accurately and effectively monitor product, customer, and channel profitability, and spend management applications, which bring together essential procurement measures across multiple dimensions of an organization to match sourcing strategies to strategic business goals.

Profitability, cost, and spend management

Information Infrastructure

All of the capabilities just listed are best deployed in any organization based on an information infrastructure that provides a set of common services to simplify the management and administration of tools, reports, and applications across end users. Key attributes of such an information infrastructure include the following elements:

> Broadcasting capabilities

> Metadata management

> Security and administration

BI User Profiles

Typical BI user profiles that you may find in any organization include executives and managers, business analysts, and information consumers (see Figure 1.8).

Figure 1.8 BI User Profiles

Executives and Managers

A key user profile for traditional BI is typically small and high level, consisting largely of two groups: executives and managers. They manage by metrics, are often in a hurry to get answers and make decisions, and don't have the time or appetite to learn how to use BI.

Business Analysts

Another key user profile for traditional BI is also fairly small, consisting of business analysts. They are technically and functionally very capable when it comes to using BI to access and interpret data to support executives and managers in their decision-making process.

Information Consumers

Last, but not least, the user profile with the largest potential user base consists of general information consumers. Most of those people are not at the executive and managerial, or analytical level. They typically rely on operational reporting for their day-to-day operational needs. Information consumers are underserved by traditional BI due to its inherent complexity.

The Future of Business Intelligence

Crystal ball BI has significantly evolved over time. It has certainly gained more prominence recently, and many industry analysts, experts, and various stakeholders have their own opinions on how it will evolve in the foreseeable future. Of course, there is no crystal ball, but there is general consensus about the following trends and development themes in the BI market.

 Did You Know?

A 2009 Gartner paper predicts that because of lack of information, processes, and tools, through 2012, more than 35% of the top 5,000 global companies will regularly fail to make insightful decisions about significant changes in their businesses and markets.

Enterprise BI Deployments

After DBMSs in the 1980s and 1990s and business process automation applications in the 1990s and 2000s, BI is expected to be the next big wave of pervasive enterprise applications.

Business user requirements for BI haven't significantly evolved since early BI systems. However, thanks to drastic improvements to information technology (IT), the ability to deliver solutions for these requirements to a wide scale *is* dramatically changing.

Pervasive BI solutions

IT teams are now enabled to service BI to all business users across the enterprise allowing the users to work directly with the data in the way they need which results in a lowered total cost of ownership (TCO). This ability to deploy pervasive BI solutions will lead more often to very large adoption across the enterprise beyond the happy few who have access to BI today.

Total cost of ownership

BI Standardization

The significant trend toward BI standardization not only enables enterprise BI deployments but also saves time and money. BI standardization is aimed at reducing the number of BI tools and technologies in use in an organization to a reasonable number and consolidating into a portfolio of products with as little overlap as possible.

BI standardization addresses issues with complexity and cost in learning and administering various tools and technologies. It also enables you to bring together information from disparate sources — thus offering a more holistic view of the business performance — more efficiently than with various tools and technologies.

Holistic view of the business performance

Convergence of BI and Performance Management

BI and performance management (PM), as well as governance, risk, and compliance (GRC), have been disparate disciplines in the past. Their convergence into a single, complete, and integrated solution that addresses business user's demands for broader insight from multiple sources, aligned strategic decision-making across teams, optimized operational decisions, and flawless execution across operational systems

GRC

will deliver new ability to manage and track integrated performance and risk indicators to optimize business performance.

Search-Based BI

With Google and other search engines putting masses of information at the fingertips of all consumers in an easily searchable and usable fashion thanks to the Web 2.0 user experience, users are beginning to expect enterprise applications to work in the same way, with the same ease of use and information access.

Google-like search interface The ability to search with high-performance both structured and unstructured data sources and map them into dimensions and key figures that users can easily and quickly navigate and explore using a Google-like search interface will become prominent in the future.

Collaborative BI

The nature of how people work is changing. Enterprise applications supporting individual contributors within a functional silo is no longer sufficient. Business users need support for how they really get things done — collaborating in teams and communicating across departmental and global geographic boundaries in a very specific business context.

 Tip

Studies show that people who collaborate with peers and team members make better decisions than those who work in isolation.

Providing functionality for business users to collaborate on the decision-making process will be an important feature of future BI solutions.

BI Mash-Ups

Another effect of the broad adoption of the Web 2.0 user experience is that today's business users expect to be self-sufficient and to create and customize their own solution environments, rather than always relying on IT. The ability to build mash-ups to easily combine and enhance data streams with web applications will offer a new BI experience.

Ex Example

The SAP 5O5 World Championship is a perfect example of how a better user experience to track your performance can profoundly change the way you work and help you achieve your goals — whether in the athletic or business arena.

For the first time, sailors can use an intuitive and interactive mash-up of Google maps, GPS data, information on winds and currents, and a sailing-planning application to create a model of the best possible route for each day's race and employ it for competitive advantage (see Figure 1.9).

As in business, the more information and insight athletes have at their disposal, the smarter their decisions and the stronger their performance.

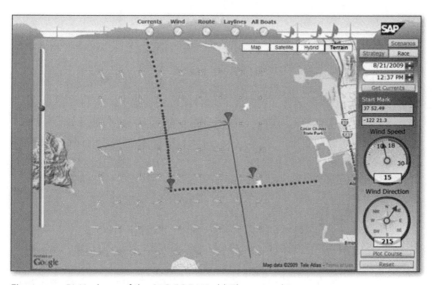

Figure 1.9   BI Mash-up of the SAP 5O5 World Championship

BI on Unstructured Data

The nature of information is changing. Managing your business using only structured information generated within four walls is no longer possible. All information, whether structured or unstructured, from inside or outside the organization, needs to be brought together in a way that is relevant for business decisions.

Emails and office documents

Unlocking the information currently hidden away in emails, office documents, and the sea of data available on the Internet is just the first step. Sorting through this mountain of information to generate trusted, relevant insight for a decision maker — and delivering this insight with business context — will see more adoption in the future.

In-Memory BI

The speed of mainstream BI will increase many times thanks to in-memory processing on specialized hardware and software rather than by thrashing hard drives. Memory is significantly cheaper than a few years ago, processor speeds have consistently improved, and 64-bit servers are already common, which allow you to put larger data sets directly into memory.

High-performance

Modern data management technology eliminates the need to build data models that are expensive to define, tune, and maintain; they enable you to just load raw transaction data into memory to enable high-performance and near-to-real-time BI. Coupled with in-memory processing, these technologies will deliver dramatic improvements to mainstream BI in the future.

OnDemand BI

SaaS

BI deployment models are also changing with expectations that software should be instantly available, up and running in hours, not days, weeks, or months, at a controlled TCO. OnDemand BI, which preserves capital, minimizes risk, and delivers value quickly thanks to the software as a service (SaaS) model for licensing and delivery, is addressing these expectations.

The overall increase in business executive influence over BI buying decisions will drive more OnDemand BI adoption. Also OnDemand applications in core business areas such as HR and CRM lack good BI, and market surveys indicate that BI is perceived to be the best suited for OnDemand delivery among other technologies.

Summary

In this first chapter, you've learned about the context and key information for understanding the value of BI by considering the following:

> An introduction to the BI fact gap
> A simple definition for BI
> Information about how BI can help your organization
> An overview of key BI functionality in the market today as well as typical BI user profiles
> A quick outlook to the future of BI

In Chapter 2, you'll learn more about the history of Business Objects. We'll describe core products and innovative technologies that enabled Business Objects to pioneer and lead the BI market.

Business Objects: A Historical Perspective

In this chapter, you'll learn more about the history of Business Objects through a look back at the core products and innovative technologies that enabled Business Objects to pioneer and lead the BI market for almost 20 years.

A Good Idea Can Go a Long Way

Business Objects was founded in Paris in August 1990 by two colleagues from the French subsidiary of Oracle — the clear database market leader in the 1980s. Recognizing the need for empowering business users with effective ways to access data locked inside corporate databases and enterprise application suites, Bernard Liautaud and Denis Payre, then aged 29 and 28, respectively, set up in a small office in the Parisian suburb with start-up capital of merely 10,000 Euros (less than $14,000).

Business Objects founded in 1990

Before 1990, the relational technology at the core of relational database management systems (RDBMSs) was supposed to relieve end users from the technicalities of data storage to enable easy access. The Structured Query Language (SQL), which allowed query writing, was called the first language that was understandable and usable by end users. Relational technology was promoted with this new ease-of-use paradigm, but ironically, the first implementations failed miserably to prove the concept.

While still with Oracle, Liautaud and Payre had come across software written by an independent developer, Jean-Michel Cambot, which provided a simpler means of working with Oracle databases with no SQL knowledge required. Liautaud and Payre immediately recognized the potential of this technology that no one had seen before. Liautaud and Payre purchased the software from Cambot, after they had both left Oracle, and started their new business with a strong technology already in hand.

Business Objects universes

This innovative technology, which eventually became known as Business Objects' universes, enabled Business Objects to pioneer and lead the BI market. These universes are patented and are still core in the SAP BusinessObjects BI solutions.

These business objects were designed to insulate end users from having to understand complex database structures and terminologies, such as tables, columns, and joins, in order to formulate data query requests using the SQL syntaxes demanded by RDBMSs.

Instead, the IT department just creates a series of graphical metadata objects representing SQL keywords, providing the end user with a point-and-click interface tailored to the user's business term needs. These business objects — hence the name of the company — are grouped in universes that form a semantic layer (Figure 2.1). Objects in a universe can be combined to build highly specific data query requests; the results can then be easily presented in table and graphical charts. With Business Objects' universes the database learns the business of the end user and not vice versa.

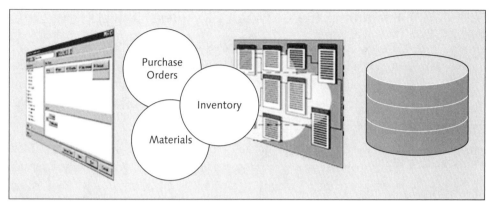

Figure 2.1   Business Objects' Semantic Layer with Universes for Purchase Orders, Inventory, and Materials

Universes give end users autonomy from the IT department, so they can build queries and reports to answer their own business questions from their data using familiar business terms. Universes also increase user productivity via reusable business logic, such as calculations and report elements. From an IT perspective, universes ensure reliable and controlled data access.

Autonomy from the IT department

 ### Remembering the World Before Business Objects' Universes

> Hi Mr. IT, I need to know how many containers are available in New York and Boston.
>
> (And I need it right now....)
>
> Hi Mr. Shipshandler, no problem, I'll build a query and a report for you. (I mean... when I have a moment!)
>
> A couple of days later...
>
> Hi Mr. Shipshandler, here's your report. There is no container available in New York and Boston. (Oops... I messed up my SQL query with an AND....)
>
> OK, thank you Mr. IT, I couldn't wait, so I've placed a couple of calls already. (I'm not working with this IT guy anymore!)

Examining the Growth of Business Objects

Liautaud and Payre's experience with Oracle's RDBMS, as well as their understanding of the outstandingly successful Silicon Valley business model (Liautaud received a Master's in management from Stanford University) marked Business Objects' business development from the beginning.

Business Objects business model

Business Objects had adopted a business model similar to its Silicon Valley counterparts, including an aggressive, internationally oriented recruitment policy, salaries boosted by stock options, and an initial public offering in September 1994. So the partners hired an international team, many of whom also had worked for Oracle, giving the company not only a strong technical and commercial base but also a working knowledge of its target customers' needs.

Business Objects also benefited from Oracles disinterest in pursuing this new market with its own resources, giving its tacit support to the development of a product that, by making Oracle databases more accessible, would also make them more attractive.

Internationalization

Liautaud and Payre adopted another particularity of the Silicon Valley business model by quickly opening up the company's capital. Almost immediately after opening Business Objects' offices, they began making the rounds to investment firms in New York, Paris, and San Francisco. Aided by Liautaud's father-in-law, former American Electronics Association President, Arnold Silverman, the pair succeeded in attracting investment interest not only in France but also among the crucial Silicon Valley investor community. The internationalization of the company's capital proved critical for enabling Business Objects to penetrate the crucial U.S. market, which immediately played a key role in Business Objects' business development and strategy. Although founded in France, Business Objects had from the start taken a distinctly international approach.

The Early Days

The market readily embraced Business Objects and its groundbreaking technology. By 1993, the company had already wooed more than

1,000 clients worldwide and achieved a growth of more than 400% since 1991. At the same time, with the growth of new client/server technology in the early 1990s, analysts had begun estimating that the niche market Business Objects had created, then worth some U.S. $90 million worldwide, could near U.S. $800 million by the late 1990s.

Indeed, Business Objects' product had come at the right time. The collapse of the international economy during the 1990s and the lingering effects of the recession, which would last into the middle of the decade, coupled with the increasing globalization of business competition, had driven corporations to search for new means not only to increase efficiency but also to achieve more accurate business forecasting models. By placing the technology used to conduct database queries and generate reports into the hands of the corporate users, Business Objects had created an important — and eagerly embraced — solution for these corporations.

Business Objects quickly expanded, opening multiple offices in the United States, the United Kingdom, the Netherlands, and Germany, as well as in Tokyo where it began translating its software into Japanese.

United States, United Kingdom, the Netherlands, Germany, and Japan

In 1994, Business Objects took the next step toward corporate respectability when it went public and was listed on the NASDAQ stock exchange. Business Objects was the first independent European company ever to do so. The choice to go public, and to list on an American exchange, gave the company the appearance of stability necessary to attract the world's largest corporations to its product line. At the same time, the company's IPO was one of the year's most successful and garnered favorable publicity for its products.

By 1995, sales had doubled over the previous year, and more than 70% of its sales were made internationally, with 35% of its revenues coming from the United States alone. The company, though maintaining its headquarters and, in particular, its development activities in France, was nonetheless shifting more and more of its efforts to the all-important American market.

After several years of doubling sales annually; however, revenue growth and profit slipped dramatically in 1996 due to the troubled launch of the new version 4.0, which no longer worked on Windows 3.1. This crippled the development of sales. The company's difficulties continued into 1997 because competitors had made inroads into the business-decision market, and had taken market share from Business Objects. Nevertheless, the company — and market analysts — found cause to remain optimistic with the launch of several new products, including Web Intelligence, which enabled truly web-based deployments.

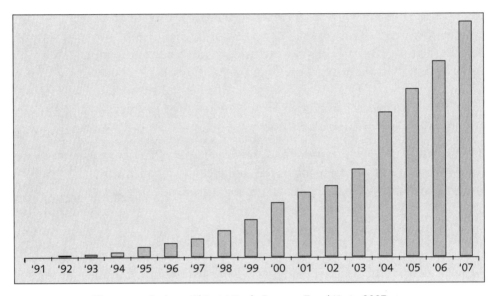

Figure 2.2   Business Objects' Yearly Revenue Trend Up to 2007

 Did You Know?

> › Business Objects — with a space between Business and Objects — was the name of the company before SAP's acquisition.
> › BusinessObjects — without a space — was the name of the legacy client/server product. It was renamed to Desktop Intelligence after its last version 6.5.
> › SAP BusinessObjects — without a space — is the correct name of the new portfolio of SAP solutions for business users.

A Story of Innovation

The universe technology that was at the origin of Business Objects' success in the market wasn't the only innovative technology introduced by the company. Over the years, Business Objects had received many industry awards for its innovative portfolio of technologies and solutions, including the following:

> **The central repository in 1993**
> To make the system administration as simple, secure, and scalable as possible, the central repository was introduced in 1993. Thanks to its RDBMS storage, the central repository addressed challenges with easy access and sharing of resources such as universes and reports with the appropriate security controls. That was a first in the BI market where file sharing used to be the norm.

> **Integrated query, reporting, and analysis in 1996**
> The company released several major innovations in 1996 with version 4 of BusinessObjects.
>
> One of them was the integration of query, reporting, and analysis in a single user interface. Previously, end users needed multiple tools for fulfilling casual query, reporting, and analysis requirements. With such an integrated environment, end users only needed to learn one tool and could easily move from query to reporting to analysis with the same information for maximum insight.

> **The dynamic microcube in 1996**
> Another major innovation of the 1996 release was the introduction of the dynamic microcube. End users could build multidimensional cubes on the fly, whereas previously IT had to build and maintain cubes, which was a long and labor-intensive task.

> **Access to multiple data sources in 1996**
> Also introduced with the 1996 release was the ability for end users to access any information source wherever it was throughout the enterprise and to easily combine all information together in reports and analyses. This was a major improvement for most business users who often needed to access multiple sources of information.

> **Thin client for the Web in 1997**
> In 1997, while the Web was still nascent from a corporate user

point of view, the integrated query, reporting, and analysis experience of BusinessObjects started to evolve from pure client/server deployments to also support Internet architectures. Web Intelligence was born, allowing a dramatic reduction of TCO for Business Objects' customers.

Successful Merger and Acquisitions

To build a very strong product portfolio that covered all the spectrum of BI requirements with best-of-breed solutions, enable Business Objects to enjoy an accelerated market uptake and penetration, and reinforce its leading position in the market, the company also successfully seized multiple merger and acquisition (M&A) opportunities in the 2000s.

Major milestones | There were also several major milestones in terms of technology and business impact, including the following:

> **Acta, 2002**
> Acta was a well-known leader in the data integration market, and its best-of-breed ETL technologies were added to the Business Objects' portfolio as BusinessObjects Data Integrator.

> **Crystal Decisions, 2003**
> Crystal Decisions was the clear leader in the enterprise reporting market segment with the Crystal Reports brand. The Crystal Decisions M&A was one of the major milestones in the history of Business Objects. Not only did the Crystal Reports product became Business Objects' strategic offering for enterprise reporting to complement its classic integrated reporting, query, and analysis products but also Crystal Enterprise information infrastructure software became the technology foundation for BusinessObjects Enterprise XI released in 2004.

> **Mediance, 2005**
> Mediance was an innovative startup in the enterprise information integration (EII) space. Mediance's strong data federation technology was integrated to the Business Objects' information management portfolio as BusinessObjects' Data Federator.

> **Infomersion, 2005**
> Excelsius | Infomersion was another very innovative startup that provided high-end interactive visualization capabilities for Microsoft Excel.

Infomersion's innovative solution became integrated to Business Objects' dashboarding and visualization offering as BusinessObjects Xcelsius.

> **FirstLogic, 2006**

FirstLogic was a well-established vendor of data quality management solutions. Its core technology joined the Business Objects' information management portfolio as BusinessObjects Data Quality Management.

Data Quality Management

> **ALG, 2006**

ALG Software was a provider of profitability management and activity-based costing solutions. ALG solutions joined the Business Objects' portfolio of enterprise performance management (EPM) applications as BusinessObjects Profitability and Cost Management.

BusinessObjects Profitability and Cost Management

> **Cartesis, 2007**

Cartesis was a clear leader in the EPM space with best-of-breed applications for financial consolidation. The Cartesis M&A was another very important milestone in the Business Objects history. It enabled the company to extend further its leading BI platform with a complete suite of EPM applications for the office of the Chief Financial Officer (CFO).

> **InXight, 2007**

InXight Software was a leading provider of software solutions for unstructured information discovery. Its text analytics and federated search solutions joined the Business Objects' portfolio of information management solutions as BusinessObjects Text Analysis and BusinessObjects Intelligent Search.

BusinessObjects Intelligent Search

Business Objects in 2007

As of 2007, Business Objects had achieved market leadership as number one in total BI revenues with 45,000 customers, 75,000 on-demand subscribers, and 3,000+ channel partners. The company had query, analysis and reporting, data integration/data quality, and performance/analytic applications, as well as a broad industry presence.

In addition, the company was truly a global organization with global brand recognition, including the following:

> 1,750 developers

> 700 quota-carrying sales reps

> 50% of revenue driven by channel sales

> 1,000 consulting/training professionals worldwide

> 700 global support staff, 24/7 support

Clearly, Business Objects had become the leader in the BI industry. So for obvious reasons, SAP, the leader in business processes, was interested in merging with Business Objects, the leader in BI.

Summary

This chapter gave you a historical look at the development of Business Objects, the company, as well as the technology behind it. Through innovative product development and savvy acquisitions, Business Objects quickly became the BI market leader.

Today, as part of SAP, it continues to offer cutting-edge tools and technologies that will benefit users and the industry for years to come.

In the next chapter, we'll look at the synergy between SAP and Business Objects, and learn why it really is the "perfect match."

SAP and Business Objects: The Perfect Match

The merging of SAP and Business Objects is an ideal pairing not only for the respective companies but also for the respective customers. The SAP software suite has historically had a proven excellence in business process applications. And the Business Objects suite has historically proven excellence in business intelligence. The combined organization brings a solution to a problem that many ERP implementations face. That is, now that all of the business processes and enterprise data have been centralized in one system, how do we pull that data out to make faster, more accurate, and more effective decisions?

Complementary Products

Let's take a look at how the two platforms fit together, as illustrated in Figure 3.1.

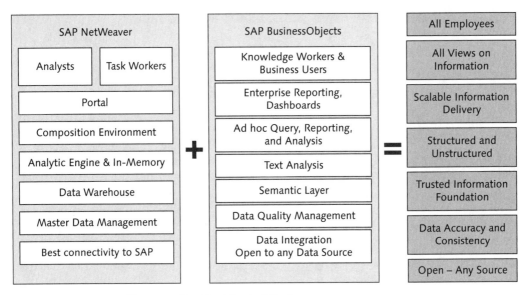

Figure 3.1   Combined Product Stacks

SAP ERP

The core of the SAP
Business Suite

SAP ERP is the core of the SAP Business Suite. It comprises a variety of applications and processes that work interactively for core business process execution. Those applications and processes for SAP ERP are shown in Tables 3.1 through 3.8.

Talent Management	Workforce Process Management
Competency Management	Employee Administration
Recruiting	Organization Management
Employee Performance Management	Global Employment
Talent Review and Collaboration	Benefits Management
Employee Development	Healthcare Cost Management
Learning	Time and Attendance
Succession Management	Payroll and Legal Reporting

Table 3.1 SAP ERP Human Capital Management (SAP ERP HCM)

Talent Management	Workforce Process Management
Compensation Management	HCM Processes and Forms
Talent Management Analytics	Employee Self-Service
	Manager Self-Service
	Employee Interaction Center
	Workforce Planning
	Workforce Cost Planning & Simulation
	Workforce Benchmarking
	Workforce Process Analytics & Measurement
	Strategic Alignment
Workforce Deployment	**Travel Management**
Project Resource Planning	Travel Request and Pre-trip approval
Resource and Program Management	Travel Planning – Online Booking
Retail Scheduling	Travel and Expense Management
	Global Travel Policy Compliance
	Travel and Expense Analytics

Table 3.1 SAP ERP Human Capital Management (SAP ERP HCM) (Cont.)

Financial Supply Chain Management	Treasury
Electronic Bill Presentment and Payment	Treasury and Risk Management
Collections Management	Cash and Liquidity Management
Credit Management	In-House Cash
Dispute Management	Bank Communication Management

Table 3.2 SAP ERP Financials

Financial Accounting	Management Accounting
General Ledger	Profit Center Accounting
Accounts Receivable	Cost Center and Internal Order Accounting
Accounts Payable	Project Accounting
Contract Accounting	Investment Management
Fixed Assets Accounting	Product Cost Accounting
Bank Accounting	Profitability Accounting
Cash Journal Accounting	Transfer Pricing
Inventory Accounting	
Tax Accounting	
Accrual Accounting	
Local Close	
Financial Statements	
Travel Management	
Corporate Governance	
Audit Information System	
Management of Internal Controls	
Risk Management	
Whistle Blower Complaints	
Segregation of Duties	

Table 3.2 SAP ERP Financials (Cont.)

Product Development and Collaboration

Product Development	Product Data Management
Product Development	Product Structure Management
Development Collaboration	Recipe Management
	Specification Management
	Change and Configuration Management

Table 3.3 SAP Collaborative Product Development

Product Intelligence	Product Compliance
Product-Centric View	Product Compliance
	REACH Compliance
Document Management	**Tool and Workgroup Integration**
Document Management	CAD Integration

Table 3.3 SAP Collaborative Product Development (Cont.)

Purchase Requisition Management	Operational Sourcing
Purchase Requisition Processing	Sourcing
	Purchase Optimization
	Compliance Management
Purchase Order Management	**Contract Management**
Purchase Order Processing	Operational Contract Processing
Delivery Schedule Processing	Scheduling Agreement
Commodity Management	Trading Contracts
Invoice Management	
Invoice Processing	
SAP Invoice Management by Open Text	
Flexible Invoice Reconciliation	

Table 3.4 Procurement

Sales Order Management	Aftermarket Sales and Service
Account Processing	Service Sales
Internet Sales	Service Contract Management
Managing Auctions	Customer Service and Support
Inquiry Processing	Installed Base Management
Quotation Processing	Warranty & Claims Management

Table 3.5 Operations: Sales and Customer Service

61

Sales Order Management	Aftermarket Sales and Service
Trading Contract Management	Field Service
Sales Order Processing	Depot Repair
Contract Processing	
Billing	
Incentive and Commission Management	
Returnable Packaging Management	
Consignment	
Commodity Management	

Table 3.5 Operations: Sales and Customer Service (Cont.)

Production Planning	Manufacturing Execution
Production Planning	Manufacturing Execution
Capacity Planning	Shop Floor Integration
Lean Planning	Supervision and Control
	Manufacturing Analytics
Manufacturing Collaboration	
External Processing	
Quality Collaboration	

Table 3.6 Operations: Manufacturing

Investment Planning and Design	Procurement and Construction
Business Planning	Supplier Qualification and Candidate Selection
Investment Management	Bidding and Contract Management
Asset Portfolio Management	Procurement Process
Collaborative Specification & Design	Document Management
Maintenance Engineering	Project Management

Table 3.7 Enterprise Asset Management

	Collaborative Construction
Interfacing CAD systems	
Project Management	Project and Investment Controlling
	MRO and Services Procurement
Maintenance and Operations	**Decommission & Disposal**
Technical Assets Management	Asset Transfer & Disposal
Workforce Management	Document Management
Preventive and Predictive Maintenance	Collaborative Disposal Management
Maintenance Planning and Scheduling	Project Management
Work Order Management	Waste Management
Approval Processing	Asset Compliance
Contractor Management	Asset Remarketing
Refurbishment	
Mobile Asset Management including RFID enablement	
Service Parts & Inventory Management	
Interfacing CAD, GIS, and SCADA Systems	
Work Clearance Management	
Shutdown Planning	
Asset Tracking with RFID	
Takeover/Handover for Technical Objects	
Asset Analytics & Performance Optimization	**Real Estate Management**
Integrated Asset Accounting	Portfolio Management
Asset and Maintenance Reporting	Commercial Real Estate Management

Table 3.7 Enterprise Asset Management (Cont.)

Asset Analytics & Performance Optimization	Real Estate Management
Asset Performance Management	Corporate Real Estate Management
Reliability Centered Maintenance	Facilities Management
Asset Life-Cycle Costing	Support Processes
Damage Analytics	
Object Statistics	
Spend and Supplier Performance Analytics	
Predictive Condition Monitoring	
Operator Dashboards	
Budget Tracking	
Maintenance Cost Planning	
Fleet Management	
Fleet Administration	
Fleet Maintenance	
Transportation Logistics	
Capacity Planning	
Fleet Analysis	

Table 3.7 Enterprise Asset Management (Cont.)

Quality Management	Environment, Health, and Safety Compliance Management
Quality Engineering	EHS Management
Quality Assurance/Control	Recycling Administration
Quality Improvement	
Audit Management	

Table 3.8 Operations: Cross Functions

Inbound and Outbound Logistics	Inventory and Warehouse Management
Inbound Processing	Cross Docking
Outbound Processing	Warehousing and Storage
Transportation Execution	Physical Inventory
Freight Costing	
Product Classification	
Duty Calculation	
Customs Communication Service	
Trade Document Service	
Trade Preference Processing	
Global Trade Services	**Project and Portfolio Management**
Export Management	Portfolio Management
Import Management	Project Management
Trade Preference Management	Resource Management
Restitution Management	

Table 3.8 Operations: Cross Functions (Cont.)

These solutions make up the basic SAP ERP system. SAP also has in-dustry-specific versions of the SAP ERP system as well, such as SAP for Banking, SAP Aerospace & Defense, SAP for Consumer Products, SAP for Mill Products, and SAP for Oil & Gas, along with several others. See the SAP website for more information on industrial solutions. We will now take a look at SAP NetWeaver BW.

Industry-specific solutions

SAP NetWeaver Platform

The SAP NetWeaver Business Warehouse (SAP NetWeaver BW) plat-form provides the core data warehousing capabilities of the SAP Busi-ness Suite.

Primary SAP NetWeaver platform components

It has three primary components:

> The first layer is extraction, transformation, and load (ETL). This component extracts data from a specific data source, applies transformation rules, and loads the data into the PSA layer of SAP NetWeaver BW.

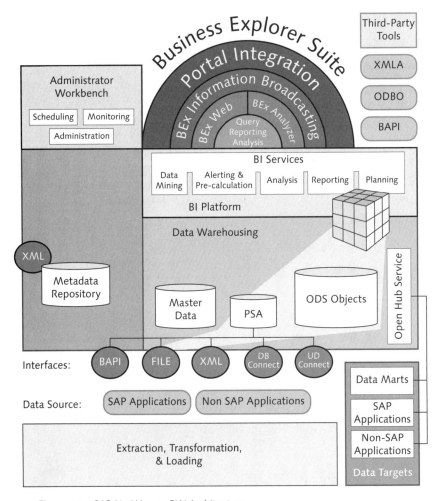

Figure 3.2 SAP NetWeaver BW Architecture

> The next layer is the Data Warehouse itself, which provides the storage layer for the various types of data structures in SAP NetWeaver BW. These structures include InfoCubes, InfoObjects, MultiProviders, and DataStore Objects (DSOs).

> The third layer is Reporting. This layer currently consists of the SAP Business Explorer (SAP BEx) toolset. The toolset consists of the following: BEx Excel analyzer, BEx query designer, BEx Web analyzer, BEx report designer, and BEx Web application designer. According to SAP, some of these tools will be retired and either replaced or enhanced by some of the SAP BusinessObjects tool suite (see Figure 3.2.) But SAP will continue to support the tools for the foreseeable future.

Next we will take a look at some of the recent acquisitions and new products that SAP has collectively placed in the SAP BusinessObjects enterprise performance management (EPM) space.

SAP BusinessObjects Enterprise Performance Management

The SAP EPM applications are designed for specific requirements that are common in the current marketplace to increase a customer's competitive edge and stay compliant with regulatory requirements. Examples of these solutions include the following:

SAP Business-Objects EPM Solutions

> **SAP BusinessObjects Strategy Management**: This solution allows companies to set goals, map strategies, and then monitor and manage performance from high-level objectives down to operational metrics.

> **SAP BusinessObjects Planning and Consolidation**: This application enables companies to increase accuracy in planning at all levels in an organization while reducing budget cycles and associated costs. The introduction of these capabilities to an organization speed up and improve financial and management reporting and decision making.

> **SAP BusinessObjects Financial Consolidation**: This application allows customers to complete financial consolidations and reporting cycles faster with a higher degree of confidence in the underlying data.

67

> **SAP BusinessObjects XBRL Publishing application by UBmatrix:** This application enables customers to leverage data in SAP BusinessObjects Planning and Consolidation, SAP Business Objects Financial Consolidation, and SAP Business Suite to create XBRL documents. The eXtensible Business Reporting Language (XBRL) is the new global standard for exchanging financial and business information.

> **SAP BusinessObjects Financial Information Management:** This application gives customers the ability to access, map, and load information from multiple SAP and non-SAP systems into SAP BusinessObjects Financial Consolidation and SAP BusinessObjects Profitability and Cost Management applications.

> **SAP BusinessObjects Intercompany:** This application allows customers to accelerate their closings by enabling business units to debate and reconcile balances directly with each other and eliminate delays at the corporate and division levels.

> **SAP BusinessObjects Profitability and Cost Management**: This application enables customers to identify the causes of underperformance and take action to reduce costs and optimize profitability across dimensions such as product, customer, and channel.

> **SAP BusinessObjects Spend Performance Management**: This application gives customers the power to maximize cost savings and reduce supplier risk by giving continuous visibility into company-wide spending patterns, savings potential, and external market factors.

> **SAP BusinessObjects Supply Chain Performance Management**: This application enables customers to improve supply chain effectiveness by focusing on actionable, operational process metrics that impact supply chain performance.

> **SAP BusinessObjects Sustainability Performance Management:** This application enables customers to track and communicate sustainability performance, set goals and objectives, manage risks, and monitor activities.

The SAP BusinessObjects EPM suite extends a customer's ability to collectively optimize business performance from the SAP ERP platform or other core application software programs. Next let's take a look at the SAP BusinessObjects Business Intelligence set of solutions to see the capabilities in those applications.

SAP BusinessObjects Business Intelligence

The SAP BusinessObjects BI suite of tools is composed of the SAP BusinessObjects tool set. These tools are used to provide the core functionality that empowers end users to make decisions and consume information with relative ease. These tools cover a wide variety of capabilities:

Core functionality to empowers end users

> **Information infrastructure**: The SAP BusinessObjects Enterprise software allows customers to share and distribute information for optimal decision making. The platform is built on a service-oriented architecture, which supports a variety of tools that allow IT departments to extend BI to any application or process.

> **Advanced analytics**: This set of applications is designed for financial and business analysts to use sophisticated analytic engines to access both numeric and text data. The customer can interrogate complex historical data to look for trends, outliers, and patterns through a visual interface.

> **Dashboards and visualizations:** SAP BusinessObjects Xcelsius Enterprise enables customers to create sophisticated visualizations of process and performance data. End users can perform what-if analysis with these dashboards to make better informed decisions.

> **Query, reporting, and analysis**: This set of applications allows end users to interact with data and perform ad hoc analysis. They support query generation and integrated analysis, as well as basic web-based and client-based report authoring.

> **Reporting**: The SAP Crystal Reports tool allows customers to connect to virtually any data source, design and format interactive reports, and share them both internally and externally using the SAP BusinessObjects Enterprise platform. Crystal Reports has native connectivity to the SAP ERP and SAP NetWeaver BW applications.

> **Search and exploration**: The SAP BusinessObjects Explorer application provides a simple interface to allow end users to search

and explore data to provide quick, easy answers to on-the-fly questions. The solution comes in both SAP and non-SAP versions. The SAP version of the Explorer platform is integrated with the SAP NetWeaver BW and the SAP NetWeaver BW accelerated version for ease of implementation and use.

These tools make up the SAP BusinessObjects suite. They complement the SAP ERP and SAP NetWeaver BW applications by seamlessly providing the basic reporting, ad hoc, search, and delivery capabilities that are needed by customers using those solutions. Next, let's take a look at the set of SAP BusinessObjects enterprise information management (EIM) tools that are now available to customers.

SAP BusinessObjects Enterprise Information Management

Completely integrated EIM solution

The SAP EIM products provide customers with a world-class set of ETL tools that allow IT to build a completely integrated EIM solution that spreads across the organization and encompasses both SAP and non-SAP data sources. Those solutions include the following:

> **Data Integration**: The SAP BusinessObjects Data Integration set of tools allows customers to access all types of structured and unstructured data from virtually any source, from databases to web forums. They allow the integration and delivery of data in real time or batch mode using flexible approaches through data federation or ETL.

> **SAP BusinessObjects Data Quality Management**: This software enables customers to verify that data is correct, consistent, and complete. The software also includes data profiling, parsing, cleansing, standardization, and matching capabilities that increase trust in data and the decisions that are made on that data.

> **SAP BusinessObjects Data Services**: This software provides customers with an enterprise class data integration and data quality solution. It provides one development, run time, and management environment that allows users to integrate, transform, improve, and deliver data to any target with any type of frequency.

> **SAP NetWeaver Master Data Management:** This component is an enabling foundation for EIM. It provides a single version of master data for supplier, product, customer, or user-defined data objects in heterogeneous environments.

> **SAP BusinessObjects Metadata Management**: This software allows customers to consolidate and integrate data metadata into an open and relational repository. It consolidates and audits metadata, enables users to view and analyze the integrated metadata, and provides a "metapedia" or encyclopedia that translates the metadata into business definitions for easier navigation and data discovery.

The combined set of classic SAP and SAP BusinessObjects applications provides customers with a robust, complete solution that is flexible enough to fit any need or requirement, as shown in Figure 3.3.

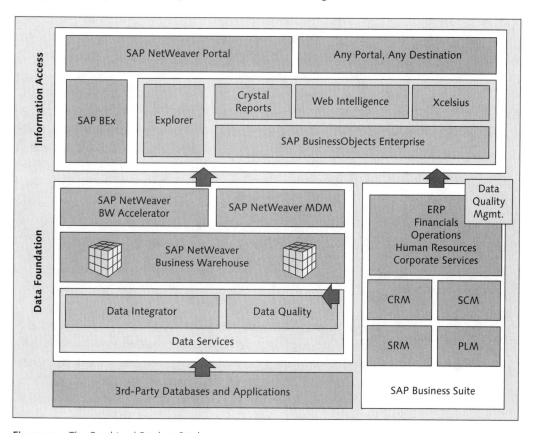

Figure 3.3 The Combined Product Stack

Now let's take a brief look at the history of the integration of the products.

Long-Time Product Integration

SAP Integration Kit   The SAP and SAP BusinessObjects products have a long history of integration. The first iteration of the SAP Integration Kit was in place with Seagate Software on the Seagate Info 7.5 platform. The Integration Kit allowed Crystal developers to connect to the underlying SAP tables in R/3. Future iterations of the SAP Integration Kit expanded the footprint of Crystal Reports in SAP implementations.

Crystal Enterprise/mySAP Integration Kit

Crystal Enterprise   The powerful Crystal Enterprise platform was the basis for the Crystal
SAP Edition   Enterprise SAP Edition. This product was Original Equipment Manufactured (OEM'd) with SAP BW in 2001. It included more than 100 Crystal Report templates that were embedded in SAP BW Business Content. This edition allowed customers to configure and modify up to 10 reports from the Crystal Report templates. It allowed consumption of reports from either the Crystal Enterprise ePortfolio application or Enterprise Portal by any SAP user. The OEM edition provided access to SAP BW data only and was limited to 1 CPU. This platform provided a leverage point for Crystal Decisions to introduce the Crystal Enterprise Enhanced SAP Edition, which allowed unlimited use of the Crystal Report templates, unlimited access to SAP systems (including R/3, SAP NetWeaver BW, SAP CRM, and SAP APO) and non-SAP systems (Oracle, SQL Server, Informix, etc.), and no CPU limitations.

SAP BusinessObjects Enterprise/SAP Integration Kit

The release of the SAP Business Objects XI platform in 2004 saw a corresponding release of the SAP Integration Kit. This version of the SAP Integration Kit saw the extension of the drivers to include the addition of a DSO (DataStore Object) driver (connects to operational DataStores) and support for personalization. It also saw the integration of SAP BusinessObjects Web Intelligence and SAP BusinessObjects Voyager into the Integration Kit. This version of the SAP Integration

Kit has provided the basis for the most current available version SAP BusinessObjects XI 3.1.

Now that we have done a high-level overview of the different SAP solutions and the history of the integration, let's talk about how these combined solutions make SAP so important in today's business landscape.

A Clear Market Leader

The combined companies with their respective strengths represent a clear market leader in the business software and business performance and optimization space. With SAP's acquisition of Business Objects, the company provides end-to-end solutions that benefit customers in the small, medium, and large enterprise spaces. SAP has more than 12 million users worldwide. There are more than 91,500 installations across 120 countries. SAP has 48,500 employees spread across 50 countries. The company has a long history of working with customers and consultants to build stronger business best practices in the respective industrial solutions that it offers. SAP is the third largest independent software vendor in the world, behind Microsoft and IBM.

Customers in small, medium, and large businesses

So what are the benefits of this integrated product offering to existing Business Objects customers and existing SAP customers?

Benefits to existing Business Objects and SAP customers

> **Benefits to Business Objects Customers**

- Added value of SAP: openness, high capacity, protected investment

- Availability of SAP's leading edge portfolio

- Broader portfolio: TREX/in-memory, BW, flow (Process Integration (PI), Business Process Management (BPM), Composition Environment (CE)) and MDM capabilities

- Analytics deeply enriched by the business process and vertical domain expertise

> **Benefits to SAP Customers**

- Wall-to-wall business user offering (innovation, usability, ease-of-use)

- Closed-loop — decision support — process (embedded analytics, homogenous best-in-class BI platform)
- Added value of Business Objects: deep analytics and technical know-how, accelerated innovation, vertical competence

> **Benefits to Joint Customers**

- On-demand reporting
- Embedded analytics applications
- EIM: non-SAP application access that delivers extraction and semantic layer
- Lower TCO: one lifecycle management, one ID management
- Great midmarket synergy potential, expanded market leadership in the Subject Matter Exert (SME) space

Summary

In this chapter, we've outlined, at a high level, the different types of solutions that are available from SAP and its acquisition of Business Objects. The key components include the following:

> SAP ERP

> SAP NetWeaver Business Warehouse

> SAP BusinessObjects enterprise performance management solutions

> SAP BusinessObjects business intelligence solutions

> SAP BusinessObjects enterprise information management (EIM) solutions

When combined, these different applications represent the overall solutions offered by SAP and SAP BusinessObjects to customers. For the purposes of this book, we will be taking a deeper look at the last three bullet points: SAP EPM, SAP BusinessObjects BI, and SAP BusinessObjects EIM, as well as the SAP BusinessObjects governance, risk, and compliance (GRC) solutions.

PART II
SAP BusinessObjects Portfolio Solutions

4

Closing the Gap Between Strategy and Execution

In this chapter, we'll look at the gap that exists between a company's intended strategy and the actual execution of that strategy. This is an issue with most customers, whether they are for-profit or non-profit. Through some of its recent purchases, including OutlookSoft, Pilot, and Business Objects, SAP is looking to bridge that gap for users not only of SAP ERP but also of other products as well.

Intended strategy versus actual execution

Your Organization's Performance: The Humbling Statistics

Some business statistics about various organizations' performance from the *Harvard Business Review* are very revealing:

Surprising statistics

> 90% of organizations fail to execute on their strategies.

> 95% of any given workforce does not understand its organization's strategy.

> 70% of companies do not link the incentives of middle management to strategy.

> 60% of organizations do not link budget to strategy. [Kaplan05]

Ask yourself this... These numbers come as quite a shock to most people. If you attempt to ask yourself the following questions, your answers will probably hit home pretty quickly:

> Did your organization succeed in executing on the strategies or strategic goals last year? Do you know if your organization failed and by how much?

> Do you understand your organization's strategic goals for this year, and are you able to effectively communicate them to others in your organization?

> Are your incentives linked to the strategic goals for the organization for the year? Are you able to easily find out how the organization is doing and how you are doing?

> Do you have access to budget decisions? If so, how did you incorporate your organization's strategies into the budget?

The most telling number is that 9 out of 10 companies are not executing on their strategies. The reality is that a large number of factors come into play against the success of a company's strategy. Technologies evolve, regulations shift, customers make surprising choices, macroeconomic variables fluctuate, and competitors thwart the best-laid plans [Sull07].

Other internal factors come into play as well: Executives don't have all the data they need, company data is locked into silos, and goals aren't clearly communicated to employees. All of these factors combine together to cause organizations to fail against their strategies.

Higher brain function jobs This seems counter-intuitive when you consider how the skill set of the average worker has changed in the past 40 years. Recent research shows that people are moving into "higher brain function" jobs, as illustrated in Figure 4.1.

Contributing to productivity These jobs indicate that the relative worker or employee in an organization is growing smarter and better able to contribute productively. A large part of this change can be attributed to the introduction of complex application computer systems such as SAP ERP. These applications require end users to be fully versed in the processes of the organization and how they fit into the organization as a whole. So the question lies in how organizations are able to close the gap between strategy and execution.

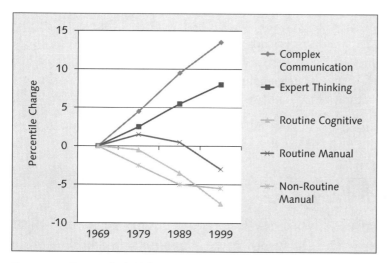

Figure 4.1 Change of Job Skill Set 1969 to 1999 [Levy05]

How Organizations Close the Gap Between Strategy and Execution

The solution is to first take a hard look at how strategy is being worked on in your organization. Generally, organizations work from a linear process when looking at strategy. The solution is to look at strategy as a loop as opposed to a line. This allows you to avoid the potentially fatal flaw of not incorporating new data into the strategy and avoid commitment to a failed strategy. In a linear strategy approach, the plan is developed at the beginning of a cycle and not revisited. The organization continues to sink resources into meeting the targets of the unrevised strategic plan, which leads to the further deterioration of the organization.

The solution loop is an iterative process that solves the flaws of the linear approach to strategy. It allows your organization to align strategy and execution across the entire business by strategic formulation across the organization at every level. Risks are identified initially, and potential solutions are documented. That formulation is translated

Solution loop

79

into plans that are communicated to all stakeholders. From there, the plans are monitored in real time, as well as against historical data on an internal and external level. Real-time insights are channeled back to managers to take action on. Unexpected events and risks that occur are identified and factored into updated strategic plans. This is a closed-loop process that relies on trusted data and insights that come out of performance management solutions, business intelligence applications, and information management strategies to be successful.

Let's take a look at how the SAP BusinessObjects set of solutions provide this for both SAP and non-SAP system customers.

The SAP Advantage

Addressing the gap between strategy and execution

The SAP BusinessObjects suite includes a broad range of tools to help customers with every aspect of the solution loop to close the gap between strategy and execution. This is where the SAP advantage is located in the marketplace for organizations. SAP has robust and proven solutions in each of the four primary disciplines that are required to successfully close the gap between strategy and execution. Those four disciplines are as follows:

> Business intelligence (BI)

> Enterprise information management

> Governance, risk, and compliance

> Enterprise performance management

Lower costs and higher ROI

These four disciplines are tightly integrated in the SAP solution. This tight integration means that organizations can implement the solutions and not be concerned with compatibility issues that can arise when trying to integrate multiple distinct solutions, which translates into lower cost and higher added ROI.

SAP has a long history of focusing on the needs of organizations standardizing on enterprise-wide BI and PM. Key factors that set SAP apart from the other BI vendors include the following:

> **Number one in the industry:** According to an IDC market study, SAP is ranked as the number one vendor of BI products in the world. More consultants, strategic integrators, and potential employees know SAP's products better than those of any other vendor. This ubiquity means that its products can integrate more easily with a customer's existing systems, at a lower cost.

> **Wide product portfolio:** SAP has one of the broadest set of BI products available in the market today, covering the following:

  - **All information:** From SAP and non-SAP business applications, data warehouses, OLAP databases, unstructured information, and real-time information feeds.

  - **All people:** From operational reporting all the way to dynamic dashboards, and from the factory floor to the financial analyst and the executive suite.

  - **All Systems:** A single, integrated platform.

In addition, the SAP BusinessObjects portfolio includes performance optimization applications that leverage these BI products:

> Performance management applications that handle strategy management; financial budgeting, planning, and consolidation; profitability and costing; and spend analysis

> Governance, risk, and compliance solutions that include risk management, process controls, global trade services, and environmental health and safety

Finally, SAP offers deep standardization experience. SAP has extensive experience in helping organizations around the world implement BI standards. The company has dedicated consulting teams that have helped organizations with strategic BI projects, working with users to get buy-in from business units and avoid the typical challenges companies face with BI projects.

An approach to how SAP sees the strategy loop is illustrated in Figure 4.2.

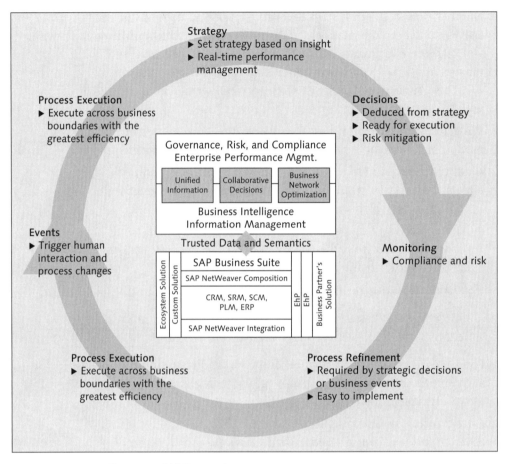

Figure 4.2 SAP Strategy Loop

As you can see, there are various stages and elements to each stage, including the following:

> **Strategy:** Set strategy based on insight and real-time performance management.

> **Insight:** Gained from reliable enterprise data.

> **Events:** Triggered by human interaction and process changes.

> **Process Execution:** Executed across business boundaries with the greatest efficiency.

> **Process Refinement:** Required by strategic decisions or business events, and easily implemented.

> **Monitoring:** Compliance and risk.

> **Decision:** Reduced from strategy, these are ready for execution with risk mitigation in mind.

Case Study

One of the largest U.S. insurance organizations, with more than 40,000 employees, had grown through acquisitions, and each business unit had retained responsibility for BI projects within its area. The decentralized operations made it hard for senior management to get a global overview of operations. To position for the future, the company decided to standardize its information systems at a corporate level and to implement a new enterprise data warehouse using the SAP NetWeaver Business Warehouse (SAP NetWeaver BW) component. In addition, the company established a Business Intelligence Competency Center (BICC) to manage its overall BI strategy, to rationalize systems, to eliminate duplicate information, and to have more control over metadata.

The BICC was staffed using resources from the previously fragmented management reporting systems. Charged with consolidating existing BI software deployments, the BICC chose the SAP BusinessObjects portfolio as a single solution for both operational and analytical projects across the company. The BICC has focused on simplification, compliance and security, and BI governance. It uses the iterative model approach to continually improve content. The group spends time ensuring that different business units, with many different points of view, all understand and buy in to the high-level BI strategy.

The company believes that it has reduced the cost of purchasing and deploying BI applications by up to 25%, resulting in annual savings of several million dollars. In addition, the IT organization is more easily able to support the rising demand for access and analysis of data from the company's applications from SAP and other vendors. A common set of business rules and metadata definitions are now used across the organization.

Key success factors for this insurance company's BI initiative included executive sponsorship, the ability to enforce central standards, and knowledge of the businesses served. By standardizing on SAP BusinessObjects solutions, the company has reduced the risk of data quality and integrity issues, conflicting reports, and inaccurate measurements of critical business metrics.

Summary

In this chapter we have taken a look at some of the key driving BI elements that set SAP apart in the marketplace. The discussion of why customers are having issues with the gap between strategy and execution helps to frame the reasoning behind why SAP is making some of the acquisition decisions of recent years. We have also taken a deeper look at how SAP is solving those issues with the integration of the four main disciplines of the SAP BusinessObjects framework. Now, let's move on to the business intelligence platform in Chapter 5.

Business Intelligence and On Demand Solutions

In this chapter, we'll look at the business intelligence (BI) and On Demand solutions. BI solutions are often associated with enterprise information management (EIM) covered in Chapter 6, because there can't be any reliable and meaningful business intelligence without good and trusted data.

To achieve the best level of integration and ensure the lowest cost of ownership, SAP chose the strategy of developing a platform, commonly referred to as the *business intelligence platform*, or BI platform for short, that provides a set of common services to the various pieces of the solution.

An integrated BI platform is becoming the norm

The Need for a Business Intelligence Platform

Historically, BI has been a patchwork of disparate technology solutions and vendors. Recent technology advances, greater integration, and industry consolidation have brought about significant change to the industry. A standard integrated BI platform is becoming the norm as opposed to the exception.

Figure 5.1 illustrates the evolution of BI since the 1990s.

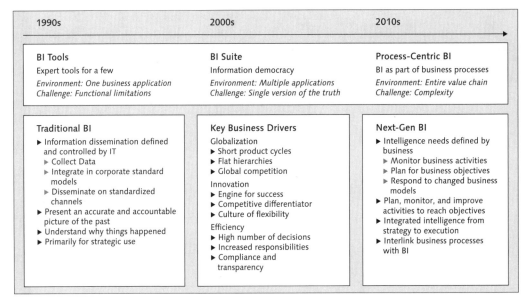

Figure 5.1   Evolution of Business Intelligence

The BI application of today must provide all of the information that decision makers, analysts, and business users need — when they need it. The application must be able to connect seamlessly to multiple systems, databases, office tools, and various web standards to get the data. That data can be in a structured format, such as a database table, or in an unstructured format. The BI application must be able to meet each of the tiers of the Business Intelligence pyramid. This concept has been around for several years. In essence, the pyramid is a visualization of the needs for BI within an organization and a representation of the prevalence of the respective requirements, as illustrated in Figure 5.2. As we've noted in earlier chapters, EPM (shown at the top of the pyramid) stands for *enterprise performance management*. We will develop that concept and related solutions in the next chapter.

Figure 5.2 Business Intelligence Pyramid

 Tip

The user segments represented by the pyramid may be different from one project to another. A specific user segmentation does not apply across your entire company. For example, the analysis segment is likely to be larger in finance, as opposed to shipping operations that rely on quite a few operational reports.

To cover all those business objectives and address specific user needs, a suite of tools is required. Not all users have the same needs or the same level of proficiency with BI, and although a wide-ranging tool may address the majority of users, some will need something more specialized.

Although one strategy is to shop and implement disparate solutions from various vendors, this can quickly lead to interoperability problems as well as additional costs of ownership. Very specialized but disparate tools mean specific training, specific administration, specific licensing, multiple customer support centers, and so on. This strategy has some pros, but in most cases, companies choose an integrated solution.

This is where the BI platform comes into play. The SAP Business-Objects BI platform offers a number of services that are common to all BI tools and ensures some degree of interoperability. For example, the content created by the BI clients operating on the platform is stored

The SAP Business-Objects platform provides a common set of services leveraged by all BI tools and secured in a central repository. There's a central place to manage users and security across the suite of specialized tools.

 Naming Convention

> SAP BusinessObjects XI is the commonly used name for the BI platform. XI refers to the platform although it was dropped from the name in version 4.0.

Let's review the main services provided by the BI platform.

Security

The platform provides a single point for managing security for both the BI tools and the BI content. Administrators use the Central Management Console (CMC) interface to define users and groups and grant them access to the features and functions of the various BI clients you decided to include in your solution. Likewise, the content created by users is secured.

Existing enterprise directories can be leveraged

The SAP BusinessObjects platform can obviously integrate with existing enterprise directories or leverage the security of SAP systems. In terms of data security, it's possible to surface the security defined at the database level.

Typically, large enterprises have a limited number of super-administrators who have access to the entire system, and they often belong to the center of excellence while a number of local administrators are delegated administration rights for their groups.

 Business Intelligence Center of Excellence

> The center of excellence is a team that puts together the strategy, best practices and governance related to business intelligence in the company. This team also consists of the tools experts and usually provides the first level of support to the internal users.

Storage, Publishing, and Distribution

The SAP BusinessObjects BI platform provides a central repository where the BI content created with any BI tool from the suite can be published securely or sent directly to other users.

InfoView portal was renamed BI Launch pad in version XI 4.0

Although you can integrate your BI content with your existing enterprise portal, you may also decide to use the portal that comes with the platform: InfoView in versions up to XI 3.x and renamed to BI Launch pad in verison 4.0.

InfoView or BI Launch pad is a web desktop, shown in Figure 5.3, that allows you to access Crystal Reports, Voyager workspaces, Web Intelligence documents, and other objects, and organizes them to fit the needs of each individual user.

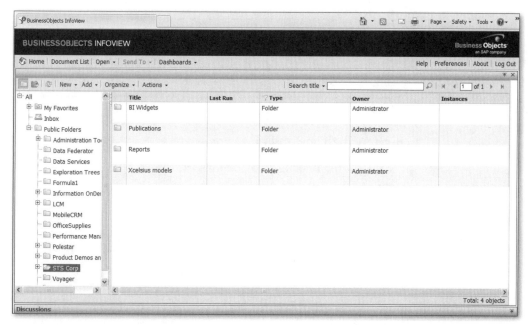

Figure 5.3 SAP BusinessObjects InfoView

Auditing and Monitoring

The auditing service records numerous events related to the use and administration of the system, and the information collected can then be viewed and analyzed by using the reporting tools against the audit database. In most deployments, audit is mandatory to verify compliance with standards such as Sarbanes Oxley (SOX). Audit is also largely used by administrators to understand the use of the platform, double-check who has access to what content, and make the necessary adjustments or plan for system maintenance.

Monitoring allows for improved availability of the BI solution

Monitoring is a newer capability introduced with version 4 of the BI platform. It captures in real-time a series of key system metrics and measures to control the health of the platform and BI services. Monitoring is critical to a good availability of the system, allowing for early detection of problems, preventive maintenance, planning for growth, and root cause analysis of possible problems.

 Tip

The implementation of memory and performance thresholds in your monitoring solution can help you detect runaway processes and take appropriate actions to avoid service interruptions. This translates into fewer support calls and higher customer satisfaction.

High Availability and Performances

Looking at the BI landscape architecture, the SAP BusinessObjects Enterprise platform was designed to provide high availability and performance in any size deployment.

The platform architecture allows for vertical or horizontal scaling

The platform is composed of multiple services (daemons in UNIX) that can be scaled both vertically and horizontally. *Vertical scaling* means that the services can all run on a single server, or additional instances of the services can be added to take advantage of all of the processing power that is available. *Horizontal scaling* means that the services can be run across multiple servers to provide a fault-tolerant, highly scalable solution as shown in Figure 5.4.

Example

A large retail bank operates on Windows servers per is IT standards. To support its growing number of BI projects, the company decided to use clustered four-CPU servers. Each time a new project starts, the company assesses the need for processing power and purchases the servers to be added to the cluster. Each new server is clustered with the existing ones. This is horizontal scaling.

On the other hand, a European government agency is standardized on very large IBM servers. The system is not clustered; the SAP Business-Objects instance runs on a subset of a 64-CPUs server. When the demand grows, additional CPUs get allocated to SAP BusinessObjects. This is vertical scalability.

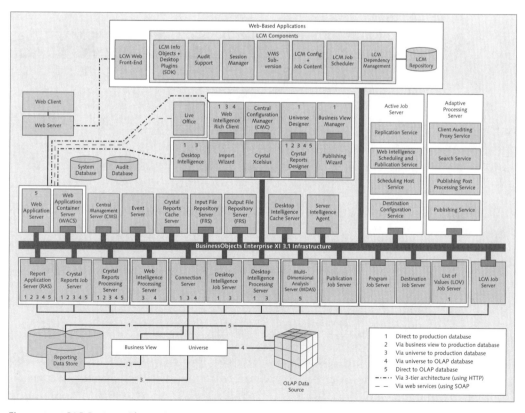

Figure 5.4 SAP BusinessObjects Enterprise Services

The enterprise infrastructure provides the basic messaging mechanism needed for SAP BusinessObjects Enterprise components to communicate with one another. This series of services are designed to communicate via CORBA (Common Object Request Broker Architecture), which runs over TCP/IP.

General Administration

The *Central Management Console (CMC)* is a web-based tool used to perform administrative tasks, including content, user, and server management. It allows administrators to publish, organize, and set security levels for all of the content in the SAP BusinessObjects Enterprise system (Figure 5.5).

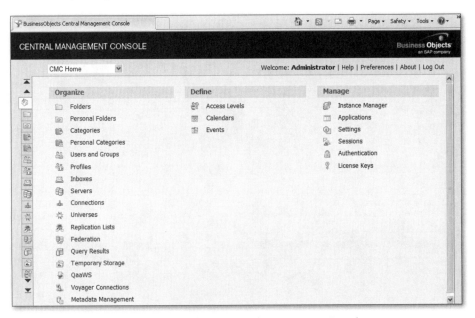

Figure 5.5 SAP BusinessObjects Central Management Console

In SAP Business-Objects XI 4.0, audit and monitoring are controlled from the CMC

Controlling audit and monitoring

Starting with the SAP BusinessObjects BI 4.0 version, the CMC also provides a central place to control audit (although audit was available in previous versions) and a central place to control monitoring (see details of those capabilities earlier in Section 5.1.3, Auditing and Monitoring).

Thanks to the design of the platform, security model, and CMC, administration tasks can be delegated at various levels so there can be multiple administrators.

 Example

> In shared deployments, multiple departments or businesses share the same BI platform. Although a general administrator sits in IT and oversees the entire platform, each business has its own administrators who only see and deal with their group of users in the system. This allows for a very flexible and decentralized model.

Lifecycle Management

Proper lifecycle management is key to the availability of the BI applications and compliance with standards and regulations. Most often, updates or additions to BI applications are not done directly to the production system. They have to be verified and accepted prior to being deployed in production.

The *SAP BusinessObjects LifeCycle Manager* is the web-based tool that enables organizations to move BI content from one system to another system. The tool also allows organizations to manage BI resource dependencies, manage different versions of BI objects, and roll back a promoted resource to restore the destination system to its previous state.

SAP Business-
Objects LifeCycle
Manager

 Example

> Let's assume a project leader asks the administrator to promote a new dashboard from the test environment to the production environment. However, for an undetermined reason, the dashboard failed to open while in production. In this case, the administrator can roll back the promotion and restore the previous version of the dashboard in just a few clicks — avoiding a major business disruption.

Figure 5.6 shows the SAP BusinessObjects LifeCycle Manager.

Figure 5.6 SAP BusinessObjects LifeCycle Manager

Upgrade and Migration

During the life of your BI system, chances are that you will need to upgrade the system at least once, if not more often, to introduce new capabilities or keep up with the versions in support.

The Import Wizard is available in SAP Business-Objects versions prior to XI 4.0

In SAP BusinessObjects versions prior to 4.0, the *Import Wizard* (shown in Figure 5.7) is a Windows application that enables administrators to import objects, users, groups, folders, events, server groups, repository objects, and calendars from one environment to another.

Figure 5.7 Import Wizard

It also allows administrators to create Business Intelligence Archive Resource (BIAR) files, which can be used for disaster recovery or migration purposes.

Starting with version 4.0, upgrade was simplified by introducing the *Upgrade Management tool*, shown in Figure 5.8, which provides simple wizard-based workflows to move all of the security and BI content from an existing system to a newer system version.

> The Upgrade Management tool replaces the Import Wizard

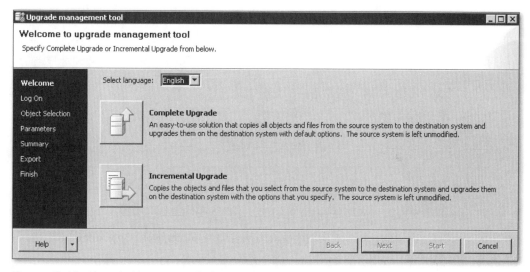

Figure 5.8   The Upgrade Management Tool in BI 4.0

Now that we've covered the need for a BI platform, we're ready to move on to detailing the SAP BusinessObjects BI solutions.

SAP BusinessObjects Business Intelligence Solutions

The SAP BusinessObjects BI solution covers the entire range of the Business Intelligence pyramid. In the previous section, you saw how the BI platform provides the underlying technical architecture to orchestrate the full solution and ensure the best economy of scale. Now let's take a deeper look at the different client components of the SAP BusinessObjects BI solution and how they fit together to deliver an enterprise class solution. Figure 5.9 shows the overall structure of the portfolio. At the bottom, in blue, you see the various data sources that can be accessed. The enterprise platform that we just discussed provides the common services to the BI solutions. Then, at the top, the reporting tools are organized by segment, which we're going to discuss in detail in this chapter.

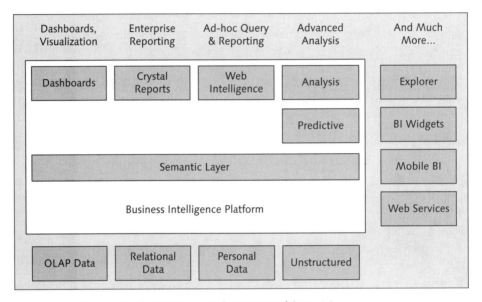

Figure 5.9 The SAP BusinessObjects BI Portfolio in 4.0

The Semantic Layer

The concept of the semantic layer materialized through the universes remains one of the most important concepts in the SAP Business-Objects BI solution. It is key to the objective of extending the reach of information to all users in the organization while allowing them self-service access.

Ex Example

Imagine a user who wants to create a report with email address from cus-tomers. Without a semantic layer, the user would have to know that the email address is stored in the column SMTP_ADDR of Table ADR6 and issue the corresponding SQL statement. This is obviously out of reach for most business users, which limits self-service access to information.

The role of the semantic layer is to abstract the complexity of the data structure, tables, columns, technical names, and so on, to represent those data items in a way that is meaningful to a business user, that is, through the use of *business objects*.

The universe exposes items relevant to the user's business and allows the user to build a query

 The Previous Example Revisited

The business user sees an object "email" in the list of available objects, drags and drops it along with the object "customer," and the corresponding query is automatically generated. We now have a self-service solution where business users directly access the data they need when they need it.

Additionally, the semantic layer provides a number of services that allow very advanced queries to be performed through aggregations, projections, calculations, contexts, security, and merging data.

The business objects just defined are grouped into classes. Objects and classes are both visible to SAP BusinessObjects Web Intelligence users.

Classes, which represent a category of objects, are logical groupings of objects within a universe. The name of a class should indicate the category of the objects that it contains. A class can be divided hierarchically into subclasses, for example, "Store" and "Store Details" in Figure 5.10.

The name of an object should be drawn from the business vocabulary of the targeted user group. Objects used in a universe, shown in Figure 5.10, by a product manager could be Product, Lifecycle, or Release Date. A universe for a financial analyst could contain objects such as Revenue, Profit Margin, or Return on Investment.

Objects can be qualified into three different types:

> Dimension
> Detail
> Measure

Figure 5.10 and Table 5.1 illustrate and provide more detail on the objects and their descriptions.

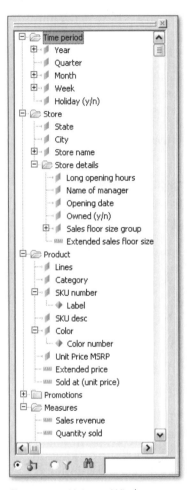

Figure 5.10   Universe Window

Universes are typically designed by a team technically competent with the database structure and with the business meaning of the data. Most often this is a virtual team between the business and IT.

Object Type	Description
Dimension	Provide parameters for analysis. Dimensions typically relate to a hierarchy such as geography, product, or time. Example: Last Name and City_ID.
Detail	Provide a description of a dimension but are not the focus for analysis. Example: Phone Number.
Measure	Convey numeric information that is used to quantify a dimension object. Example: Sales Revenue.

Table 5.1 Object Types

The Universe Designer, as shown in Figure 5.11, is the Windows client tool used to design and publish the universes in SAP Business-Objects XI 3.x and below. It also ships with version 4.0 under the name of the Universe Design Tool. Both those tools produce a file with the historical .unv extension, which is still fully relevant and useable in the newer release.

Universe Design Tool designs new universes in SAP Business-Objects BI 4.0

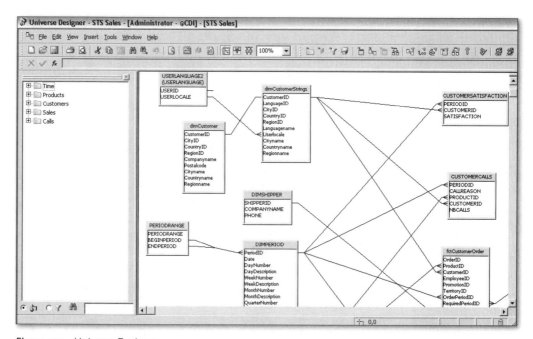

Figure 5.11 Universe Designer

Starting with SAP BusinessObjects BI 4.0, a new universe format was introduced, producing a file with the .unx extension. The new format is generated using the Windows client tool named *Information Design Tool* and introduces powerful new features such as the full native support of hierarchical data and the in-memory merging of multiple data sources.

 Note

> For a smooth transition and investment protection, SAP ships both tools so that existing customers can upgrade to the new platform without disruption and adopt the new universe features at their own pace.

Enterprise Reporting

Crystal Reports is the enterprise reporting tool of choice

Crystal Reports provides the reporting component of SAP BusinessObjects. Crystal Reports is designed to work with almost any database currently in existence. The tool makes it easy to create not only simple reports but also complex or specialized reports. It is also the SAP standard reporting tool for all SAP products ranging from SAP Business One to the SAP Business Suite. Let's take a look at some of the capabilities of Crystal Reports.

Report Creation Wizards

Crystal Reports comes with four different report creation wizards. These wizards can be used to create and build the report or to build the base and then allow for advanced editing. They all contain several screens that walk users through the process of building the respective report.

> **Standard:** This creation wizard, shown in Figure 5.12, is the most generic of the report makers. It allows you to select the tables and fields from a data source. From there, you can specify grouping, summarization, and sorting criteria. Finally, it allows you to add a chart and select records.

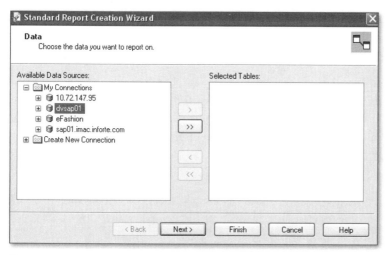

Figure 5.12   Standard Report Creation Wizard

> **Crosstab:** This creation wizard guides you through the creation and formatting of a crosstab report.

> **Mailing Label:** This creation wizard helps you create mailing labels. You can select a commercial type of label or define your own.

> **OLAP:** This creation wizard guides you through the creation of an online analytical processing report where the data is displayed as a grid object. It is similar to the Crosstab wizard, but designed specifically for connecting to OLAP data.

Record Selection

Crystal Reports can also select records from the data source. This means that the data returned to the report when it is run does not include all values in the database but just the specific ones required by you, the end user. For example, you may not want to see all of the sales records for the whole company but only the ones that apply to your region. Record selection only pulls the relevant records from the database.

Sorting, Grouping, and Totaling

Sorting refers to putting the data in some kind of meaningful order.   Sorting
Sorting can occur in two directions: ascending order, in which records

5

are sorted smallest to largest (1 to 9, A to Z, False to True), or descending order, in which records are sorted largest to smallest (9 to 1, Z to A, True to False).

Grouping data

Grouping allows an end user to sort and break up the data records into meaningful groups. For example, you might want to group customers or vendors into regions. Grouping can also be sorted in ascending and descending order, and can also be sorted in a user-specified order or in the original order in which the data records are stored in the database.

Totaling

Totaling allows end users to insert summaries or calculations into the report object based on groupings and overall totals. Running totals are also possible with Crystal Reports.

Formatting

Formatting is one of the most powerful capabilities of Crystal Reports because it allows you to generate pixel-perfect reports that can be used for a variety of purposes. Formatting can be absolute, or it can be set conditionally by using formulas in the Crystal Report. Absolute formatting always remains as defined, whereas conditional formatting changes depending on the value in the report.

Ex Example

An example of absolute formatting is a report defined so that headers are in bold font and table cells have a gray background. The same report using conditional formatting can be defined so that headers are still bold and will remain bold. But table cells will be all gray except when a negative figure is displayed. In that case, this particular cell background turns red.

Formulas

Formulas are another prominent feature that enables organizations to build powerful reports. Some examples of common uses of formulas in Crystal Reports are listed here:

> Creating calculated fields for the report

> Formatting text on the report

> Pulling out a portion, or portions, of a text string

> Extracting parts of a date

> Using custom-built functions

 Note

Although we've described the most commonly used capabilities in Crystal Reports, it doesn't stop there. Additional capabilities include the following:

> Multiple Section reports

> Charting

> Mapping

> OLE

> Building custom queries

> Report alerts

> Parameter fields and prompting

> Subreports

The release of Crystal Reports 2008 has seen some additional capabilities added to the powerful report-authoring tool. Crystal Reports 2008 supports the embedding of Adobe Flash files (SWF) into the report object, which means that organizations can build "flashier" reports and provide additional capabilities. For example, you could use the SWF file to do database write-back, as shown in Figure 5.13.

Crystal Reports 2008 comes with additional capabilities

Crystal Reports 2008 also includes the Parameter Panel, as shown in Figure 5.14. This functionality allows end users to set parameter values on the report, without refreshing the data that can change the report formatting, sorting, and filtering.

The Parameter Panel allows users to change report parameters

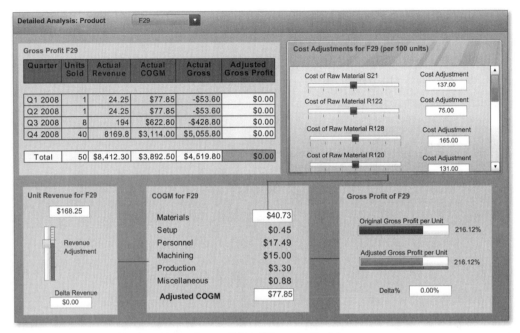

Figure 5.13   On-Report What-If Scenario Model

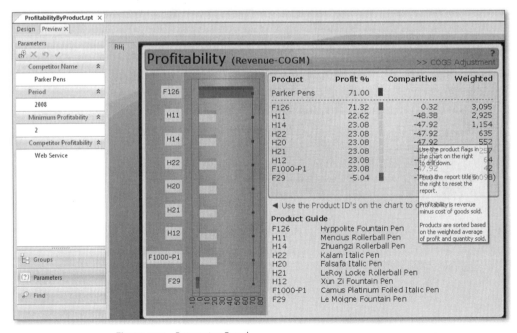

Figure 5.14   Parameter Panel

Finally, Crystal Reports 2008 has added the ability to consume data from XML and Web services with a dedicated database driver. Web services created with Simple Object Access Protocol (SOAP) 1.2 are accessible to Crystal Reports. This includes newer architectures, such as .NET 3.0 and ADO.NET Dataset, and also supports the integration of third-party mapping tools such as ESRI, as shown in Figure 5.15.

XML and Web services

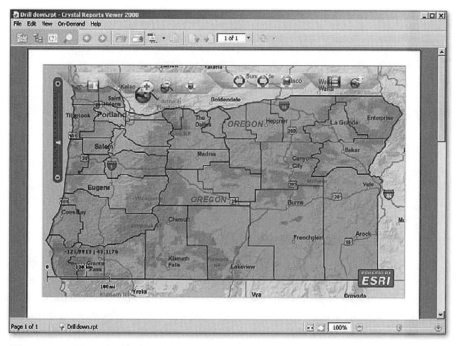

Figure 5.15   ESRI Embedded in a Crystal Report

In short, Crystal Reports is the de facto reporting tool from SAP BusinessObjects. It provides organizations with the capability to create highly formatted, interactive, and professional quality reports using a complete set of layout tools and design controls.

Now that we've covered enterprise reporting, let's take a look at the SAP BusinessObjects solutions for ad hoc reporting.

Ad Hoc Reporting and Analysis

Organizations need access to ad hoc information every day. Many times, users across the enterprise need access to look at information that is not contained in standard operational reports or visualizations. Requests for additional views of data or for up-to-date information often result in user frustration and report backlog with IT.

SAP BusinessObjects Web Intelligence provides end users with self-service access to data, reporting, and intuitive information analysis.

Depending on the business needs and the administration constraints, multiple choices are available for deploying interactive analysis:

> A full HTML interface with zero footprint or download to the client machine provides an already rich ad hoc experience.
> A Java panel allows for more features and functions while requiring a runtime and applet on the client.
> The Rich Client is a Windows client that offers all of the features of the Java panel plus the ability to work disconnected from the BI platform.

In the typical ad hoc scenario, if you are given the report authoring privileges, you are presented with a list of universes that you have access to per your security settings (as we touched on in Section 5.2.1, The Semantic Layer).

The query panel, as shown in Figure 5.16, allows you to drag and drop the components relevant to your query and create the associated report.

 Example

Figure 5.16 displays on the left panel a tree structure of the objects available in an inventory management universe. The objects "Line," "Category," "Product Name," "Stock Level," "Min Stock Level," "Max Stock Level," "Year-Month," and others were selected by the business user and now appear on the top-right panel. Upon execution, this query will generate a report giving the evolution of stocks per product/product category/product line.

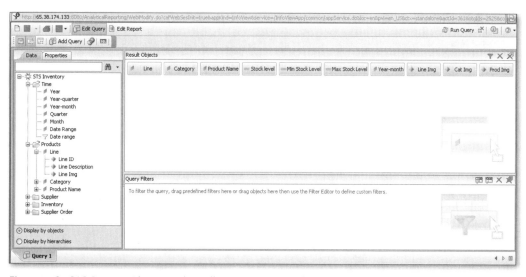

Figure 5.16 SAP BusinessObjects Web Intelligence Query Panel

After the query is built and executed, the tool fetches the data and creates a *microcube,* which is a local storage of the data embedded within the report file. The microcube is used to navigate and interact with the report without the need to re-query the data warehouse.

The microcube stores the data within the report

The microcube is also the key element of the technology allowing for offline (disconnected from the network) view and interaction with the reports.

The Web Intelligence report panel (Figure 5.17) is very rich and interactive depending on the deployment option you choose. The new version, introduced with SAP BusinessObjects 4.0, brings a brand new charting engine among numerous other improvements (see the What's New guide that comes with the release documentation, also available through the SAP Support Portal at *http://service.sap.com/support*).

The capabilities that SAP BusinessObjects Web Intelligence extends to business users include the following:

> View report metadata

> View, edit, and remove report, section, or block filters

> Format and resize cells, tables, and charts

107

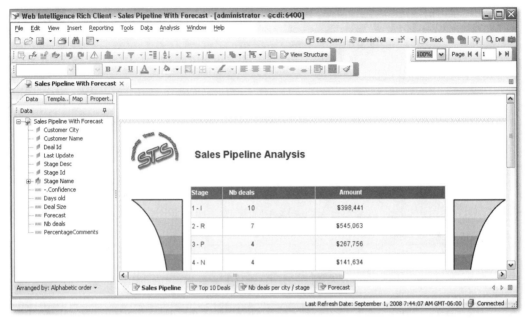

Figure 5.17 Web Intelligence Report Panel

> Recombine report objects and variables in tables and charts

> Set breaks and sorts

> Insert calculations

> Add rows and columns to tables

> Create and duplicate tables and charts

> Turn a grid into a chart or a chart into a grid

> Create formulas and variables

> Edit cell formulas in place

Administrators and universe designers have many options to fine-tune what ad hoc query users can actually do to limit unexpected impact on the underlying data warehouse.

SAP BusinessObjects Web Intelligence introduces a new BI component to SAP customers.

But Web Intelligence, now Interactive Analysis, is more than just an ad hoc query tool. It generates a format that remains highly interactive at viewing time and is widely used to publish interactive data to a larger population of report consumers.

Interactivity of the final report with consumers is a key value to Interactive Analysis

 Example

We typically see a smaller number of advanced business users build reports that can be used by a larger population provided there is some built-in flexibility, such as filters, swapping columns, sorting, and so on, which report consumers can easily perform without being report authors or accessing the authoring tools.

In addition, *Query as a Web Service* (QaaWS) allows BI content to be delivered to any interface that can process Web services. Users can define their own query from a universe and then easily and securely publish that query as a standalone Web service (Figure 5.18).

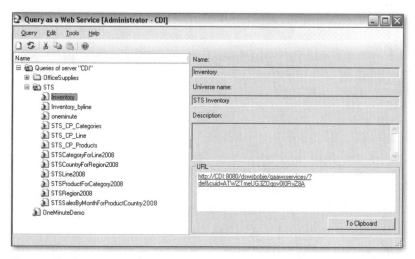

Figure 5.18 Query as a Web Service

Advanced Analytics

The advanced analytics solutions from SAP BusinessObjects went through a major revamping following the integration into the SAP system, so let's take a look at the roadmap for each.

SAP BusinessObjects Voyager

Voyager is replaced by Advanced Analysis

Available up to the SAP BusinessObjects XI 3.x version, SAP Business-Objects Voyager enables business analysts to explore and use online analytical processing (OLAP) data to answer business questions, discover trends, and share that analysis with others in the organization. You can create a workspace in a web-based application, add crosstab and chart objects, connect those objects to OLAP data sources, and then interactively define the queries to explore the data, as shown in Figure 5.19.

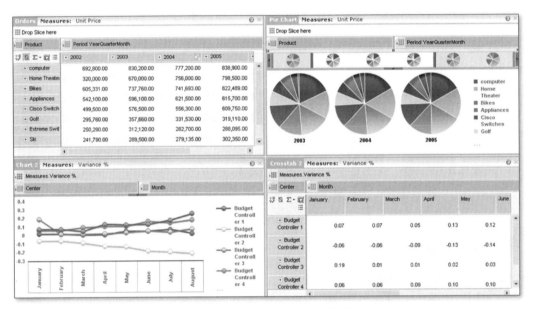

Figure 5.19 SAP BusinessObjects Voyager Workspace

OLAP data cubes are used in solving more BI requirements.

 OLAP Example

> An example of one of those requirements is to give an analyst the ability to view periods between Q1 and Q4 in any financial year and look at the trends that exist in sales of different products in different regions.

These trends and the complex patterns they contain can be represented in different types of visualizations, as shown in Figure 5.20.

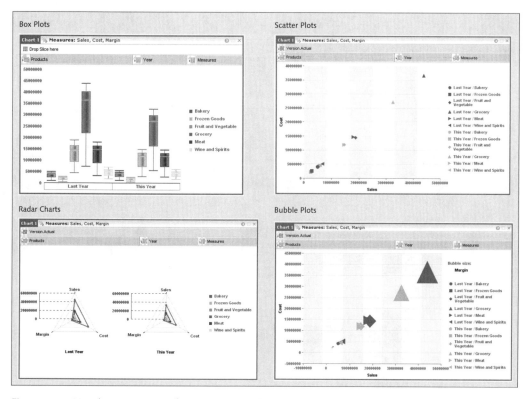

Figure 5.20 Visualization Options for SAP BusinessObjects Voyager

Voyager can simultaneously show multiple views of the same OLAP cube or of different OLAP cubes within the same workspace. For example, an analyst can look at sales data from an SAP NetWeaver BW cube on the same page as plan data from an Oracle Hyperion Essbase cube (Figure 5.21).

SAP BusinessObjects Voyager supports the data sources listed in Table 5.2.

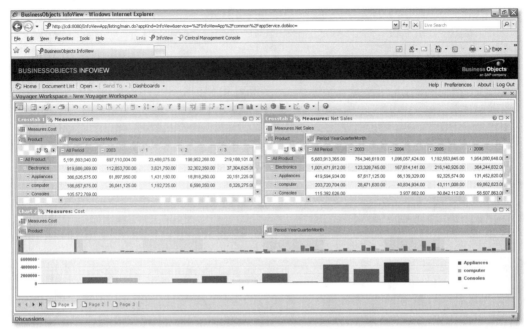

Figure 5.21 Simultaneous Access to Multiple OLAP Cubes

Provider Name	Data Connector
EPM MDX Connector	BusinessObjects EPM Profitability MDX Connector
Hyperion Essbase Server 7.1.x	Hyperion Essbase API 7.1.x
Hyperion System 9	Hyperion Essbase Client 9.0 Hyperion Essbase Client 9.2 Hyperion Essbase Client 9.3
Microsoft SQL Server Analysis Services 2000 SP4	Microsoft SQL Server 2000 Analysis 8.0 OLE DB Provider SP4
Microsoft SQL Server Analysis Services 2005 SP1	Microsoft SQL Server 2005 Analysis 9.0 OLE DB Provider SP1
Microsoft SQL Server Analysis Services 2005 SP2	Microsoft SQL Server 2005 Analysis 9.0 OLE DB Provider SP2

Table 5.2 Data Sources Supported by Voyager

Provider Name	Data Connector
Microsoft SQL Server Analysis Services 2008	Microsoft SQL Server 2008 Analysis 10.0 OLE DB Provider
SAP BW 3.5	
SAP NetWeaver BI 7.0	
SAP NetWeaver BI 7.02	

Table 5.2 Data Sources Supported by Voyager (Cont.)

SAP BusinessObjects Analysis

SAP BusinessObjects Analysis is the new generation OLAP analysis tool from SAP BusinessObjects. As such, it shares the same objectives as Voyager (discussed in the previous section) and brings together the best of the technology inherited from Business Objects, the ad hoc, interactive design of Voyager, with the advanced OLAP exploration concepts from SAP Business Explorer.

SAP Business-Objects Analysis is the new generation OLAP tool

SAP BusinessObjects Analysis ships in two versions:

> **SAP BusinessObjects Analysis, edition for Microsoft Office**: As shown in Figure 5.22, this is a Microsoft Excel add-in geared toward analysts who spend most of their time in Microsoft Office. It is also positioned by SAP as the premium alternative to SAP BEx Analyzer for SAP customers. The edition for Microsoft Office is compatible with the SAP BusinessObjects XI 3.1 platform, so it doesn't require the newer BI 4.0.

> **SAP BusinessObjects Analysis, edition for OLAP**: This is the web-based version of SAP BusinessObjects Analysis shown in Figure 5.23. It is recommended to business analysts who need to run ad hoc OLAP analysis or share OLAP workspaces with others as explained in the previous section, SAP BusinessObjects Voyager. The Web edition ships with SAP BusinessObjects BI 4.0.

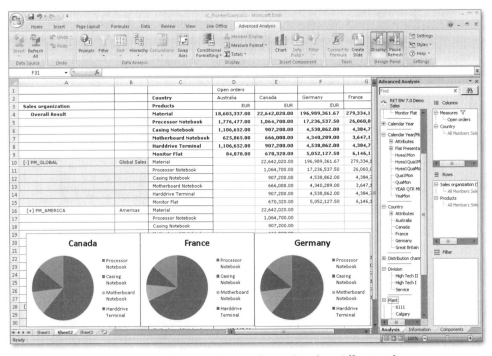

Figure 5.22   SAP BusinessObjects Advanced Analysis Office Interface

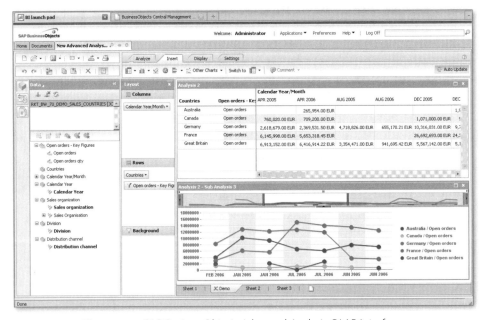

Figure 5.23   SAP BusinessObjects Advanced Analysis OLAP Interface

In the common use case where an analyst wants to present the result of his analysis to a wider audience that may not have access to the OLAP tools, SAP BusinessObjects Analysis provides multiple options:

> If using the edition for Microsoft Office, the business analyst benefits from the charting capabilities of Excel and the options to use the data and charts in PowerPoint.

> When using the edition for Microsoft Office or the Web edition, the business analyst can also save the query resulting from the analysis to consume it in a Crystal Report or SAP BusinessObjects Web Intelligence report and thus getting access to the reporting and interactivity power of those tools from the suite.

If you already use SAP and have a large investment in SAP BEx, you should note that SAP BusinessObjects Analysis can leverage existing SAP BEx queries as a data source.

SAP BusinessObjects Advanced Analysis protects existing investments in SAP BEx queries

SAP BusinessObjects Predictive Workbench

SAP BusinessObjects Predictive Workbench software by IBM allows data analysts as well as business users to mine data and perform statistical analysis. The application is based on SPSS Clementine 12.0.1.

The application allows SAP BusinessObjects to use universes as data sources, whether they use relational or OLAP databases. The SAP BusinessObjects Predictive Workbench allows users to mine data for many different types of business scenarios. For example, you can define and execute predictive analysis by building a model that analyzes a data set to identify the variables that affect customer loss.

Predictive analysis can also be embedded in BI applications to recommend sales opportunities based on market analysis. Some examples of other types of data mining applications include the following:

Mine data for different types of business scenarios

> **Direct mail:** Determine which demographic groups have the highest response rate. Use this information to maximize the response to future mailing.

> **Credit scoring:** Use an individual's credit history to make credit decisions.

> **Human resources:** Understand past hiring practices and create decision rules to streamline the hiring process.

> **Medical research:** Create decision rules that suggest appropriate procedures based on medical evidence.

> **Market analysis:** Determine which variables, such as geography, price, and customer characteristics, are associated with sales.

> **Quality control:** Analyze data from product manufacturing and identify variables determining product defects.

> **Policy studies:** Use survey data to formulate policy by applying decision rules to select the most important variables.

> **Health care:** Combine user surveys and clinical data to discover variables that contribute to health.

SAP BusinessObjects SET Analysis

SAP BusinessObjects SET Analysis is an application that ships up to SAP BusinessObjects XI 3.1 and then is being retired. We do not recommend starting any new project with this tool. However, you should understand the application because SAP BusinessObjects XI 3.1 is widely deployed and maintained until 2015 (2017 with extended maintenance).

SAP Business-
Objects SET Analysis
is being retired
after version 3.1

SAP BusinessObjects SET Analysis allows data analysts to define complex selections and custom groupings of customers, products, or other individual items in a database. They allow for the identification and targeting of groups of clients based on different criteria. For example, you might want to target all clients that live in a certain geographical region, who rent apartments, above a certain age, and don't have children. The subject identifies the central theme for the sets that are based on it. Customers, clients, and vendors can be classified, analyzed, and treated in different ways using set techniques.

Sets have the following attributes:

> Sets contain items based on a single subject that determines the primary key.

> Sets are uniquely identified by name, folder, and author.

> Sets can have a description.

> Sets have a last modified date.

> Sets are allocated to a folder.

> Sets contain a count of the members if the set has been built; otherwise, it just has a definition.

> Sets contain members that can accumulate a score based on the weightings a user defines.

> Sets can be processed from many steps, with each step based on a single table or view.

Sets help organizations understand how groups and segments contribute to overall performance by simplifying and accelerating the data segmentation process. They are able to address the following types of business questions:

> Turnover

> Cross-selling

> Customer scoring (ranking)

> Data sampling

> Segment interaction

> List management

> Marketing stratification

Dashboards and Visualization

The SAP BusinessObjects dashboarding and visualization tool set allows organizations to transform their data into visual representations of key metrics and information.

Transform data into visual representations of key metrics and information

These dashboards and visualizations can be as simple as a series of metrics to as complex as a "what-if" scenario. Used in conjunction with SAP BusinessObjects Enterprise, these visualizations can be pulled from multiple data sources to provide a holistic view of the organization and how it's performing. Let's take a look at some of these tools.

SAP Business-Objects dashboarding and visualization

SAP BusinessObjects Xcelsius Enterprise

SAP BusinessObjects Xcelsius Enterprise, which may also appear under the new name of SAP BusinessObjects Dashboards, is a data visualization software tool that enables users to create dynamic and interactive models that can be added to dashboards and exported for delivery in a variety of formats.

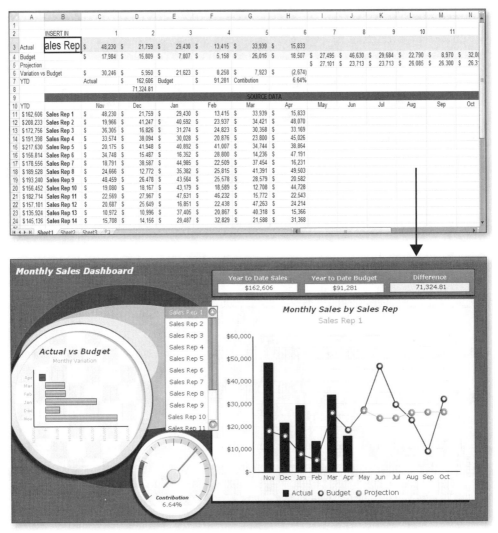

Figure 5.24 Excel to SAP BusinessObjects Xcelsius Enterprise Visualization

The software includes a fully functional Excel spreadsheet. Data and formulas can be imported or entered directly into the embedded spreadsheet and then modified as required. Figure 5.24 shows an Excel to SAP BusinessObjects Xcelsius Enterprise visualization.

Users simply place components on the canvas and link them to the data in a spreadsheet. SAP BusinessObjects Xcelsius Enterprise offers a wide range of components, including dials, gauges, charts, maps, picklists, and sliders. These components can be configured to display data directly from the spreadsheet, to write data to the spreadsheet so that it can be used by other components, or to accept data from end users when the model is running (Figure 5.25).

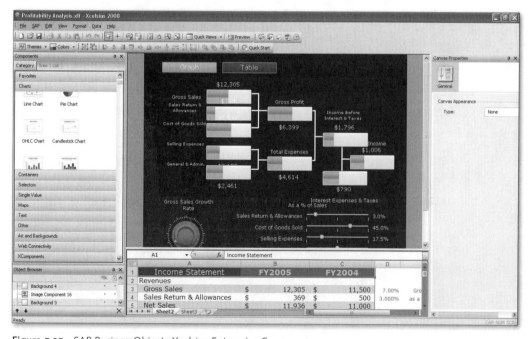

Figure 5.25 SAP BusinessObjects Xcelsius Enterprise Canvas

A commonly used approach with this software is the *what-if*, which is a mathematical model that is built on and accepts quantitative inputs to determine the effect on the model.

For example, a profitability what-if model might look at the costs of raw materials for a product. The model can be set up to look at how

Microsoft Excel to SAP Business-Objects Xcelsius Enterprise visualization

What-if analysis allows dynamic visualization of various scenarios

variations in the cost of the raw materials will affect the gross profit of the product, as shown in Figures 5.26 and 5.27.

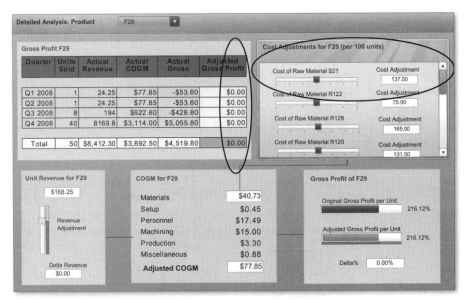

Figure 5.26   What-If Analysis 1

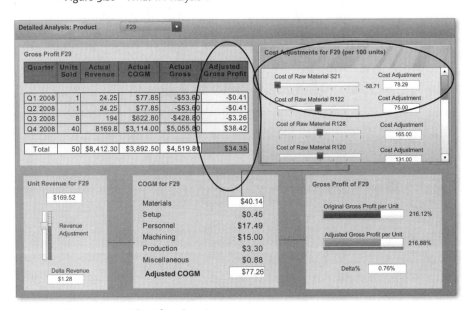

Figure 5.27   What-If Analysis 2

SAP BusinessObjects Xcelsius Enterprise models conform to the Shockwave Flash (SWF) file format. SWF is a vector-based graphics format designed to run in the Adobe Flash Player. Because a Shockwave file is vector-based, its graphics are scalable and play back smoothly on any screen size and across multiple platforms.

Vector-based files usually have a smaller file size than other types of animations. These models are extremely powerful and can be used to represent even operational data in an easy-to-read format. Figure 5.28 illustrates this in an SAP BusinessObjects Xcelsius Enterprise Consolidated Statement of Income.

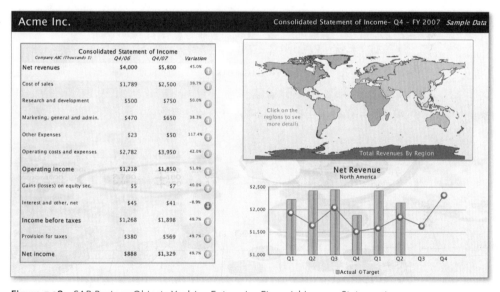

Figure 5.28 SAP BusinessObjects Xcelsius Enterprise Financial Income Statement

The SAP BusinessObjects Xcelsius Enterprise models can be exported into a variety of formats, such as Flash, PowerPoint, PDF, AIR, Outlook, and HTML. These models retain their full interactivity and only require Adobe Flash Player to play.

Using SAP BusinessObjects Enterprise, these models can be configured with live data updates from external sources such as XML, portals, Web services, SAP BusinessObjects Live Office, Query as a Web Service, SAP BusinessObjects Explorer queries, and SAP BusinessObjects BI consumer services.

SAP Business-Objects Xcelsius Enterprise publishes dashboards in Flash

SAP Business-Objects Xcelsius Enterprise models can rely on live data when combined with the BI platform

SAP BusinessObjects Dashboard Builder and BI Workspace

The SAP BusinessObjects Dashboard Builder as we know it in versions up to SAP BusinessObjects XI 3.1 is being replaced by BI Workspaces in version 4.0.

The SAP BusinessObjects Dashboard Builder or BI Workspace allows end users to create dashboards that provide visibility into business activities across the organization. It offers dashboard management capabilities. Dashboards in SAP BusinessObjects Enterprise can include the following types of objects:

> SAP BusinessObjects Xcelsius Enterprise (SWF)
> SAP BusinessObjects Web Intelligence
> SAP Crystal Reports
> Adobe Reader PDF documents
> Microsoft Excel spreadsheets
> Microsoft Word documents
> Text files
> Rich Text files
> Microsoft PowerPoint presentations
> Hyperlinks

End users can create, customize, and view the following types of dashboards:

> **Corporate dashboards:** Corporate dashboards contain analytics created either via InfoView or in the corporate dashboards menu for public viewing. A corporate dashboard can have several tabs and subtabs.

With SAP Business-Objects Dashboard Builder, users create their personal portal

> **Personal dashboards:** Personal dashboards incorporate a concept known as "My Dashboards" in SAP BusinessObjects Enterprise. My Dashboard stores end users' personal dashboard tabs, which can contain personal analytics and corporate analytics whose parameters can be modified for the respective end user's personal view. Personal dashboards can contain one or more tabs.

Search and Exploration

Organizations have a need for a simple search and exploration tool. The proliferation of search tools on the Internet, such as Google, has created a skilled group of users that want to quickly answer questions and use a web-based paradigm to do the searching.

The issue that most organizations face when it comes to doing this type of activity is that their internal data is not exposed and indexed by the Google search engine.

This is where the SAP BusinessObjects Explorer solution comes in. Originally known as Polestar, this recently rebranded product combines the simplicity and speed of the Internet with high performance and instant response times. Users can find relevant information that lies hidden in both SAP and non-SAP data sources.

SAP Business-Objects Explorer changes the paradigm to data access

Data sources and metadata are pre-indexed so that enterprise data sources such as operational systems and data warehouses can be searched with almost instantaneous speeds. The overall end user experience is as easy as browsing an online retailer. The added benefit is that no preexisting reports or metrics need to be built. They are all encapsulated within the SAP BusinessObjects Explorer interface.

The first step for a user is to search for a term, as shown in Figure 5.29, in the SAP BusinessObjects Explorer Search Panel.

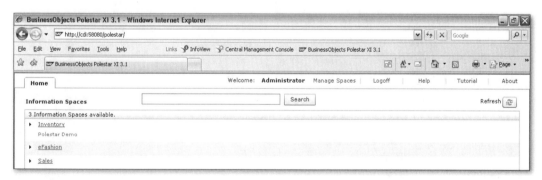

Figure 5.29 SAP BusinessObjects Explorer Search Panel

All relevant hits are then returned to the user, as shown in Figure 5.30.

Figure 5.30   SAP BusinessObjects Explorer Search Result Panel

The user can then view the resulting information in the Exploration Panel, as shown in Figure 5.31.

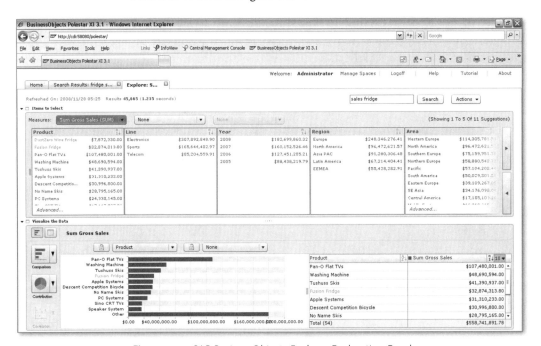

Figure 5.31   SAP BusinessObjects Explorer Exploration Panel

SAP BusinessObjects Explorer allows end users to search across all data sources and perform contextual exploration. It provides automated relevancy and chart generation, as well as high performance and scalability. SAP BusinessObjects Explorer is an ideal addition for customers in SAP and non-SAP environments to provide a Google-like interface as a BI solution.

The Exploration Panel displays a default layout chosen by the tool as the most pertinent

SAP StreamWork and SAP BusinessObjects BI OnDemand

Software as a Service (SaaS) has been a growing market over the past couple years. The business model pioneered by SalesForce.com is based on a technical platform fully hosted by the vendor while businesses subscribe to the service as needed.

SAP StreamWork and SAP BusinessObjects BI OnDemand constitute the SaaS offering in the SAP BusinessObjects portfolio. This model offers a couple advantages and is worth considering in complement with the traditional on-premise model:

> The platform is completely hosted and maintained by the vendor. This eliminates hidden costs and lets the vendor manage the availability.

> Solutions can be subscribed and unsubscribed as needed. No upfront cost needs to be amortized over the years

> Businesses can often use operational budgets to subscribe to these services, giving them more control and flexibility over both the solution and their investments choice.

> Upon subscription, the solution is immediately available to the business. No installation, deployment, or other configuration is needed from IT.

> Enterprise versions bridge the on-demand world with the on-premise world and allow the solutions to benefit from corporate data and user authentication services.

Let's review the services offered by SAP StreamWork and SAP BusinessObjects BI OnDemand.

SAP StreamWork

SAP StreamWork in the next step in BI

SAP StreamWork is very specific because it is more a collaboration tool than a pure BI player. SAP StreamWork is actually the next step in BI. While BI starts with collecting data and analyzing it, the next step in the process is often to make decisions based on the findings. Decisions are usually discussed and made by a group of people rather than a single individual, which is where SAP StreamWork helps by allowing people to collaborate.

 Example

> Let's assume someone needs to involve a couple of stakeholders to make a decision on a new product feature. Instead of calling a meeting, they could open a SAP StreamWork activity, invite all stakeholders to this activity, attach all of the relevant material and references, and then use the numerous widgets to have a discussion online in SAP StreamWork. Eventually, a decision is made. Stakeholders can sign off in SAP Stream-Work, and the activity is closed but kept in the archive for a full track of record.

Activities are the work entities in SAP StreamWork, somewhat like a report or a document in other tools

Let's now look at the capabilities of the solution. Upon logon in SAP StreamWork, you are presented with your list of activities as shown in Figure 5.32. Each activity represents a specific decision or discussion item that is by nature limited in time and involves a group of people. By default, activities are sorted so the most recently updated appears first.

You can quickly determine if you have pending action items on a specific activity through the action item column as represented by the number 1 in the first activity of Figure 5.32.

 Tip

> You can sign up for free and try the solution. A free account may open up to five activities and 125MB of storage space. Just connect to *https://streamwork.com/*, create an account, and try it with a couple of coworkers.

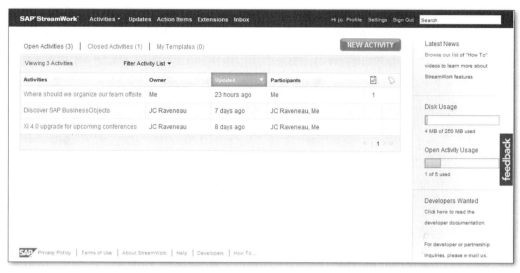

Figure 5.32 SAP StreamWork Activity Page

Each activity can be built by the owner and participants out of a collection of widgets called *tools* in SAP StreamWork and that embed the best practices of collaboration and decision making. Although SAP StreamWork was often compared to Google Wave, the tools and best practices in SAP StreamWork make its value.

New tools are being developed regularly by both SAP and partners. At this time the collection includes the following:

> Agenda uses SAP StreamWork in support of a live meeting with collaboratively creating an agenda and following up on it.

> Time Management graphically represents the urgency and importance of your tasks and helps you define priorities.

> Timeline displays milestones on a calendar.

> Analysis matrix include SWOT, Product Portfolio, Cost/Benefits, PICK and Stakeholders analysis.

> A number of tools, including voting widgets, pro-con tables, and ranking to structure the decision-making process.

> Basic plain text and threaded discussions for free-form exchanges.

Tools in SAP StreamWork provide guidance and best practices for the collaboration and decision process

Figure 5.33 shows a decision activity. The owner used a text tool at the top as a readme, and then a pro-con table to discuss the possible locations for a team offsite.

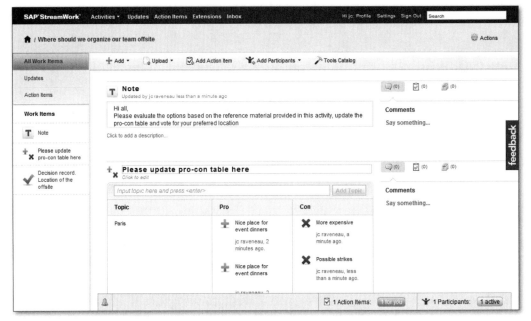

Figure 5.33 Typical Structure for a SAP StreamWork Activity

As you can see in Figure 5.33, the left-hand panel displays the overall structure of the activity and allows for quick access to each item. Comments and action items can be associated with each tool in the activity to encourage the discussion and collaboration.

SAP StreamWork includes a highly customizable notification system — Users can define their email notification preferences for each event generated by the application such as when a contributor comments in an activity, accepts an invitation to collaborate, or votes in a poll.

 Go Personal

SAP StreamWork is also great to organize your personal social events, so you may want to consider creating a personal account as well.

Documents such as PowerPoint presentations and Excel spreadsheets can be attached in support of the discussion. You can also upload and actually embed a fully functional SAP BusinessObjects Xcelsius Enterprise dashboard as shown in Figure 5.34. This gives you an idea of what the solution could become when you include any of the SAP BusinessObjects BI content in the SAP StreamWork decision process.

SAP Business-Objects Xcelsius Enterprise dashboards can be embedded while waiting for more BI content in the future

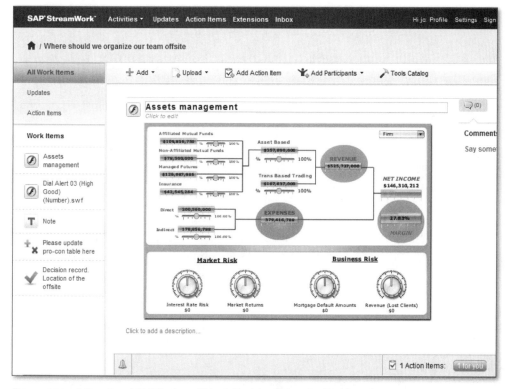

Figure 5.34 A Functional SAP BusinessObjects Xcelsius Enterprise Dashboard Embedded in SAP StreamWork

One key value of the SAP StreamWork solution is the persistence of the information and decision process. The classic meetings hardly track some action items and decisions via meeting minutes, and most of the process is lost along with valuable knowledge. With SAP StreamWork, a closed activity is retained for future reference:

SAP StreamWork captures the decision process as an additional asset to the business

> Anyone who is invited to join a decision group after it started has the full track of record and supporting material to quickly catch-up with the group. This avoids time consuming ramp-up and re-discussion of closed items.

> SAP StreamWork ensures full transparency in the decision process so there is less questioning and re-opening of decisions and more trust overall.

Overall, SAP StreamWork delivers the following:

> A fully hosted collaborative decision-making platform

> Best practices for a guided and more efficient decision process

> Reusable decision processes as an asset to your business

> Transparency and trust for a more efficient business

Now that we looked at SAP StreamWork, let's review the second SaaS solution from the SAP BusinessObjects portfolio: SAP BI OnDemand.

SAP BusinessObjects BI OnDemand

Compared to SAP StreamWork, SAP BusinessObjects BI OnDemand is more of a classic BI tool in the sense that it uses some of the concepts from the rest of the BI portfolio. The technical platform is actually based on the SAP BusinessObjects BI platform already discussed in this book.

SAP Business-Objects BI OnDemand is a full BI solution hosted and ready to go

SAP BusinessObjects BI OnDemand uses the same business model as SAP StreamWork:

> A fully hosted technical platform managed by the vendor

> Ready-to-use — no installation or configuration on the client side

> The option to have an enterprise plug-in to benefit from user authentication and corporate data access (requires on-premise installation by IT)

> A free account to get you started with the solution and see how it works for you

> A subscription-based model for an immediate return on investment

Tip

> If you have an SAP StreamWork account, you can use it with SAP Business-Objects BI OnDemand. Connect at *www.ondemand.com/businessintelligence/*.

Let's look at the capabilities:

Datasets

Datasets refer to the collection of data on which you would want to use BI to discover trends, find patterns, and do some exploration. The data may come from different systems and need to be uploaded to SAP BusinessObjects BI OnDemand so it is visible and useable by the application. Currently, datasets can be created from the following sources:

> Excel or .csv files can be uploaded to the SAP BusinessObjects BI OnDemand system to create a dataset.

> Users that have the proper license and universe in place may extract data from a database.

> Other sources such as Saledforce.com and RSS feeds are also available.

> Users can input data manually into the application by populating a blank table

Once uploaded to the application, multiple datasets can be combined if they offer a common dimension.

 Example

> A user creates a dataset from an Excel spreadsheet that contains the date, customer ID, product ordered, quantity, and total value. Then the user creates another dataset from a second Excel spreadsheet that contains the customer ID, company name, and address. Now the user can combine those two datasets in SAP BusinessObjects BI OnDemand, using the item customer ID as the common dimension. This allows the user to associate the company name and address with the orders in reports, charts, and exploration.

Organize and Publish

SAP BusinessObjects BI OnDemand allows you to upload all sorts of content and organize it in a folder structure as shown in Figure 5.35. You can customize the folders at will and apply security to allow you to share some content with a selected set of coworkers.

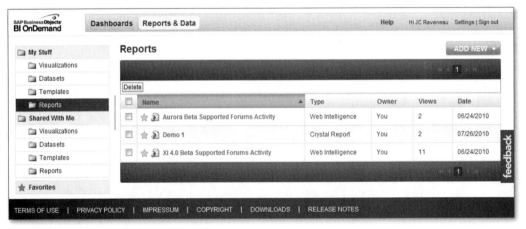

Figure 5.35   SAP BusinessObjects BI OnDemand Main Screen

SAP Business-Objects BI OnDemand can process BI content created with other SAP Business-Objects BI tools

Report

The content you upload can be of any type, but more specifically, you can upload and process in SAP BusinessObjects BI OnDemand Crystal Reports and SAP BusinessObjects Web Intelligence files. This allows you to securely share BI content with others and start collaborating. Users that are licensed and connected to their corporate data via a universe can also create a SAP BusinessObjects Web Intelligence report directly in SAP BusinessObjects BI OnDemand. The SAP BusinessObjects OnDemand Web Intelligence design environment offers most of the features from SAP BusinessObjects Web Intelligence, this includes the following:

> Design tables and charts

> Sections and breaks

> Sorting and calculations

> Full formula language for the creation of advanced variables
> Layout and formatting
> Full interactivity of the final report through toolbar, contextual menu, and input controls

Figure 5.36 shows the SAP BusinessObjects Web Intelligence design environment with an open contextual menu.

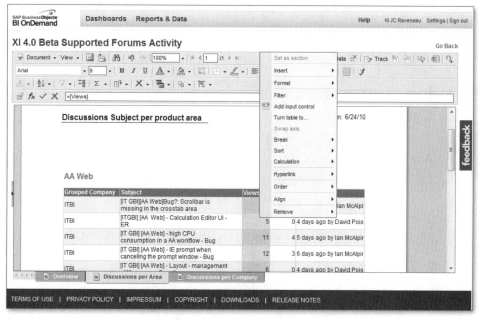

Figure 5.36 SAP BusinessObjects Web Intelligence design in SAP BusinessObjects BI OnDemand

Explore

SAP BusinessObjects BI OnDemand includes a version of SAP Business-Objects Explorer already covered in detail earlier in this chapter. It allows users to upload their Excel spreadsheets and start exploring the data right away. When a user clicks on the Explore tab in the interface, the product parses the content of the spreadsheet and comes back with a suggested starting point as shown in Figure 5.37.

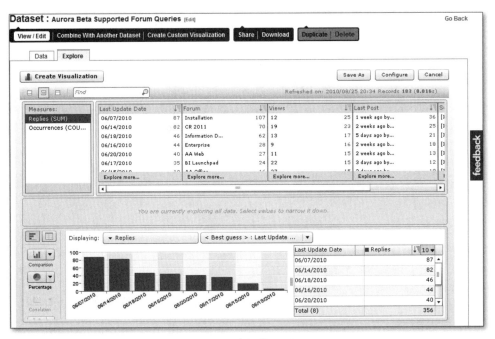

Figure 5.37 "Best Guess" Initial Explorer View

From there, users can start to refine their exploration through the facets, sorting, and charting options. For example, while the initial best guess from the tool was that we wanted to see the number of forum replies per date, we were actually looking for the activity of each forum as a percentage of the total. Consequently we refined the exploration as displayed in Figure 5.38 (pie chart)

Visualizations help you save a graphic snapshot of your exploration

Visualize

After your data exploration leads to the discovery of some trends or pattern that you want to capture, the Create Visualization button allows you to capture the final exploration chart as shown in Figure 5.39. The visualization can be saved as such, along with the underlying data, to be shared with coworkers to support discussions and decisions.

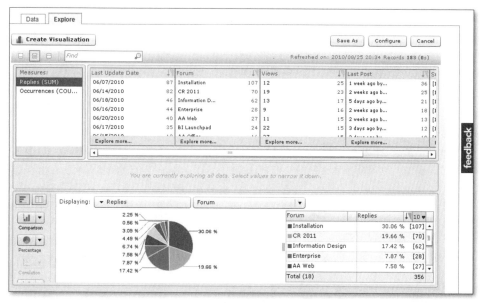

Figure 5.38   Refined Exploration

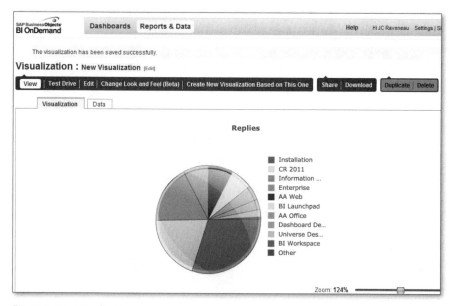

Figure 5.39   Visualization

Additionally, SAP BusinessObjects BI OnDemand can create advanced visualizations similar to the SAP BusinessObjects Xcelsius Enterprise dashboards. We recommend that you refer to Section 5.3.1, SAP BusinessObjects Xcelsius Enterprise, for more details. Users familiar with SAP BusinessObjects Xcelsius Enterprise will recognize the familiar design environment in SAP BusinessObjects BI OnDemand as shown in Figure 5.40.

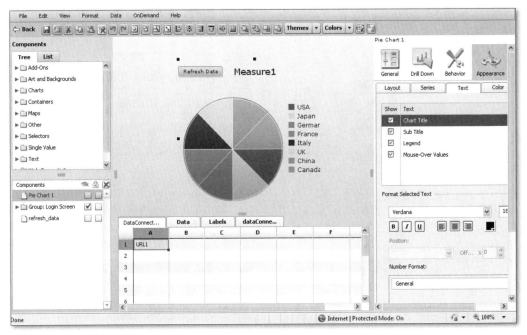

Figure 5.40 Advanced Visualization Design Environment

Dashboards

SAP BusinessObjects BI OnDemand offers the possibility to design your own dashboards in the sense of displaying on one page content from multiple sources, just like a customized portal. This is useful to users who need to have an overview of their business with key indicators that they'll check regularly. Instead of having to open sequentially a series of reports or visualizations, they can put a dashboard layout together and see them all in one place. Dashboards are easily created in a design mode. Figure 5.41 shows the design environment and associated menus. Portlets (each content container) can be resized and organized, and templates offer a couple of common layouts to start with. You may design multiple dashboards that will display on the screen via multiple tabs as shown on Figure 5.41. In design mode, you can drag and drop content to the dashboard from a content toolbox. Only the content in SAP BusinessObjects BI OnDemand may be added to dashboards currently.

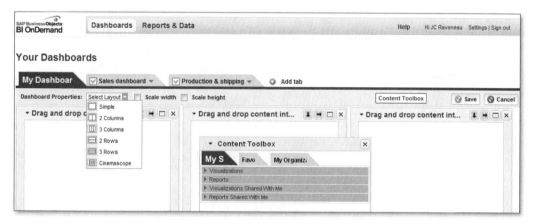

Figure 5.41 Dashboards in Design Mode

In the example of Figure 5.42, we created a dashboard from an SAP BusinessObjects Web Intelligence report and an SAP BusinessObjects Explorer visualization, each displayed in its own portlet.

Add content to a dashboard via the content toolbox

Scheduling

Scheduling allows you to refresh and publish reports automatically. Each time a report gets refreshed with scheduling, it creates a report *instance* that constitutes a snapshot in time of the report. Users can browse and view instances to get historic views of the report. Scheduled refresh offers the options (from the online help) provided in Table 5.3.

Scheduling and instances allow you to take a snapshot of the report and retain historical data

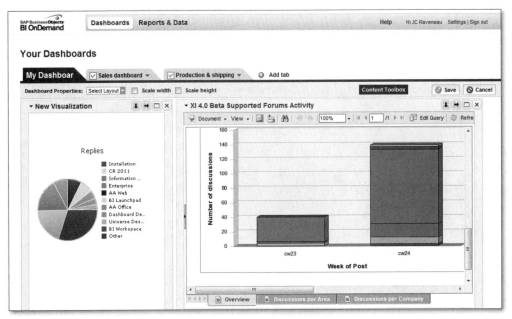

Figure 5.42   Example of SAP BusinessObjects BI OnDemand Dashboard

Recurrence Pattern	Description
Now	The report will be run as soon as you click Schedule.
Once	The report will be run only once. It can be run now or in the future.
Hourly	The report will be run every hour. You can specify at what time it will start, as well as a start and end date.
Daily	The report will be run every day. It can be run once or several times a day. You can specify at what time it will run, as well as a start and end date.
Weekly	The report will be run every week. It can be run once a week or several times a week. You can specify on which days and at what time it will run, as well as and a start and end date.
Monthly	The report will be run every month or every several months. You can specify on which days of the month and at what time it will run, as well as a start and end date.

Table 5.3 Scheduling Options

Tip: Output Formats

> Scheduled reports can be saved in a new format for easy consumption. SAP BusinessObjects Web Intelligence reports can be published as PDF files. SAP Crystal Reports can be published as PDF or CSV. Both can obviously also retain their original format.

Overall SAP BusinessObjects BI OnDemand capabilities make it a fully featured BI platform with the flexibility and accessibility of the SaaS business model.

Summary

The SAP BusinessObjects Enterprise helps organizations unlock and access all corporate information, both structured and unstructured, and provides a unified view for more confident decision making. It includes a complete suite of enterprise-level BI tools that are required for strategic, corporate BI initiatives and for aligning teams and business networks. It brings all this functionality integrated into one flexible and unified BI platform. The portfolio also sees the emergence of new trends in BI around collaborative BI and on-demand SaaS BI suites.

In the next chapter, we will move on to look at the foundation of any enterprise BI platform: information management.

SAP BusinessObjects Enterprise Information Management Solutions

The SAP BusinessObjects Enterprise Information Management (EIM) solutions set of applications provides a customer with comprehensive information management functionality that helps organizations deliver integrated, accurate, and timely data across the enterprise. The data can either be in a structured or unstructured format. These solutions allow organizations to provide trusted data for key initiatives, such as business transaction processing, BI, data warehousing, and master data management applications. Let's take a deeper look at each of them.

SAP BusinessObjects Data Services

SAP BusinessObjects Data Services is a unification of the SAP Business-Objects Data Integrator and SAP BusinessObjects Data Quality Management platforms in a single solution. This unification helps organizations move, transform, and improve quality in any type of

SAP Business-Objects Data Integrator and SAP BusinessObjects Data Quality Management data at any frequency. It provides a single environment for the development, runtime, management, security, and data connectivity components. Organizations benefit from increased agility, access to trusted information, operational excellence, and enterprise-class performance. Let's take a deeper look into this:

> **Agility**

  – **Faster time to market:** Customers will have a faster time to market based on a single development and runtime environment.

  – **Reuse and collaboration:** Developers will have higher rates of reuse and collaboration of data integration and data quality components.

  – **Unified set of developer skills:** Organizations will be able to leverage a unified set of skills for developing SAP BusinessObjects Data Integrator and SAP BusinessObjects Data Quality Management jobs.

> **Trusted Information**

  – **Data governance:** The application provides support for data governance with transparency via lineage, change management, security, and controls.

  – **Global data support:** Multinational organizations have complete global data support.

  – **End-to-end data management:** Organizations can quickly understand the impact of a change, from source to report, with end-to-end metadata management

> **Operational Excellence**

  – **Single repository:** Customers can leverage a single development, administration, and metadata repository.

  – **Single platform:** The use of a single platform reduces resources and costs for installing, maintaining, and supporting multiple applications.

  – **Multiplatform support:** SAP BusinessObjects Data Services offers support for 64-bit, UNIX, Linux, and Microsoft Windows operating systems.

> **Enterprise-Class Performance**

- **Scalable performance:** SAP BusinessObjects Data Services offers a highly scalable platform that supports both parallelization and grid computing.

- **Enterprise connectivity:** Organizations have a tool that supports enterprise connectivity with support for any data source.

- **Services enabled:** The SAP BusinessObjects Data Service application supports service-oriented architecture (SOA) requirements.

Now that we've talked about the overall SAP BusinessObjects Data Services platform, let's take a deeper look at the two primary components SAP BusinessObjects Data Integrator and SAP BusinessObjects Data Quality Management. These two products are included together in SAP BusinessObjects Data Services but can still be purchased separately if so desired.

SAP BusinessObjects Data Integrator

SAP BusinessObjects Data Integrator provides customers with a robust enterprise class data integration tool that allows them to explore, extract, transform, and deliver data anywhere, at any frequency. Organizations can unite their diverse set of enterprise data sources to generate a strategic advantage. The application enables them to integrate their various data sources, ensure data integrity, and build an agile and trusted data foundation to rapidly respond to information demands. Following are some of the benefits of using SAP BusinessObjects Data Integrator:

Generating a strategic advantage

> **Reduce TCO:** Organizations will be able to reduce the costs associated with managing data consolidation, operational reports, and analytics.

> **Increase ROI:** Business users will get a greater return on investment by being able to more quickly leverage information assets that are generally trapped in enterprise applications and data warehouses.

> **Decrease change management costs:** Customers will be able to lower the costs associated with evolving data source types, instances, and versions.

> **Speed development and delivery:** IT organizations will be able to speed execution on BI and data warehousing projects.

> **Facilitate compliance:** Organizations will be able to ease the complexity of compliance with corporate and data governance policies

> **Optimize merger and acquisition activities:** Companies will be able to accelerate consolidation and speed to value activities associated with mergers and acquisitions.

> **Empower executives and employees:** Organizations will be able to give users fast access to trusted, accurate, and timely information that they can act on more confidently.

Enterprise data quality

SAP BusinessObjects Data Integrator ensures the quality of an organization's enterprise data with advanced data profiling, which allows users to understand the content, structure, quality, and relationships between tables in source data. The data validation feature helps customers build a firewall between their source and target systems, so they can filter out unwanted data based on their business rules. Throughout the extraction, transformation, and load (ETL) process, SAP BusinessObjects Data Integrator audits data to verify the integrity of the data; additional data quality functionality to cleanse the data of any operational domain (such as customer, product, or service) is accessible with SAP BusinessObjects Data Services.

Metadata integration provides end-to-end impact analysis

From an IT perspective, SAP BusinessObjects Data Integrator enables you to see how a change in source data can affect downstream processes and systems through metadata analysis. The software is unique in its ability to offer out-of-the-box integration with metadata from the SAP BusinessObjects software BI layer. This allows organizations to see the effect of changes in the source systems down to the BI reports. As a result, they can more easily manage change in the entire ETL and BI environment.

From a business perspective, a huge benefit of metadata integration is data lineage, which allows information consumers to view the context of data in their reports. The software allows users to see when data was updated, how it was computed, and where it came from — all the way back to the original transactional source. This visibility is critical in helping users gain better trust in their information and meet compliance requirements.

SAP BusinessObjects Data Services Designer software, shown in Figure 6.1, provides an intuitive thick client-based tool for ETL mapping, helping to more easily manage the design phase of an ETL job. Organizations can use SAP BusinessObjects Data Services Designer to collaborate with a team to gather business requirements, profile the source data, build ETL mappings, validate the accuracy of the design, generate data integration jobs, and document the project.

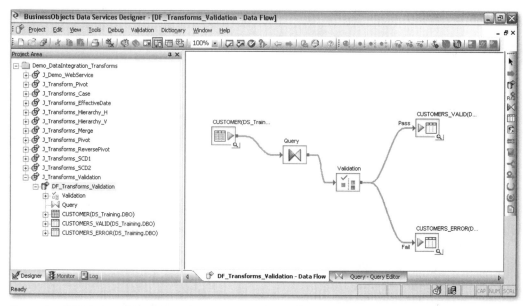

Figure 6.1 SAP BusinessObjects Data Services Designer

SAP BusinessObjects Data Integrator helps to accelerate and simplify development efforts by building and managing data integration jobs within a single graphical environment. The drag-and-drop user interface allows customers to quickly build jobs that profile, validate, audit, cleanse, transform, and move data. Advanced debugging features enable organizations to analyze problematic data through the entire ETL process. The smart documentation functionality saves time from not having to manually document the design work.

Drag-and-drop user interface

The integration software lets designers perform a complete range of data transformations. They can choose from a library of powerful, extensible, and reusable transforms for operations, such as unstructured data (via SAP BusinessObjects Text Analysis software), hierarchy flattening for XML files, XML pipelining, pivot and reverse-pivot of rows and columns, slowly changing dimensions, change data capture, data validation, and data cleansing (via SAP BusinessObjects Data Services software).

Team-based development

SAP BusinessObjects Data Integrator offers team-based development functionality. Users can check work in and out of a central metadata repository securely. They can share and version their work to accelerate development, and they can easily compare differences between objects.

Jobs can be ported to different database types, versions, and instances, so developers can design an ETL job once and port it to any database environment, further accelerating deployment.

As volumes of data rise and accepted delays drop, customers need to be able to rely on a high-performance, scalable data integration solution. SAP BusinessObjects Data Integrator delivers extreme ETL scalability with support for parallel processing, grid computing, real-time data movement, and broad source and target support. This open and services-based architecture allows users to integrate with third-party products using industry standard protocols such as CWM, XML, HTTP/HTTPS, JMS, SNMP, and Web services.

Scalability requirements for increasing data volumes and shrinking data load windows

The software's performance architecture meets scalability requirements for ever-increasing data volumes and shrinking data load windows. It provides intelligent threading, which enables parallelization in several ways. Within a single data transformation, it can dynamically launch multiple threads. In a single job, multiple transformations and job steps can run in parallel. Multiple jobs can run simultaneously through multiple instances of the SAP BusinessObjects Data Integrator job engine. Through a grid computing implementation, multiple job servers can run concurrently to balance workload and maintain high system availability.

SAP BusinessObjects Data Integrator maximizes data integration performance by intelligently pushing the processing down to the database or mainframe platforms. The software leverages your database server to aggregate functions at the source level without moving the data to the SAP BusinessObjects Data Integrator server. With the ability to distribute processing to the source systems, the software minimizes unnecessary data movement across a customer's network to optimize data integration performance.

SAP BusinessObjects Data Integrator can help connect to any data (structured or unstructured) whether it resides in a relational database, mainframe system, or enterprise application. Through SAP BusinessObjects Data Integrator, users can take a text string and extract it to a structured format via SAP BusinessObjects Text Analysis. In addition, the software provides deep metadata-based connectivity to packaged applications from SAP, Siebel, PeopleSoft, J.E. Edwards, and Oracle applications. Native connectivity is available for virtually all database types or through ODBC (open database connectivity). Customers can access legacy mainframe applications. SAP BusinessObjects Data Integrator also supports flat files, XML, and Web services. For proprietary applications, customers can connect to SAP BusinessObjects Data Integrator using a Java software development kit (SDK).

The data integration software also offers comprehensive support for Web services and is Web Services Interoperability (WS-I) compliant. It can publish or call a batch or real-time data integration job via Web services. The platform also calls Web service-enabled applications to access virtually any data. Web services can be used to get job status (e.g., running, success, or error); access logging information (e.g., trace, monitor, and error); and start or stop a real-time service.

Web Services Interoperability compliant

Next, let's take a look at the other component of SAP BusinessObjects Data Services that is also offered as a standalone product.

SAP BusinessObjects Data Quality Management

SAP BusinessObjects Data Quality Management software helps customers analyze, measure, standardize, cleanse, and match all types of data — from products or customers — to ensure that their information

SAP Business-Objects Data Quality Management

is reliable, complete, and timely. The software is built on Web services to provide a flexible solution that you can use within a wide variety of applications, platforms, and databases, including SAP, SAP Business-Objects, third-party, or proprietary software. SAP BusinessObjects Data Quality Management provides users with the following:

> **Data analysis and measurement:** Understand data defects and the impact of those defects on the business.

> **Data cleansing:** Parse all data elements, standardize the data to ensure a consistent format throughout all records, and correct the data based on secondary sources.

> **Data enhancement:** Target customers and prospects more effectively and take advantage of cross-selling opportunities.

> **Data matching and consolidation:** Identify multiple occurrences of a customer or a unique field within a record, and consolidate the information to create and maintain data relationships.

> **Data volume management:** Efficient management of massive data volumes from disparate sources and effective use of limited IT resources.

> **Accelerated response:** Quick reaction to data changes and standardized business rules for data quality.

> **Highest quality of BI:** Improved decision making and enhanced regulatory compliance.

A carefully planned data quality initiative is essential to any successful information management program — whether it's a BI project, the creation of a single client view through a master data management system, or a new data warehouse or data mart. Ensuring that the data is reliable and complete can also reduce operational costs within an enterprise.

Data quality assessment is the inspection, measurement, and analysis of data to help business users understand data defects and the impact of those defects upon the business. Data-profiling features within SAP BusinessObjects Data Quality Management automatically recognize business rules and data relationships (across columns or fields) that might otherwise go unnoticed. Customers can perform the profiling directly within a current data warehouse or data store, or they can load the data into the software and profile the data from there.

The software lets users establish data range parameters and create automated alerts that notify them if the analysis results exceed a specific parameter. The software, as shown in Figure 6.2, offers a robust set of graphic and dashboard reports, including Venn diagrams, summary profiles, frequency distributions, and referential integrity reports, to help users quickly identify data problems.

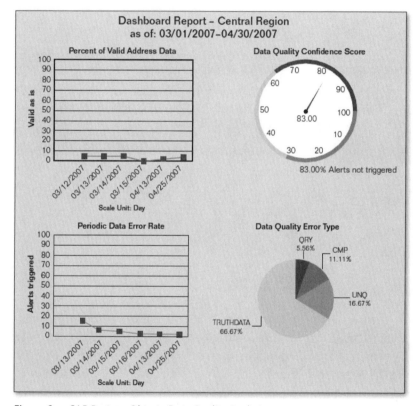

Figure 6.2 SAP BusinessObjects Data Quality Analysis

The data-cleansing process parses all data elements, standardizes the data to ensure a consistent format throughout all records, and corrects the data based on secondary sources. SAP BusinessObjects Data Quality Management can identify, standardize, and correct global data from

Data-cleansing process

more than 190 countries. It offers specific packages for Arabic, French, Portuguese, Spanish, Dutch, Italian, and German that provide cleansing for an individual's name, title, and firm.

You can identify customer information, such as email addresses, phone numbers, and Social Security numbers, and verify that this information is properly formatted. The software can also parse and standardize product-data elements such as part numbers, product codes, purchase orders, SKUs, and customer identification numbers. It can handle semistructured data and properly parse data into appropriate fields.

Enhancement options
SAP BusinessObjects Data Quality Management offers a variety of data enhancement options to help organizations more effectively target customers and prospects, take advantage of cross-selling opportunities, and successfully meet the requirements of a data quality strategy. These options include the following:

> Geocoding for marketing initiatives that are geographically or demographically based
> Geospatial assignment of customer addresses for tax jurisdictions, insurance-rating territories, and insurance hazards
> Appending a name, address, or phone number in telephone records
> Delivery-point validation, move update, and interfaces with USPS LACSLink and USPS ANKLink

Multiple occurrences of a customer
A sophisticated matching process in SAP BusinessObjects Data Quality Management helps users identify multiple occurrences of a customer or even a unique field within a record. After users have defined what the business considers a match, they can consolidate information to create and maintain data relationships. The software can match any writing script that is supported by the Unicode standard and offers advanced matching functionality for data in the Japanese, Chinese, Taiwanese, or Korean writing systems. A match wizard helps users identify members of the same household or employees from a single company or department.

Note

Customers can selectively choose data on a field-by-field basis to build a consolidated record based on the most up-to-date and reliable data. The software assigns a unique identification number for each record to create relationships between distinctly different sets of data. It can then combine records by matching different forms of the same name or firm, such as Beth and Elizabeth or AT&T, ATT, and att.

SAP BusinessObjects Data Quality Management recognizes matches within different sources of data to create a unified view. Users can match and consolidate internal account records, as well as records that are purchased externally. The software offers thousands of predefined business-rule templates that can be easily modified for fast deployment. It can process multiple sets of business rules to uncover hidden relationships in a company's data, as shown in Figure 6.3.

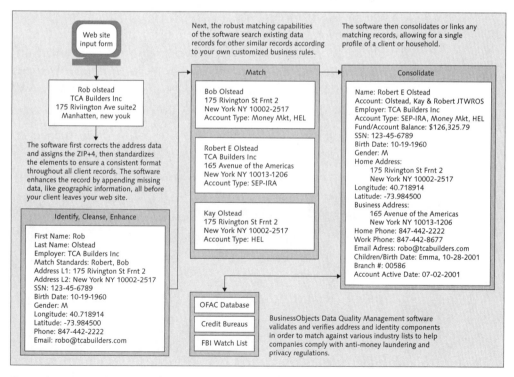

Figure 6.3 How SAP BusinessObjects Data Quality Management Improves Information Quality

Gaining confidence
in your data

The software also helps integrate disparate customer, product, and other data into a single view that supports data warehousing, customer data integration, and master data initiatives. In addition, executives and management gain the confidence that the data they provide in compliance reports for government regulations is both accurate and timely.

Remember, both SAP BusinessObjects Data Integrator and SAP BusinessObjects Data Quality Management can be purchased in one package (SAP BusinessObjects Data Services) or separately. Let's continue our look at the SAP BusinessObjects EIM platform with a look at SAP BusinessObjects Universal Data Cleanse.

SAP BusinessObjects Universal Data Cleanse

SAP BusinessObjects Universal Data Cleanse is an add-on product to SAP BusinessObjects Data Quality Management software. It can automatically adjust data to match region-specific and industry data standards. The software can tailor data cleansing to accommodate different standards, the building of custom dictionaries, and business rules. It can also process mixed language product descriptions. SAP BusinessObjects Universal Data Cleanse provides the following:

> Support for industry standards for greater assurance of data quality across business applications and operations

> Support for key organizational initiatives to extend data quality across the enterprise

> Greater efficiency for IT users who no longer need to guess at discerning the appropriate business rules

> Automated data standardization solutions that helps identify and correct data anomalies

> Greater visibility with a single, reliable, panoramic view of products, supply chains, and other vital business information

Every company struggles with a wide range of product and customer data that often is represented in several different ways across disparate systems or departments.

Ex **Example**

A product name such as "LIGHT BULB-120 VOLT 100 WATT" may appear in an organization's data sources multiple times with different capitalization, spelling, numbers, abbreviations, and hyphenation, which results in costly inefficiencies. An organization loses time because it is forced to cross check databases, find the defective data, and weed out discrepancies to ensure effective business operations. SAP BusinessObjects Universal Data Cleanse software increases an organization's confidence that its data — regardless of what type it is or where it is stored — is clean, reliable, and actionable.

SAP BusinessObjects Universal Data Cleanse greatly eliminates data duplication or discrepancies introduced by noncustomer or regional-specific data sources. With this software, customers can access an automated data standardization solution that helps identify abnormalities that those processing the data might not even imagine. The data cleansing option enables an enterprise to obtain a single, reliable, panoramic view of products, supply chains, and other vital business information.

Most data quality initiatives focus almost exclusively on structured data, which represents only a fraction of the data that exists in an organization. However, there is increasing interest in leveraging the value of unstructured data in both master data and BI applications. This is especially the case for customer and product data, which may be managed in unstructured files or encapsulated in a single field with a structured file or database. To be useful, this unstructured data must be cleansed and transformed into a semistructured (XML, for example) or structured format. Cleansing and transforming unstructured data improves operational efficiency and can add significant value to existing decision-making applications.

SAP BusinessObjects Universal Data Cleanse extends data cleansing capabilities beyond customer information, enabling customers to include any type of data their organization needs to process. Industries such as financial, pharmaceutical, and manufacturing can now process custom data sets and get a 360-degree view of products, supply chains, and vendors. SAP BusinessObjects Universal Data Cleanse functionality allows users to do the following:

> **Process bulk loads:** Incorporate product specifications coming directly from business analysts.

> **Add new classifications:** Create industry-specific or region-specific identifiers.

> **Add custom output:** Communicate results in the local language.

> **Store product data specifications in repository:** Support the master data management goals of the organization.

> **Use preloaded dictionaries:** Access colors, sizes (in English, French, German, Italian, Portuguese, Spanish), and weights (U.S. and metric).

Supporting structured and semistructured data processing

One typical use-case scenario of SAP BusinessObjects Universal Data Cleanse is to support structured and semistructured data processing. For example, a typical goal for a manufacturer may be to obtain more consistency between the descriptions of items on the web site and items in the catalog. To achieve consistency, the company needs to parse out the descriptions of each item and understand the relationships between the items so it can take out any duplicate entries and consolidate to a consistent format. Figure 6.4 illustrates the complex input text and parsing routine for the sample company.

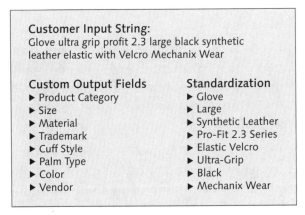

Figure 6.4 Complex Input Text and Parsing Routine

Another common use-case scenario of SAP BusinessObjects Universal Data Cleanse is the processing of international data. For an increasing number of organizations, it's important to be able to create intelligent parsing standardization processes — regardless of which language the original data is in. Equally important is the ability to present data in the local language and in the appropriate fields. With SAP BusinessObjects Universal Data Cleanse, not only are the fields named appropriately but also users can modify the rules and new names to optimize the process for the organization's specific region or language. The SAP BusinessObjects Universal Data Cleanse supported standards and initiatives are listed in Table 6.1.

International data

Support for Industry Standards	
Electronic Commerce Code Management Association Open Technical Directory (eOTD)	National Stock Number (NSN) - Military
Export Control Classification Number (ECCN)	North American Industry Classification System (NAICS)
International Organization for Standardization (ISO)	United Nations Standard Products and Services Code (UNSPSC)
International Standard for the Classification of Product and Services (eCL@ss)	And more!
Support for Organizational Initiatives	
Global Coding Systems	Mergers and Acquisitions
International Data Processing	Spend Analysis
Master Data Management	Unstructured and Semistructured Data Processing

Table 6.1 SAP BusinessObjects Universal Data Cleanse Supported Standards and Initiatives

Now that we have seen the value that SAP BusinessObjects Universal Data Cleanse brings to customers, let's take a look at another facet of the EIM solution with SAP BusinessObjects Text Analysis.

SAP BusinessObjects Text Analysis

Text-based
data sources

SAP BusinessObjects Text Analysis gives organizations a 360-degree view of their business by extracting information from text-based data sources and converting it to a useful, structured format. Powerful natural language processing derives meaning, integrating previously inaccessible information from unstructured data sources with broader information management, BI, and decision-making frameworks. SAP BusinessObjects Text Analysis offers the following:

> **Text analysis:** Extract hidden content in all major file formats and in more than 30 languages.

> **Text parsing and identification:** Extract, categorize, and summarize free-form text to discern concepts, sentiments, people, organizations, and places.

> **Workbench:** Employ a hybrid learn-by-example and rules-based approach, and create and test custom definitions for entities, relationships, and event patterns.

> **Relevant data:** Extract and analyze key sentences to summarize any document or set of documents.

> **Improved BI:** Enhanced market intelligence and decision making with details on competitor strengths, weaknesses, and improved access to intellectual capital and best practices.

> **Increased quality:** Improved quality of service and customer retention with early warning on product defects and service issues.

> **Improved marketing activities:** Enhanced campaign effectiveness, messaging, and lead generation with insight to market perceptions on company, products, brand, and industry events.

> **Increased fraud and compliance:** Improved compliance efforts, protect ongoing revenues through early detection of potential violations, proof of adherence to regulations, and support for root-cause analysis.

In a challenging economy, companies can't afford to make costly mistakes regarding strategy, product development, customer care, and operations. Too often in the pursuit of agility, companies make assumptions on what their customers truly want or where they can improve products and services and be more competitive. However, correct decisions and effective strategy development require a complete and accurate understanding of customers, markets, and the business landscape.

Unfortunately, some of the most compelling and powerful information about evolving customer needs, product pain points, and recurring service issues is locked away and inaccessible to the decision makers who need it most. Up to 80% of all corporate data is locked away in unstructured text sources such as emails, documents, notes fields, and web content. For example, as businesses seek to improve customer satisfaction, important information on customer frustrations, opinions, and feedback remains hidden in customer relationship management (CRM) comment fields, blog sites, survey notes, and email. And for organizations working to ensure compliance to regulations, textual information that includes risk-related issues lies hidden in documents, records, and contracts.

 Did You Know?

> According to Gartner, unstructured data doubles every three months, and 7 million web pages are added every day. Most companies don't have the time, resources, or outsourcing budget to tackle this overwhelming amount of data using a heavyweight, manual approach. The paradox is that businesses can't afford to ignore this information either.

SAP BusinessObjects Text Analysis software processes, classifies, and summarizes vast amounts of text-based information — helping organizations gain better insight into their business so that they can empower those initiatives that directly improve the bottom line. With SAP BusinessObjects Text Analysis, customers are able to open a window to all of the information needed to achieve a 360-degree view of their organization, their customers, their market, and their competitors.

Gain better insight into your business

SAP BusinessObjects Text Analysis can help you accomplish the following:

> Unlock critical insights hidden in online forums, call-center logs, CRM systems, and survey data, such as customers' sentiments about an organization's brand, products, and services.

> Complement structured BI with the wisdom buried in unstructured text sources by accessing and deriving meaning from hundreds of thousands of text documents in a variety of file formats and in more than 30 major languages.

> Deploy powerful extraction, categorization, and summarization of free-form text information to quickly identify and understand the concepts, people, organizations, places, and other information that only exists in these sources.

> Incorporate valuable information from unstructured data sources into an organization's decision-making framework. Add SAP BusinessObjects Text Analysis to the portfolio alongside the SAP NetWeaver technology platform, SAP BusinessObjects Enterprise software deployment, or SAP BusinessObjects Data Integrator software environment.

As you can see in Figure 6.5, SAP BusinessObjects Text Analysis gets integrated into the decision framework.

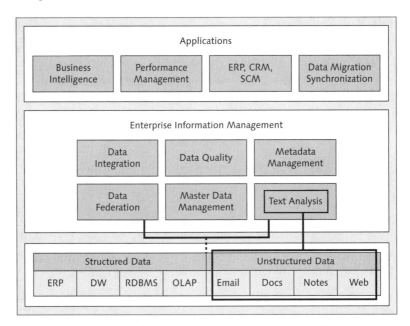

Figure 6.5   SAP BusinessObjects Text Analysis Integrated into the Decision Framework

The Internet affords individuals an unlimited ability to share their opinions with the world, and this in turn has given customers tremendous power in their collective voices. Innovative companies realize the value of this information as a competitive advantage but struggle to find a way to access useful information from the impenetrable mountain of raw data.

Power with the collective voice

SAP BusinessObjects Text Analysis allows organizations to gain meaning from customer communications by extracting and quantifying sentiment from both web-based and internal customer feedback sources such as product review sites, social networking sites, customer surveys, and CRM notes, as you can see in Figure 6.6.

Web-based and internal customer feedback

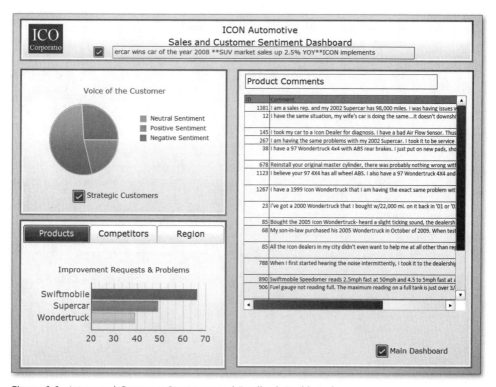

Figure 6.6 Integrated Customer Sentiment and Feedback Dashboard

After sentiment data is extracted and converted to a structured format, it can be used to identify unmet market needs and drive new product development. Customer complaints can be accessed to provide early warning of product and service issues, speeding problem resolution and enhancing customer retention. Marketing teams can improve effectiveness of campaigns and promotions by identifying feedback and needs across various segments and tracking buzz tied to communications and events over time.

Advanced linguistics capabilities

The software's advanced linguistics capabilities read and "understand" documents in more than 30 major languages. Through sophisticated natural language processing, SAP BusinessObjects Text Analysis knows how verbs, nouns, and other language structures interact. In essence, it understands the meaning and context of information — not just the words themselves.

Entity-extraction functionality is the foundation of SAP BusinessObjects Text Analysis. Powerful extraction parses large volumes of documents, identifying "entities" such as customers, products, locations, and financial information relevant to the organization. Entity extraction is complemented by categorization capabilities that can apply company-specific or industry-specific taxonomies to the text for subject-level classification, and summarization capabilities that create abstracts that are readily understood. See Table 6.2 for the extractable entities of SAP BusinessObjects Text Analysis.

Extractable Entities	
Who	People
	Job title
	Social Security numbers
What	Companies
	Organizations
	Financial indexes
	Products

Table 6.2 Extractable Entities

Extractable Entities	
When	Dates
	Days
	Holidays
	Months
	Years
	Times
	Time periods
Where	Location
	City
	State
	Country
Quantity	Currencies
	Measures
Concepts	Concept design
Relations and Events	Membership in an organization
	Person's acquaintances
	Travel
	Merger and acquisition
Categories	Business
	Terrorism
	Custom
Customizable	Industry

Table 6.2 Extractable Entities (Cont.)

With support for all major entity types, including out-of-the-box entities, relations, and events preconfigured with the system, SAP BusinessObjects Text Analysis automatically extracts key information — including people, places, companies, dates, measurements, currency figures, and email addresses — and reveals important relations and events occurring between those data items. Relationships that may not be explicit in one document or source are uncovered because SAP BusinessObjects Text Analysis identifies statements that imply relationships and converts this information to structured data that can be aggregated and visualized to put the disparate bits and pieces together, as illustrated in Figure 6.7.

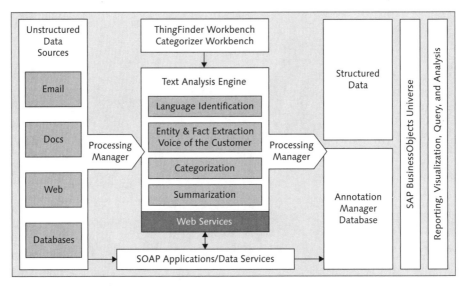

Figure 6.7   SAP BusinessObjects Text Analysis Architecture

SAP BusinessObjects Text Analysis can be extended to recognize custom entities and entity types, such as stock keeping unit (SKU) numbers, project names, special relationships and events, and specific phrases for sentiment analysis.

 Note

> SAP BusinessObjects Text Analysis provides taxonomy-based, document-level classification of information that isn't explicit within documents. For example, your document may belong to a customer complaint category, even though the word "complaint" never appears in the text. But any document that talks about dissatisfaction, for instance, is certainly a complaint-related document, regardless of whether "complaint" occurs in the document. SAP BusinessObjects Text Analysis understands these types of conceptual relationships and automatically classifies your information in the right category.

SAP BusinessObjects Text Analysis extracts and analyzes the most relevant sentences to create a summary of any document or set of documents. The best way to look at it is as an "automated abstract creator" that reads the information and creates an executive summary on the content. SAP BusinessObjects Text Analysis comprehends the general substance of the information by using a system of weighted sentences, generally giving more weight to the first and last sentences of a paragraph, for example, along with the specific query parameters of the search.

This capability to extract relevant data is important because one person may be investigating weather phenomenon and be interested in "snow," whereas someone else may use the same document to investigate transportation patterns of long-haul trucks. SAP BusinessObjects Text Analysis understands the specific requirements and weights the summary differently depending on the respective area of interest.

Now that we have a good understanding of the power of SAP Business-Objects Text Analysis, let's take a look at the federated query tool called SAP BusinessObjects Data Federator.

SAP BusinessObjects Data Federator

SAP BusinessObjects Data Federator software enables you to leverage your current infrastructure and available data sources to create a unified view of your data sources in a fast, flexible, and easily accessible way. Providing real-time, on-demand access to diverse data sources, the software allows you to quickly introduce new data sources to your BI solutions and adapt to changing data integration requirements. SAP BusinessObjects Data Federator offers the following:

> **Fast and flexible solution:** Access real-time information from multiple data sources using data federation.

> **Sophisticated query optimizer:** Get fast information access from operational systems.

> **Wide range of information systems:** Use support from relational and nonrelational sources such as Oracle, IBM, Microsoft, SAP

NetWeaver Business Warehouse, SAS, Teradata, Web services, and XML.

> **Deep integration:** Integration with SAP BusinessObjects Metadata Management software enables data lineage and analysis from report to data source.

> **Complete overview:** Gain a complete view of business information with access to multiple data sources.

> **Quicker value add:** Meet information requirements with faster agility and speed.

> **Increased trust:** Improve user trust in information with data lineage and impact analysis.

Data fragmentation and information redundancy

For many organizations, data is scattered across the enterprise within multiple systems and applications. The result is data fragmentation and information redundancy, making useful business analysis difficult. Although data warehousing can help, many organizations need a faster, lightweight solution that can be rolled out in days. Today's challenges may prevent organizations from achieving goals such as producing holistic reports in a timely manner, querying operational data in real time, and ensuring that reports contain the most accurate, up-to-date information.

Data federation

Data federation is a data integration style that allows IT departments greater flexibility and agility in providing business users with a complete view of information from multiple sources. It does this by accessing and unifying data models from disparate sources. And it generates dynamic, on-demand queries for real-time views to information.

Unlike the data integration style of ETL, which physically replicates data from disparate sources into a target system such as a data warehouse, SAP BusinessObjects Data Federator pulls information on demand based on the business application requirement, such as when running a report.

Single semantic layer, a.k.a. universe

SAP BusinessObjects Data Federator software helps you create a unified view of data and metadata from multiple sources in a fast, flexible, and easily accessible way. It allows a single semantic layer (also known as a *universe*) to connect to multiple data sources and provide a 360-degree view of the business, as illustrated in Figure 6.8.

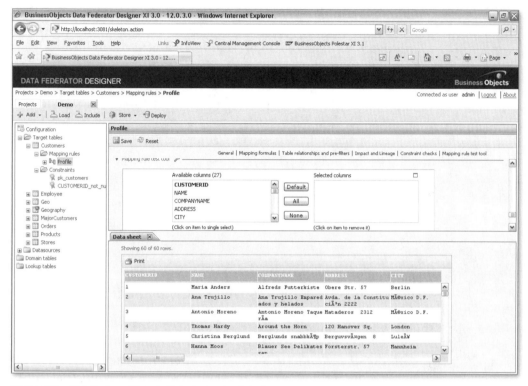

Figure 6.8 SAP BusinessObjects Data Federator Interface

With SAP BusinessObjects Data Federator, users can integrate information without data replication or the need to learn the source system's query language.

Accessing multiple data sources for reports is more of the rule today than the exception. More than ever, today's mature and sophisticated BI deployments can benefit from the functionality that data federation software offers. SAP BusinessObjects Data Federator complements the semantic layer in SAP BusinessObjects BI solutions, allowing reliable ad hoc access to disparate data regardless of data structure and location. The data federation software is a noninvasive technology with no need for special database rights or to write back to production systems.

Unified view of data sources

Designed for flexibility and ease of use, SAP BusinessObjects Data Federator helps customers develop successful projects in a short time, leverage their existing information infrastructure, and increase their management's and end users' level of confidence in data and reports. SAP BusinessObjects Data Federator software helps customers create a unified view of their data sources. The software enables them to produce holistic reports in a timely manner, query operational data in real time, and be confident that reports contain up-to date and accurate information across multiple systems and applications.

The next tool we will take a look at in the EIM solutions is SAP BusinessObjects Metadata Management. (This is not to be confused with SAP NetWeaver MDM, which we won't be talking about in this book.)

SAP BusinessObjects Metadata Management

Change management analysis and usage auditing

SAP BusinessObjects Metadata Management software provides reliable data for change management analysis and usage auditing. The software collects and unifies metadata from disparate tools and sources into a single repository. By bringing all of an organization's metadata together to deliver reliable data, users are in a better position to meet demands for compliance and internal controls, and to support sound business strategies. The benefits of SAP BusinessObjects Metadata Management include the following:

> **Metadata integration and consolidation:** Manage disparate metadata in an open, relational repository.

> **Change impact and data lineage:** Understand the relationships among data sources, targets, and universes (and their respective documents), as well as the effect of changes to those relationships.

> **Audits of business intelligence (BI) user privileges:** Analyze the impact of data changes on users and their associated privileges and permissions.

> **Integration with an SAP BusinessObjects reporting portal:** View a data lineage diagram for any BI object directly through an SAP BusinessObjects portal.

> **Advanced searches:** Add multiple conditions to narrow your metadata search.

> **Reduced total cost of ownership:** For BI solutions through a streamlined IT workload, reductions in project outlays and improved operational efficiency.

Having reliable BI is more important than ever in today's highly competitive marketplace. Data traceability is also essential under regulations such as the U.S. Sarbanes-Oxley Act (SOX), which require the officers of public companies to confirm the accuracy of their financial statements.

Data traceability

As the demand for BI grows, so do the available data sources, data warehouses, and BI reports that customers depend on for strategic business decisions. However, separate departmental deployments of BI solutions have created silos of data, making it significantly more difficult to manage the information you need. To prevent unforeseen business impacts, data architects and report designers must proactively determine the impact that changing data sources might have on the intelligence environment.

SAP BusinessObjects Metadata Management software is an EIM solution that provides reliable metadata for change impact and data lineage analysis and usage auditing. The software collects and unifies metadata from disparate tools and sources into a single repository, as shown in Figure 6.9.

Metadata intelligence uses metadata for a given domain to discover, understand, leverage, and manage applications and resources in that domain. It involves applying metadata in a business context, not just collecting and cataloging metadata as most solutions for metadata management do. Like BI, metadata intelligence requires consolidating and relating pertinent information in a central repository for business decision making. In addition, metadata intelligence helps users understand, audit, and analyze the entire BI deployment — from data sources to BI reports. Metadata intelligence can help customers maximize scarce IT resources and minimize custom development.

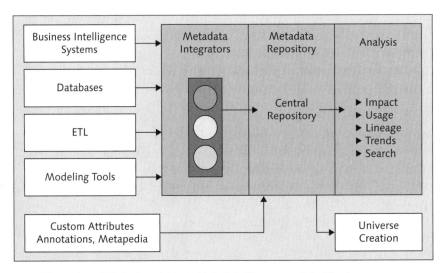

Figure 6.9   SAP BusinessObjects Metadata Management Architecture

Open, relational repository

SAP BusinessObjects Metadata Management consolidates and integrates disparate metadata into an open, relational repository. Companies can consolidate metadata from various databases, modeling tools (such as ERWin), ETL products, and BI solutions. The software can also help organizations incorporate additional business metadata with existing objects and maintain that data. It includes comprehensive functionality for metadata browsing and searching, as well as multi-anguage metadata support.

Data lineage

It's important that customers understand how changes in data sources can impact their data warehouse, reports, and BI deployment. The impact analysis functionalities in SAP BusinessObjects Metadata Management help organizations recognize the relationships among data sources, targets, and universes — and their respective documents — and thus the effect of changes to those relationships. Data lineage analysis helps users identify which sources provided the data for specific reports and see the data transformations, thereby increasing end-user confidence and providing a more accurate picture of their data architecture.

Users can trace the lineage of data from a report back to its original data source. Such visibility can help organizations make more accurate business decisions and estimate the cost-of-change impact, which, in turn, can reduce their maintenance costs.

SAP BusinessObjects Metadata Management lets customers view a data lineage diagram for any BI object directly through an SAP Business-Objects software reporting portal. They can see the data lineage diagram for any object associated with reports from SAP BusinessObjects ad hoc query and reporting tools by clicking on the lineage link for that particular object.

On the data lineage diagram shown in Figure 6.10, users can place the mouse over the object to get additional details.

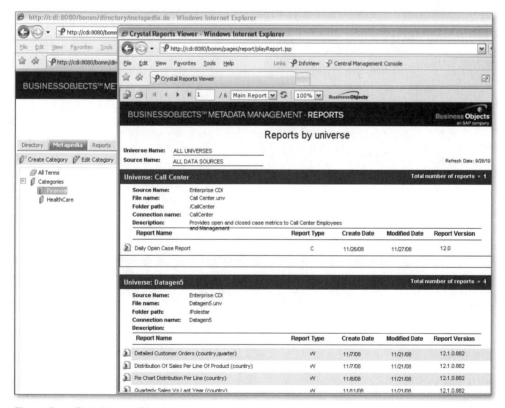

Figure 6.10 Data Lineage Diagram

Next, we'll take a look at three of the SAP BusinessObjects Rapid Marts packages. All of the SAP BusinessObjects Rapid Marts packages require SAP BusinessObjects Data Integrator as a precursor to using the respective package.

SAP BusinessObjects Rapid Marts Packages for PeopleSoft

The SAP BusinessObjects solution portfolio provides the technology, tools, and packaged data applications needed to enrich Oracle's PeopleSoft Enterprise environment with BI functionality. The SAP BusinessObjects Rapid Marts packages for PeopleSoft are additional add-ons to SAP BusinessObjects Data Services (SAP BusinessObjects Data Integrator) that provides the extractions, data structures, universes, and some reports for customers to quickly implement analysis of their PeopleSoft Enterprise Environment. There are five different SAP BusinessObjects Rapid Marts for PeopleSoft: Accounts Payable, Accounts Receivable, Asset Management, General Ledger, and HR.

SAP Business-Objects Accounts Payable Rapid Mart for PeopleSoft

The SAP BusinessObjects Accounts Payable Rapid Mart for PeopleSoft supports analysis of data in the payables module of PeopleSoft. Customers can do the following:

> Query payables transactions based on category, supplier, supplier site, supplier type, currency transaction number, General Ledger date, accounting period, and accounting chart fields such as account, alternate account, department, and operating unit.

> Calculate and analyze key accounts payables measurements such as Days Payable Outstanding (DPO).

> View on-hold invoices.

> Perform ad hoc analysis.

> View supplier paid invoice history.

> Analyze cash discounts that have been granted.

SAP Business-Objects Accounts Receivable Rapid Mart

The SAP BusinessObjects accounts receivable Rapid Mart for PeopleSoft supports analysis of data in the receivables module of PeopleSoft. Customers can do the following:

> Query receivables transactions based on category, bill-to customer, currency, transaction number, and due date.

> Calculate and analyze key account receivables measurements such as DSO and aging.

> Review information about open items.

> Perform ad hoc analysis.

> Review customer credit information.

The SAP BusinessObjects Asset Management Rapid Mart for People-Soft supports analysis of data in the asset management module of PeopleSoft. Customers can do the following:

SAP Business-Objects Asset Management Rapid Mart

> List assets by date placed in service.

> Produce asset addition reports.

> List assets by location, department, and product.

> Produce depreciation reports.

> Analyze asset movement.

> Produce retirement reports.

> Analyze capitalizations in detail.

> Compare capital budgets to actual spending.

> List associated asset books and accounting entries.

The SAP BusinessObjects General Ledger Rapid Mart for PeopleSoft supports analysis of data in the general ledger module of PeopleSoft. Customers can the following:

SAP Business-Objects General Ledger Rapid Mart

> Create and analyze financial statements.

> View multiple budget versions.

> Review financial and operational results throughout the fiscal year by drilling down to accounting transaction level.

> Investigate variances among actual, budgeted, and forecasted amounts.

> Perform ad hoc financial analysis.

> Enable analysis of cost and project accounting.

> Perform audit and control analysis.

SAP Business-
Objects HR
Rapid Mart

The SAP BusinessObjects HR Rapid Mart for PeopleSoft supports analysis of benefits, payroll, and other employment-related information. The package has the following features:

> **Job transaction:** Helps to analyze personal and employment-related information by employee or by organizational unit. This section addresses information such as age, length of service, annual salary, deadlines, and other significant dates, and includes a directory of current employees.

> **Absence history:** Enables analysis of employee absence history by absence type, employee, and organizational unit.

> **Training:** Allows analysis of training course attendance by employee and organizational unit.

> **Benefit:** Enables analysis of enrollment and use of company benefit plans. Enrollment and eligibility information can be analyzed from employee or benefit plan perspectives.

> **Payroll:** Assists in analyzing compensation by various earnings types. Compensation amounts are summarized for easy analysis. This section is currently specific to U.S. payroll.

Now that we've discussed PeopleSoft, let's move on to Siebel.

SAP BusinessObjects Rapid Marts for Siebel

SAP Business-
Objects Data
Services

The SAP BusinessObjects Rapid Marts for Siebel are additional add-ons to SAP BusinessObjects Data Services (SAP BusinessObjects Data Integrator) that provide the extractions, data structures, universes, and some reports for customers to quickly implement analysis of their Siebel applications. There are three different SAP BusinessObjects Rapid Marts for Siebel: Call Center, Campaign, and Pipeline.

SAP Business-
Objects Call Center
Rapid Mart

> The SAP BusinessObjects Call Center Rapid Mart for Siebel supports analysis of call center data in Siebel applications. Customers can do the following:

> Analyze generated service requests by campaign, sales rep, potential competitor, status, stage, and activities.

> Determine which products have defect issues, their severity, reason for failure, and resolution.

> Monitor employee skills.

> Evaluate the effectiveness of service request management.

> Monitor results of customer surveys.

> View all the activities associated with a service request.

The SAP BusinessObjects Campaign Rapid Mart for Siebel supports analysis of marketing campaign data in Siebel applications. Customers can do the following:

SAP Business-Objects Campaign Rapid Mart

> Analyze campaign programs by market segment, campaign offer, product, and wave.

> Determine which campaigns are most effective in generating further opportunities.

> Review members of households that may be targeted during a campaign program.

> Review campaign response by product, market segment, and offer.

> Monitor campaign costs.

The SAP BusinessObjects Pipeline Rapid Mart for Siebel supports analysis of pipeline data in Siebel applications. Customers can do the following:

SAP Business-Objects Pipeline Rapid Mart

> Analyze generated opportunities by campaign, sales rep, potential competitor, status, stage, and activities.

> Determine customer behavior.

> Forecast revenue by account, opportunity, product, product line, employee, partner, division, organization, sales/service agreement, or project.

> View projected margins, upside, and downside.

> Evaluate the effectiveness of sales campaigns.

> Analyze the pipeline with greater accuracy.

> Compare projected revenues with actual bookings by sales rep, opportunity, agreement, customer, contact, product, project, or internal division.

> View all of the activities associated with a particular opportunity.

> Preserve snapshots of revenue data for historical reference.

SAP BusinessObjects Rapid Marts for Oracle

SAP Business-
Objects Rapid
Marts for Oracle
applications

The SAP BusinessObjects Rapid Marts for Oracle applications are additional add-ons to SAP BusinessObjects Data Services (SAP BusinessObjects Data Integrator) that provide the extractions, data structures, universes, and some reports for customers to quickly implement analysis of their Siebel application. There are 10 different SAP BusinessObjects Rapid Mart packages for Oracle.

SAP Business-
Objects Accounts
Payable Rapid Mart

The SAP BusinessObjects Accounts Payable Rapid Mart for Oracle applications supports financial and operational analysis of payables information. Customers can do the following:

> Query payables transactions based on category, supplier, supplier site, currency, transaction number, general ledger date, due date, accounting period, and accounting flex field segments (such as account, company, product, etc.).

> Calculate and analyze key account payables measurements such as DPO and aging.

> Review unmatched items.

> View on-hold invoices.

> Perform ad hoc analysis.

> View supplier paid invoice history.

> Analyze cash discount taken trends.

> Analyze payables clerk efficiency.

> Perform audit of payables transactions posted to the general ledger.

The SAP BusinessObjects Accounts Receivable Rapid Mart for Oracle supports analysis of data in the receivables module of Oracle applications. Customers can do the following:

> Query receivables transactions based on Accounting Flex field segments, transaction category, the bill-to customer, currency, transaction number, general ledger date, due date, and the accounting period associated with the due date.

> Calculate and analyze key account receivables measurements such as DSO and aging.

> Review information about open items.

> Investigate unapplied cash receipts to ensure accuracy of the current receivables balance.

> Perform ad hoc analysis.

> Review customer credit information.

> View dunning history for a invoice, and analyze collection activities efficiency.

SAP Business-Objects Accounts Receivable Rapid Mart

The SAP BusinessObjects Contract Rapid Mart for Oracle applications supports operational and statistical analysis of contract-related information. Customers can do the following:

> View service contracts summarized by service line or detailed to the covered product level.

> List contracts expired but not renewed by the customer/product/authoring organization.

> Report on contract status.

> Analyze contract line discount and surcharge price adjustments.

> Perform quality checks on contract rules.

> Analyze contract billing activities.

> Review contract-related sales credits by sales person/customer/time period.

SAP Business-Objects Contract Rapid Mart

The SAP BusinessObjects Federal Financials Rapid Mart for Oracle applications supports analysis of data in the Oracle Applications Federal Financials suite. Customers can do the following:

SAP Business-Objects Federal Financials Rapid Mart

> View status of funds by allowee and allotee.

> Create and analyze financial statements, such as Statement of Financial Position, Statement of Net Cost, and Statement of Budgetary Resources.

> View multiple budget versions.

> Review financial and operational results throughout the fiscal year by drilling down to the accounting transaction level.

> Investigate variances among actual, budgeted, and forecasted amounts.

> Analyze commitment and obligation lifecycle.

> Perform ad hoc financial analysis.

> Perform audit and control analysis.

SAP BusinessObjects Fixed Assets Rapid Mart

The SAP BusinessObjects Fixed Assets Rapid Mart for Oracle applications supports financial and operational analysis of assets information. Customers can do the following:

> List assets by date placed in service.

> Produce asset addition reports.

> List assets by location.

> Produce depreciation reports such as accumulated depreciation balance.

> Analyze asset movement.

> Produce retirement reports.

> Analyze capitalizations in detail.

> Produce cost clearing reconciliation reports.

> Compare capital budgets to actual spending.

> Produce Capital Improvement Plan (CIP) cost balance reports.

> List associated purchase orders and invoices.

SAP BusinessObjects HR Rapid Mart

The SAP BusinessObjects HR Rapid Mart for Oracle applications supports analysis of employee assignments, benefits, payroll, training, and other employment-related information. Customers can do the following:

> Report on HR, benefits, training, and payroll activities.

> View organization hierarchies and position hierarchies.

> View the benefits structure as of certain date.

> Perform salary management analysis.

> View historical records of previous changes for employees, employee assignments, and benefits enrollment.

> Perform ad hoc analysis.

The SAP BusinessObjects Inventory Rapid Mart for Oracle supports analysis of data in the inventory module of Oracle applications. The package has the following features:

> **Material Transaction Section:** Tracks all transactions relating to items in the inventory, including receipt, transfer and issue of stock, adjustment of stock levels and cost updates.

> **Inventory Snapshot Section:** Holds aggregated current and historical daily counts of on-hand quantities of stock.

> **Physical Inventory Section:** Maintains detailed records of physical inventory counts, including rejected counts. Approved adjustments arising from these counts are posted as transactions and are included in the Material Transaction Section.

> **Reservation Section:** Contains current and future requirements of items reserved for sales orders, accounts, account aliases, inventories, or user-defined sources. The current available quantity for items can be derived by deducting the reserved quantity from the on-hand quantity stored in the Inventory Snapshot Section.

The SAP BusinessObjects Projects Rapid Mart for Oracle supports analysis of data in the projects module of Oracle applications. The package has the following features:

> **Budget Line Section:** Stores estimated cost, revenue, labor hours, and other quantities for a project and task categorized by a resource.

> **Draft Revenue Section:** Holds draft project revenue transactions prior to being transferred to other modules in Oracle applications.

SAP BusinessObjects Inventory Rapid Mart

SAP BusinessObjects Projects Rapid Mart

> **Draft Invoice Section:** Holds potential project invoices that require approval before they are officially accounted for in other Oracle applications.

> **Expenditure Section:** Contains details of expenditure items (costs and revenues) incurred by an employee or organization.

> **Event Section:** Contains summary level transactions generating revenue and/or billing activities that are not directly related to any expenditure items.

> **Project Asset Section:** Includes capital and retirement adjustment assets for capital projects.

> **Budget Summary Section:** Holds summarized inception-to-date, year-to-date, period-to-date, and prior period budget data.

> **Project Summary Section:** Stores summarized inception-to-date, year-to-date, period-to-date, and prior period project data.

> **Project Transaction Summary Section:** Contains summarized project data at the lowest level of detail.

SAP Business-
Objects Purchasing
Rapid Mart

The SAP BusinessObjects Purchasing Rapid Mart for Oracle e-Business Suite supports analysis of data in the purchasing module of the Oracle e-Business Suite. The package has the following features:

> **Purchase Requisition Section:** The purchasing process begins with a need or requirement for a certain material or service by a certain date. A purchase requisition document detailing the requirement goes to the purchasing organization for follow-up action. This section stores all requisitions at the purchase requisition distribution line level.

> **Purchase Order Section:** The purchase order document is the request to a supplier to supply a quantity of materials on a specific date or set of planned delivery dates. The price for the materials may be determined from contract-based pricing conditions or set at the time the purchase order is created. This section stores all purchase orders at the purchase order distribution line level.

> **Purchase Receipt Section:** Receiving is the function of accepting goods from a supplier and delivering them to their destination within the organization. Transactions are recorded at each stage of

this process, including receive, deliver, reject, and return to vendor. This section processes and stores these transactions.

> **Purchase Order History Section:** This section combines purchase requisition, purchase order, and purchase receipt details into a simple-to-use view for reporting. This view provides for analysis on the entire purchase cycle from a single query.

The SAP BusinessObjects Sales Rapid Mart for Oracle supports analysis of data in the order management, shipping execution, and accounts receivables modules of Oracle applications. Customers can do the following:

SAP Business-Objects Sales Rapid Mart

> Analyze sales trends.

> Determine customer behavior.

> Forecast product sales with greater accuracy.

> Plan product lifecycles.

> Evaluate the performance of sales representatives.

> View detailed (at the line item level) information on sales orders, returns, deliveries, invoices, and credit memos.

Case Study

A large company develops, manufactures, and markets printing and imaging systems, including laser printers, inkjet printers, and multifunction devices for homes and offices. The company also provides supplies for these devices and a variety of related services, including a distributed fleet management service that is a key competitive differentiator. Under this service, companies outsource the management of their printing operations to this company, which assures that its printing devices are continually operational and adequately stocked with necessary supplies. To provide excellence in this service and meet other strategic and operational objectives, this organization needs a reliable source of information regarding its customers, products, materials, suppliers, service staff, and much more. This information — their master data — is critically important to the company. It is the basis for the business decisions that keep the company competitive, and its reliability is crucial for optimizing efficiency and meeting compliance requirements.

Furthermore, to strengthen collaboration throughout its distributed global operations and productively engage business partners (especially those to whom this company outsources operations), this information must be readily accessible from a centralized source using common business processes. In short, master data must be managed as a strategic asset.

In the past, the company was challenged in these areas. Too often, key data elements were held locally, unavailable to the rest of the enterprise. Data cleansing was performed in reports, not at the source, and so inconsistencies remained as barriers to productivity. Call center agents often could not bring up accurate information about customers. A long-term user of SAP BusinessObjects solutions, the company wanted to reap more benefits from the software's analysis powers but could not rely on results because data quality was always held suspect.

This organization found the ideal occasion to address these challenges when it decided to replace its former enterprise resource planning software with a single instance of SAP ERP. Infecting SAP ERP with problematic data would cause many of its benefits to be lost. Therefore, concurrently with the implementation of SAP ERP, the company conducted a master data management (MDM) program. This program entailed integrating, cleansing, and consolidating master data from 15 disparate applications and creating a single, consistent, global source of master data along with a governance structure to keep it trustworthy. For tools, they relied on SAP BusinessObjects solutions, especially SAP BusinessObjects Data Services software, along with the SAP NetWeaver Master Data Management (SAP NetWeaver MDM) component, SAP NetWeaver Portal component, and SAP NetWeaver Process Integration (SAP NetWeaver PI) offering. These applications combined to provide all of the functionality required for such a massive data management undertaking — a rarity for a single vendor to offer. In addition, their tight integration with SAP ERP greatly simplified data flow throughout the software infrastructure.

The customer created a reusable framework for migrating master data. During the initial data readiness stage, the team developed an understanding of the data sources and how they are used. Next, they integrated and cleaned data, delivering only trusted information to the central repository. The team then consolidated and harmonized data elements into a uniform landscape for ready accessibility, and created metadata regarding their relationships and the business processes and applications that use them. Finally, in the data governance stage, business users followed rigorous processes to maintain quality.

Summary

Trusted information helps end users, managers, departments, and ultimately the entire organization to have confidence in their information and decisions. In the course of this chapter, we have briefly looked at the different components that make up the SAP BusinessObjects set of enterprise information management (EIM) technologies. SAP offers components that work in ETL, data quality, data marts, and data federation. SAP also has solutions that look at unstructured data both internally and externally. In the next chapter, we'll take a look at the set of solutions that make up the SAP BusinessObjects enterprise performance management (EPM) portfolio.

7

SAP BusinessObjects Enterprise Performance Management Solutions

The SAP BusinessObjects enterprise performance management solutions (EPM) enables companies to capitalize on the value of their existing data assets. With these solutions, organizations can become more agile by gaining organizational alignment, visibility, and confidence that give them optimal control and competitive advantage. These solutions can integrate with SAP BusinessObjects business intelligence (BI) solutions; SAP BusinessObjects enterprise information management (EIM) solutions; and SAP BusinessObjects governance, risk, and compliance (GRC) solutions. Users can maximize business profitability, manage risk and compliance, and optimize corporate systems, people, and processes. Let's start by taking a look at SAP BusinessObjects Planning and Consolidation.

SAP BusinessObjects Planning and Consolidation

The SAP BusinessObjects Planning and Consolidation application comes in two different flavors. There is a version for the SAP

Compliance with regulatory and financial reporting requirements

NetWeaver technology platform and a different version for the Microsoft technology platform. The application brings order to business planning processes by helping users plan, budget, and forecast more effectively. With embedded support for financial consolidation, the software facilitates compliance with regulatory and financial reporting requirements. Key features and benefits include the following:

> **Business planning and budgeting:** Gain support for top-down and bottom-up planning and budgeting, leading to timely, more accurate plans aligned with strategic goals.

> **Forecasting:** Enable continuous planning and rolling forecasts to meet rapidly changing business conditions.

> **Reporting and analysis:** Generate production and management reports (including exception reports) on the fly.

> **Consolidation:** Fulfill legal and management consolidation and reporting requirements for a faster, more compliant close.

> **Shorter time:** Reduce cycle time in creating and approving budgets by enabling finance and line of-business managers to collaborate to align budgets.

> **Empower business users:** Enable users to own and modify common business processes without IT assistance via a solution they can maintain themselves.

> **Higher productivity:** Increase business user productivity with native access to familiar tools such as Microsoft Office.

> **Diminished risk:** Minimize business and compliance risk by enabling transparent financial reporting with a fully documented audit trail from a single data repository.

Aligning operational plans with corporate goals

SAP BusinessObjects Planning and Consolidation gives end users access to reliable corporate data and streamlines planning and consolidation processes. It lets them align operational plans with corporate goals, initiatives, and metrics defined using the SAP BusinessObjects Strategy Management application. They can execute to plan, understand risk factors, and have the financial resources budgeted to support all initiatives.

Familiar Microsoft Office applications, including Excel, as well as an intuitive, 100% thin-client web interface, serve as native interfaces to the application. Business users can access Excel spreadsheets linked directly to live operational data; as data is updated, so is the spreadsheet. Working with tools they know well, business users need minimal training and are productive from day one. Business users view relevant, context-sensitive selections based on where they are in an application and their security profile, enabling them to understand what to do, when, and why.

All users can access information and create reports on the fly without help from IT. Drag-and-drop interfaces enable them to create reports intuitively. They can create custom reports or adapt the reporting templates that come with the software to meet their needs.

Drag-and-drop interfaces

Today's finance department must ensure that staff and line-of-business (LOB) managers follow consistent processes enterprise-wide. Without the right support for processes such as annual or quarterly budgeting or closing the books, even small deviations can throw off key figures. Self-service business process flows guide users through each step of a given planning or consolidation-related process, providing confidence that all relevant contributors consistently complete all required steps. Business process flows are automatically tracked and audited, and are customizable to the needs of the organization.

SAP BusinessObjects Planning and Consolidation is a single application that delivers planning, budgeting, forecasting, reporting, and financial consolidation functionality, eliminating the need to use multiple applications that require manual integration. The result is saved time and money, fewer errors, and a more consistent user experience. The centralized data repository contains up-to-date "actuals" from the user's operational systems in addition to plan data. This provides instant access to a complete picture of how their business performed and how it is expected to perform. If they need to drill into the specifics — to compare marketing expenditures last year to the budget this year, for example — they can do that from one application. Activities such as budgeting and statutory reporting are transformed into efficient, collaborative processes that foster confidence.

Save time and money, with fewer errors and a more consistent user experience

With a greater understanding of company performance, the user can make better decisions that contribute to future business results.

Users can perform bottom-up and top-down financial and operational planning with a single application and user interface. They can collaborate on plans, manage stakeholder interactions, track versions and changes, engage managers in the planning process, and enable clear ownership and accountability. Planning processes are supported by business process flows and automation that help ensure the right people participate at the right time. And organizations can incorporate unstructured data such as Microsoft Office documents and email to help tell the story behind plans.

The application supports a streamlined process for business-relevant budgets that the entire organization agrees on and that align with strategic plans. Widely distributed stakeholders can work together on spreadsheets, both online and offline. Because they start with a single, consistent version of operational and financial data — both real-time and historical — users can be confident in the integrity and accuracy of their budgets.

What-if modeling   To simplify forecasting, business process flows are tightly linked to the data and processes supporting planning and budgeting. What-if modeling and scenario-planning functions enable assessment of budgeting reasonability in real time.

SAP BusinessObjects Planning and Consolidation supports financial and operational reporting and analysis. Organizations can perform production and management reporting (including exception reports), financial and operational analysis, and multidimensional analysis. The software also provides a "park-and-go" feature that captures the data users are currently working with so they can work remotely offline when performing analysis.

Now users can meet legal and management consolidation and reporting requirements for a fast close process. Because a central data repository contains up-to-date "actuals" from the operational systems, users have instant access to harmonized charts of accounts. This shaves weeks off the consolidation process and supports compliance with regulatory mandates, such as the Sarbanes-Oxley Act (SOX). Users gain a single, centralized view of performance data and can instantly generate clear, transparent financial statements and reports relating to, for example, profit and loss, cash flows, and balance sheets. The software helps users compare budget versus "actual," automate the intercompany elimination process, gain transparency into corporate transactions at all levels, manage any number of currencies, and perform conversions, allocations, and eliminations. Automated reports support all reporting standards, including GAAP and International Financial Reporting Standards (IFRS). Finally, the software improves compliance with regulatory and financial standards and generates a fully documented audit trail.

As we mentioned at the beginning of this section, there are two different types of SAP BusinessObjects Planning and Consolidation. The first is for the SAP NetWeaver platform and plugs directly into SAP NetWeaver BW. It uses the well-known, Business Warehouse architecture as the data storage backend for the solution. The second type of SAP BusinessObjects Planning and Consolidation uses Microsoft's SQL Server as the data storage backend for the solution. The solution can therefore be used by both SAP and non-SAP users to fit their planning, forecasting, and consolidation needs.

SAP NetWeaver and Microsoft SQL Server

Next we'll look at SAP BusinessObjects Strategy Management.

SAP BusinessObjects Strategy Management

Business agility means that everyone — from C-level executives to front-line workers — needs to execute on changing strategies. Everyone needs to communicate plans clearly, translate them into priorities and tasks, and instantly monitor and report on progress to any level of detail. The SAP BusinessObjects Strategy Management application empowers business users at all levels to align resources to execute on strategies, understand risk, and drive efficiency and profitability. Some key features and benefits of SAP BusinessObjects Strategy Management include the following:

Business agility

> **Communication:** Transform written plans into living documents that can be used with employees to define, discuss, share, and update goals.

> **Collaboration:** Motivate employees and encourage greater collaboration by making performance-relevant data available in a contextually appropriate, personalized way.

> **Strategy management:** Deploy resources more efficiently by understanding interdependencies, "below horizon" objectives, risks, and the importance of initiatives to strategic goals.

> **Optimized performance:** Improve performance through greater organizational alignment and strategy adoption.

> **Greater agility:** Enjoy more effective collaboration, communication, and understanding of interdependencies, priorities, and risk.

> **Improved visibility:** See more clearly and have more control over the factors that affect the organization.

> **Higher confidence:** Be more confident in decisions and information when the entire organization works off the same data and can react quickly to changing business needs.

Set clear priorities and tasks

The SAP BusinessObjects Strategy Management application helps both LOB managers and corporate executives drive strategic execution into the planning process. By clearly linking strategic plans to initiatives, performance measures, and people, users can set clear priorities and tasks that employees can act on with confidence and purpose. Ultimately, executives gain greater visibility into and control over the factors that affect the organization's performance, which leads to more agile execution. The application addresses the needs of both the organization and individual stakeholders. It provides the tools needed to effectively communicate and manage strategic goals, initiatives, and key performance indicators (KPIs) from initial definition to completed execution. And because the software enables management to prioritize and weight initiatives based on their impact on strategic goals, employees know how to focus their daily actions. They are empowered to leverage their collective intelligence, work collaboratively toward a common mission, and understand exactly how they bring value to the business. Figure 7.1 illustrates how Strategy Management helps to close the gap between strategy and execution.

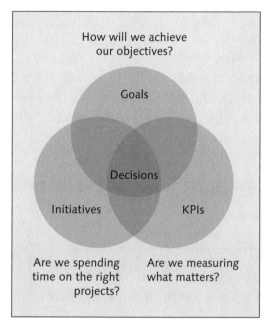

How will we achieve
our objectives?

Goals

Decisions

Initiatives KPIs

Are we spending
time on the right
projects?

Are we measuring
what matters?

Figure 7.1 Closing the Gap Between Strategy and Execution

When used with other SAP BusinessObjects EPM solutions, SAP BusinessObjects Strategy Management can help organizations close the gap between strategy and execution.

The application supports the strategy development process by transforming written plans developed by executives into living documents that can be used with employees to define, discuss, share, and update goals. These documents can include rich contextual visualizations that drive greater understanding of key objectives across your organization. For example, "pathway" diagrams depict the progressive stages and desired performance targets involved in realizing your organization's short-, medium-, and long-term vision. They help everyone understand the phases — which goals play primary roles and which goals must be prioritized. And to help gain adoption, users can import custom diagrams already used within their company and include them in strategic plans.

Visualization

SAP BusinessObjects Strategy Management makes performance-relevant data available in a contextually appropriate way. With secure, role-based access to data from across the enterprise and interdependency ("fishbone") diagrams, employees can better understand how their work affects (and is affected by) other stakeholders and departments. They can quickly measure ongoing progress toward their objectives, assess risk, and determine where efforts are most needed. This insight frees executives, managers, and analysts to spend more time executing on strategy and identifying new or more optimal opportunities for the business.

Giving everyone easier access to performance-related information increases transparency regarding activities underway in other departments and promotes greater collaboration.

Ex Example

> The vice president of sales can give the director of marketing direct access to pipeline data so they can work together on initiatives to meet revenue goals. This promotes teamwork and provides greater intelligibility.

Performance reports and operational reviews are part of every organization's activities and involve different audiences ranging from staff and board members to shareholders and the public. With SAP BusinessObjects Strategy Management, everything required to prepare for any type of operational review is centralized, consistent, and instantly available. With data in one "system of record," employees can consolidate and present relevant information and KPIs for their target audience in minutes. And because all reports are based on a single, trusted data source, concerns over data accuracy and validity are minimized.

The software enables management to prioritize and weight initiatives based on their impact on strategic goals, which enables resources to be deployed effectively and informs employees how to focus their daily actions. Via integration with the SAP BusinessObjects Risk Management application, key risk indicators can be displayed alongside KPIs, enabling proactive identification of strategies at risk. Likewise, the application can automatically detect and communicate "below horizon" objectives so that users can proactively manage exceptions and head off problems. This is especially helpful in situations where the company may appear to be performing according to plan, but in reality, there may be a danger of failure.

SAP BusinessObjects Strategy Management can be deployed by executives within their own department or business unit, not just at the corporate level, for immediate results. For example, the head of marketing can roll out the software to help ensure execution of marketing initiatives needed to drive sales and deploy it jointly with the sales department for more effective collaboration on reaching sales goals. Smaller operational implementations allow companies to quickly develop a record of success and then scale the application across the enterprise. Once deployed on a corporate level, executives can align corporate and operational strategies with ease and gain complete visibility from a performance management perspective.

The solution can be thought of as almost an umbrella control product to align and track all of the applications in an organization's environment. It can be used with both SAP and non-SAP applications.

Umbrella control product

Now that we have taken a look at the two flagship products in the SAP EPM suite, let's take a look at some of the other offerings that are available.

SAP BusinessObjects Financial Consolidation

To meet strict regulatory consolidation and reporting requirements, organizations need an application that gives control to the finance office yet is flexible enough for subsidiaries. The SAP BusinessObjects Financial Consolidation application provides users with the power, agility, and confidence to close their books quickly. Some of the key features and benefits of the solution include the following:

> **Legal consolidation and reporting:** Gain the power, financial intelligence, process control, and transparency to comply with global reporting requirements.

> **Management reporting:** Take advantage of timely and reliable information and analysis to address all of your performance management reporting requirements.

> **Power:** Get a faster close through streamlined financial consolidation and reporting processes, without sacrificing data quality.

> **Agility:** Employ a safer adaptation to changing needs without having to rebuild or destroy previous reporting scenarios, saving time and money.

> **Confidence and corporate compliance:** Enjoy greater data reliability for legal reporting and management decisions.

As an organization grows, so does the difficulty of its financial consolidation and reporting challenges. Organizations must deal with multiple currencies, various accounting standards, and a host of reporting and compliance regulations. Many grapple with the challenges brought on by mergers and acquisitions, such as the integration of new business units into the reporting chain. Through all of this, the organization must balance the need for precise financial reporting and corporate governance with the need for timeliness in meeting reporting deadlines.

Consolidation and reporting requirements aren't easy

For organizations, addressing consolidation and reporting requirements isn't easy. Too often, companies get tripped up by the intercompany reconciliation process, data quality and collection errors, weak audit trails, poor performance from consolidations applications, or a lack of automation for key processes. Then the IT department has to get involved, and the finance team spends extra time fixing errors, which causes overtime expense and longer financial close cycles. When this occurs, critical financial information isn't available when decision makers or investors need it, and the organization suffers from uninformed choices and missed opportunities.

A fast, high-quality close describes a corporation's ability to complete its accounting cycles and close its books quickly and accurately. Organizations that close fast, with the support of a powerful financial consolidation system, reap the benefits of quick access to information. They have more time for value-added analysis, improved control systems and quality, and faster reporting and statutory compliance. And they can reduce costs and strengthen investor relations.

With patented database processing technology, the SAP Business-Objects Financial Consolidation application helps users recover critical time in their closing and management reporting cycles without sacrificing any of the controls or auditing needed for today's global compliance environment.

Recover critical time in closing and management reporting

SAP BusinessObjects Financial Consolidation performs simultaneous consolidation processing directly in the database rather than at the application server. The application doesn't compromise the audit trail, and users experience fewer cycles.

The ability to automate as many financial consolidation processes as possible is vital to a fast close. Applications that centralize data and metadata management, automate interfaces with source systems, and automate business rules, such as data validation, are a start.

SAP BusinessObjects Financial Consolidation takes automation to that level. The application includes built-in rules logic that automates consolidation entries. Currency translation adjustments, minority interest and equity calculations, intercompany reconciliations, and automatic cash flows are easily set up through a standard user interface and intuitive wizards.

The application can intelligently cope with multiple reporting channels, differing charts of accounts, account flows, and numerous analysis dimensions to retain past reporting frameworks within the system. This enables finance professionals to safely adapt to changing needs without having to rebuild or destroy previous reporting scenarios, saving time and money.

Supported by powerful analytical functionality, the application delivers information to users on a near-real-time basis, with updates flowing automatically from a reliable central data source. This enables your financial analysts to evaluate data more quickly and enables your finance team to derive more definitive answers to complex business questions. Business leaders can make decisions based on the most accurate and up-to-date information and analysis. Using the advanced

Evaluate data quickly and gain definitive answers

benchmarking functionality in SAP BusinessObjects Financial Consolidation, companies can pull in key data about peers and competitors and then use that data to measure and improve performance. Scenario-creation tools help exploit this data for more accurate merger and acquisition planning.

Accurate data, reports, analysis, and simulations

SAP BusinessObjects Financial Consolidation provides access to accurate data, reports, analysis, and simulations. All processes, data, and users are connected to the application's integrated data model so that all decisions are based on consistent, reliable data, enabling an organization to report and analyze information more quickly.

The application can be integrated into both SAP and non-SAP software environments and can load source data from any general ledger application. SAP BusinessObjects Financial Consolidation is fully supported by the SAP BusinessObjects Financial Information Management application, allowing users to manage the process of accessing, mapping, and loading information from source systems. SAP BusinessObjects Financial Information Management combines ease of use with functionality that facilitates compliance, helps ensure data reliability, and builds trust. Preapproved intercompany reconciliations can be loaded directly from the SAP BusinessObjects Intercompany application into SAP BusinessObjects Financial Consolidation.

Generally accepted accounting principles

Data coming into financial consolidation applications must be intelligently checked and filtered based on the reporting framework and rules defined by central finance. Generally accepted accounting principles (GAAP) presentation, required information breakdowns, and starting and end dates are examples of automatic checkpoints. By employing SAP BusinessObjects Financial Consolidation, finance centers can help ensure data quality throughout a reporting cycle. They can be sure that incoming information not only respects the timing and expected format but also makes sense; is consistent, complete, and commented appropriately; and goes through the right auditable approval process. This leads to greater quality and a "right first time" approach to the closing cycle.

The application supports comprehensive process control, data access security, and transparent and auditable change management, including the establishment of audit trails from source to disclosure. It facilitates the publishing of eXtensible Business Reporting Language (XBRL) instance statements by working together with the SAP BusinessObjects XBRL Publishing application by UBmatrix. (We will talk more about the XBRL application in the next section.) As a result, companies are able to address the legal reporting and disclosure requirements of regulations more easily, such as International Financial Reporting Standards (IFRS) and the Sarbanes-Oxley Act (SOX).

The SAP BusinessObjects Financial Consolidation Solution is an excellent alternative for users looking for a consolidations-only solution. Let's take a look at the SAP BusinessObjects XBRL Publishing application next.

SAP BusinessObjects XBRL Publishing

The SAP BusinessObjects XBRL Publishing application enables business users to leverage data in SAP Business Suite software and SAP BusinessObjects EPM solutions and prepare XBRL documents. Designed for ease of use, speed, and flexibility, the application gives organizations greater control over the XBRL generation process for communicating financial and business data. Some of the key features and benefits of XBRL publishing include the following:

> **XBRL taxonomy navigation:** Quickly search and filter large, complex taxonomies to find tags relevant for your business data.

> **Mapping:** Map taxonomy tags to data using a drag-and-drop mapping environment.

> **Validation:** Use comprehensive validation functionality to confirm accuracy and completeness and to identify issues.

> **Disclosure inclusion:** Link to and import management discussions, disclosures, footnotes, and other narratives created in Microsoft Word to XBRL documents.

> **Taxonomy extension:** Easily extend published XBRL taxonomies to include other information.

> › **Compliance:** Be confident that your XBRL documents comply with the business rules of third-party taxonomies.

> › **Reduced time and effort:** Create XBRL documents more easily thanks to integration with Excel, taxonomy navigation tools, and drag-and-drop functions that simplify mapping.

> › **Lower audit costs:** Perform audits faster, more accurately, and at lower cost because auditors can "slice and dice" your financial data quickly and easily.

> › **Greater confidence:** Be confident in your financial disclosures because data and mappings are validated as accurate, complete, and in compliance with business rules defined by third-party taxonomies.

> › **More opportunities:** Take advantage of increased flexibility and control and lower costs by eliminating the need for XBRL outsourcing services.

The global standard for business and financial exchange

The XBRL specification has become the new global standard for exchanging financial and business information. With the U.S. Securities and Exchange Commission (SEC) joining European banking regulators, the UK tax authorities, and others in mandating its use, implementing an XBRL reporting solution is no longer an option — it's a requirement. XBRL enables all accounting jurisdictions — both U.S. and foreign — to download, codify, and analyze time-sensitive financial data in seconds. Each jurisdiction can define its own accounting taxonomy, a set of agreed-upon, computer-readable "tags" for individual data items in business reports. When a company reports a figure for annual revenues, for example, that figure can be tagged in a way that enables almost any computer to immediately recognize and categorize it as "annual revenues." A sample format is shown in Figure 7.2.

Pull data from any consolidation application

To generate an XBRL-based financial statement, organizations need to choose line items tags from a regulator's taxonomy and map them to their financial figures. Given that any one company can have thousands of data items, getting consolidated financials published as XBRL documents is no trivial task. That's why many companies have outsourced XBRL tagging and document generation. With the SAP BusinessObjects XBRL Publishing application, companies can pull data from any consolidation application (or other business software) and prepare, review, and analyze data in XBRL documents quickly and accurately. This is a more cost-effective approach that also gives users greater flexibility and control over the process.

```
<!-- (c) 2002 IASC Foundation and XBRL International -->
<!-- Date/time created: 11/8/2002 1:02:57 PM -->
- <group xsi:schemaLocation=" http://www.xbrl.org/taxonomy/int/fr/ias/ci/pfs/2002-11-15 ias-ci-pfs-2002-11-15.xsd http://www.xbrlSolutions.com/taxonomies/iso4217/2002-06-30
  http://www.xbrlsolutions.com/taxonomies/iso4217/2002-06-30/iso4217.xsd ">
    <!-- Row:10 Property, plant and equipment -->
    <iascf-pfs:PropertyPlantEquipment numericContext="Current_AsOf">540000</iascf-pfs:PropertyPlantEquipment>
    <iascf-pfs:PropertyPlantEquipment numericContext="Prior_AsOf">400000</iascf-pfs:PropertyPlantEquipment>
    <!-- Row:11 Investment property -->
    <iascf-pfs:InvestmentProperty numericContext="Current_AsOf">150000</iascf-pfs:InvestmentProperty>
    <iascf-pfs:InvestmentProperty numericContext="Prior_AsOf">150000</iascf-pfs:InvestmentProperty>
    <!-- Row:12 Goodwill -->
    <iascf-pfs:Goodwill numericContext="Current_AsOf">140000</iascf-pfs:Goodwill>
    <iascf-pfs:Goodwill numericContext="Prior_AsOf">150000</iascf-pfs:Goodwill>
    <!-- Row:13 Investments in associates -->
    <iascf-pfs:InvestmentsAssociates numericContext="Current_AsOf">60000</iascf-pfs:InvestmentsAssociates>
    <iascf-pfs:InvestmentsAssociates numericContext="Prior_AsOf">60000</iascf-pfs:InvestmentsAssociates>
    <!-- Row:16 Total Non Current Assets -->
    <iascf-pfs:NonCurrentAssets numericContext="Current_AsOf">890000</iascf-pfs:NonCurrentAssets>
    <iascf-pfs:NonCurrentAssets numericContext="Prior_AsOf">760000</iascf-pfs:NonCurrentAssets>
    <!-- Row:19 Inventories -->
    <iascf-pfs:Inventories numericContext="Current_AsOf">350000</iascf-pfs:Inventories>
    <iascf-pfs:Inventories numericContext="Prior_AsOf">175000</iascf-pfs:Inventories>
    <!-- Row:20 Trade and other receivables -->
    <iascf-pfs:TradeOtherReceivablesCurrent numericContext="Current_AsOf">490000</iascf-pfs:TradeOtherReceivablesCurrent>
    <iascf-pfs:TradeOtherReceivablesCurrent numericContext="Prior_AsOf">590000</iascf-pfs:TradeOtherReceivablesCurrent>
    <!-- Row:21 Prepayments -->
    <iascf-pfs:PrepaymentsCurrent numericContext="Current_AsOf">5000</iascf-pfs:PrepaymentsCurrent>
```

Figure 7.2   Sample XBRL Format

SAP BusinessObjects XBRL Publishing works together with SAP consolidation and financial reporting applications to enable financial staff to prepare XBRL report submissions right from their desktops. Finance and compliance teams can create, interact with, customize, and validate all kinds of XBRL documents quickly and efficiently.

Preparers first assemble financial reports using one of the following:

> The SAP BusinessObjects Planning and Consolidation application

> The SAP BusinessObjects Financial Consolidation application

> SAP Business Suite software

They can then use the SAP BusinessObjects XBRL Publishing application to tag, transform, and map this data to create XBRL-instance documents. And because SAP BusinessObjects XBRL Publishing comes with the leading XBRL engine from UBmatrix Inc., users can be confident that their documents are valid for the taxonomies used by regulatory agencies.

Integrated development environment

SAP BusinessObjects XBRL Publishing also provides an integrated development environment for building, extending, and maintaining XBRL taxonomies. This means users can incorporate custom reporting requirements, for example, to add information to financial reports needed to represent their company more favorably to investors.

Translating Microsoft Excel–based reports into XBRL using SAP BusinessObjects XBRL Publishing is fast and efficient. The application allows users to retrieve taxonomies from their desktop or from the Web. Taxonomies can be large and complex, containing thousands of elements. SAP BusinessObjects XBRL Publishing provides a search and filtering functionality that allows business users to navigate them quickly. Using mapping, search, and filter dialogs, they can browse a taxonomy hierarchy and perform a full or partial search of concepts and labels. Users can use smart filtering to limit the scope of a search to certain areas of the taxonomy, such as the income statement, and access a detailed view of mappings to confirm matches with their financial data.

Refresh without having to remap

The drag-and-drop mapping environment allows business users to map concepts, contexts, and units (such as monetary and shares) with automatic synchronization between their financial report and the mapping tool. For example, when users click on a cell in Excel, the tagged information is highlighted in the mapping dialog window. Users can also refresh reports with the latest data without having to remap.

SAP BusinessObjects XBRL Publishing provides fast, thorough validation of generated XBRL documents against the syntax of taxonomy business rules so that the right numeric values are in the right numeric fields. In addition, XBRL validates the semantics of the data, for example, to confirm that the balance sheet actually balances. Users can also access automatically generated reports that identify incomplete mappings, distinguish between actual errors and detected inconsistencies, trace errors for fast resolution, and help ensure compliance.

When creating XBRL documents, SAP BusinessObjects XBRL Publishing acts as common user interface for users of SAP Business Suite software and SAP BusinessObjects EPM solutions. Business users work in a familiar Excel–based environment and don't need to learn or work with complex XBRL syntax directly. They simply use SAP Business-Objects XBRL Publishing to meet all XBRL reporting needs, right from their desktops. XBRL instance documents containing the full XBRL syntax for each report are always available.

The software also makes it easier to incorporate into reports comple-   **Footnotes**
mentary sources of information stored in Microsoft Word, such as financial table footnotes and management discussion and analyses. Users can attach Word documents, as well as reference select content from each document when producing XBRL. Footnote entries can be reused any number of times, and multiple footnotes can be associated with a given reporting element. This approach offers the best of both worlds: Users can create financial reports in a friendly Excel environ-ment and create text using Word.

SAP BusinessObjects XBRL Publishing gives companies great flexibil-ity when creating XBRL reports. Many organizations want to extend their XBRL reporting beyond standard taxonomies, as shown in the following example.

Ex Example

To differentiate themselves from competitors, a company uses SAP BusinessObjects XBRL Publishing to provide extra information to inves-tors. The application enables the company to design and extend XBRL taxonomies using simple drag-and-drop editing functions, such as a busi-ness rules editor. The company can also define relationships across ex-tended links (created by breaking up complex links), as well as link base types (the parts of the taxonomy defining the data presentation, calcula-tions, labels, and definitions).

Because SAP BusinessObjects XBRL Publishing complies with the XBRL 2.1 specification, companies can use it to leverage the full po-tential of XBRL reporting. It supports any taxonomy in use today and has been used to model many of the world's XBRL taxonomies, such as International Financial Reporting Standards (IFRS), U.S. GAAP, and more. The application also supports basic and block-text footnotes, which is a user-friendly way to capture both plain text and formatted HTML text.

In summary, any company can use SAP BusinessObjects XBRL Publishing to fulfill XBRL reporting requirements from its respective authority. Next we'll take a look at the SAP BusinessObjects Financial Information Management Solution.

SAP BusinessObjects Financial Information Management

With the SAP BusinessObjects Financial Information Management application, users can take the risk, cost, and effort out of manual, error-prone processes to collect, map, and move data into performance management software. It integrates directly with data sources — both SAP and non-SAP — and validates that data loads correctly into and between SAP BusinessObjects EPM solutions. Some key features and benefits of this application include the following:

> **Data collection:** Connect directly to source systems to move data into or between SAP BusinessObjects EPM solutions.

> **Mapping:** Use an intuitive, wizard-driven process to define and maintain sophisticated data mappings, create mapping rules, and map accounts to multiple dimensions.

> **Loading:** Launch loading tasks and monitor task execution in real time.

> **Audit trail creation and reporting:** Automatically generate detailed mapping and loading histories for each user, and instantly drill back to source data from any consolidated number.

> **Security:** Govern user access to data needed to perform daily tasks with role-based permissions.

> **Higher capacity:** Increase productivity of finance staff by replacing manual activities with efficient, repeatable information management.

> **Increased assurance:** Enjoy higher confidence levels in financial data by reducing data integrity risk when collecting, mapping, and moving data.

> **Reduced costs:** Lower compliance costs by standardizing processes, automatically generating audit trails, enabling drill-to origin, and supporting process transparency.

> **Decrease time:** Streamline performance management processes for faster profitability reporting, more accurate planning, reduced closing cycles, and shorter audit time frames.

> **Greater business value:** Increase value through superior connectivity that supports closed-loop EPM processes and reporting.

The SAP BusinessObjects Financial Information Management application enables finance professionals to manage the process of accessing, mapping, and loading information from source systems to SAP BusinessObjects EPM solutions, which are part of the SAP BusinessObjects portfolio. The application combines ease of use with functionality that facilitates full compliance, builds trust in the data, and helps ensure data reliability — from source to report. All of this can be done without IT assistance.

The application provides connectivity with SAP and non-SAP applications, facilitating fast, robust data collection from across the enterprise. It features strong finance controls, data validation functions, and comprehensive audit ability, which enables everyone in your organization to work with trusted, up-to-date data.

Integration with and access to trusted data enables users to simultaneously improve EPM business processes and facilitate corporate compliance. With SAP BusinessObjects Financial Information Management, users gain an information management solution with powerful data integration functionality. They can load data from SAP and non-SAP sources directly into their SAP BusinessObjects EPM solutions to support their business planning, profitability, and financial consolidation processes. Through more effective information management, they can improve their EPM business processes in ways that accelerate planning, optimize profitability, reduce audit times, and facilitate easier compliance with legal and management reporting

EPM and corporate compliance

requirements. In addition, the application also supports EPM-to-EPM integration for closed-loop EPM processes, which is the key to conducting common closed-loop performance management scenarios. Figure 7.3 shows an example of a closed-loop EPM process.

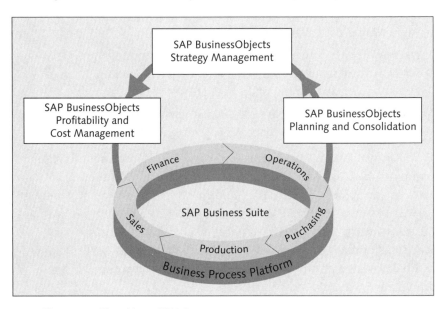

Figure 7.3   Closed Loop EPM Process

SAP BusinessObjects Financial Information Management is designed for ease of use, enabling business users to set up and use repeatable, automated processes for managing enterprise financial data. Deployment and maintenance are simpler; because the software runs in a web browser, there's no need for client installations on employees' PCs. And the application can be easily distributed and maintained for enterprise users.

The application makes it easier to access and use data; it shares a common "look and feel" with other SAP BusinessObjects EPM solutions and is launched directly from within the following applications:

> SAP BusinessObjects Financial Consolidation
> SAP BusinessObjects Planning and Consolidation
> SAP BusinessObjects Profitability and Cost Management

Once deployed, the application provides business users with a familiar environment for managing enterprise financial data, acting as a
staging room for all financial data across the enterprise. SAP Business-
Objects Financial Information Management provides an intuitive
environment for business users to define integration mappings and
load validated data to a target EPM application. No manual coding
is required; using a wizard-driven integration interface, users simply
select the source and target applications from a list. Table 7.1 provides
examples of application and database connectivity.

Application Connectivity	Database Connectivity
SAP Business Suite Software	Oracle
SAP NetWeaver Business Warehouse	DB2
JD Edwards Software	Sybase
Oracle Applications	Microsoft SQL Server
PeopleSoft Software	Informix
Siebel Software	Teradata
	Netezza

Table 7.1 Examples of Application and Database Connectivity

This user interface (Figure 7.4) dramatically simplifies and accelerates the mapping and loading processes, helping business users work
faster and more effectively.

The following key mapping activities are supported:

> Simplified mapping
> Mapping rules for automation
> Mapping data reuse
> Multiple target-dimension mapping

SAP BusinessObjects Financial Information Management helps organizations improve data accuracy and integrity while reducing risk. Users can launch and load tasks at will and monitor task execution in
real time to verify a quick and successful integration, complete with

validated results for auditing purposes. By reducing the need for manual intervention, there is less opportunity for human error to creep into the process (a common problem with other approaches to data integration), which can increase complexity and costs.

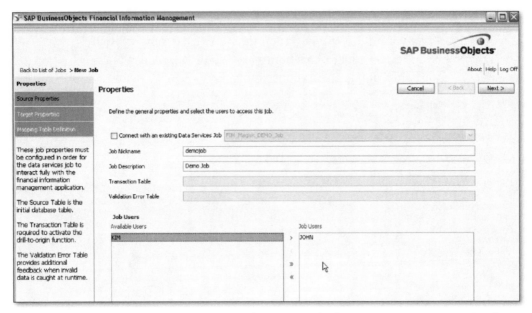

Figure 7.4 SAP BusinessObjects Financial Information Management User Interface

The application supports a standardized process for EPM data integration that enables accurate, consistent, and repeatable information management across the enterprise. The result is easier access to trusted financial information, regardless of the source system or target EPM application. Due to the consistent integration approach the software supports, users can easily reuse and modify any integration process created using the application's wizard-driven environment.

Process
transparency

The application also enables process transparency, resulting in greater clarity and confidence in integrated data, increased data accuracy, and faster auditing time frames — all while lowering compliance costs.

As data is mapped, the software automatically creates an easily accessible audit trail for every data move. Users can capture full mapping details, including the "from" and "to" values with timestamps for all affected dimensions. In addition, the audit trail tracks all details of the launch and load task, including task name, start and end timestamps, user, status, and detailed task feedback. Business users can see their own audit trail, according to their role-based permissions, complete with mapping and load histories. Audit users can see the audit history of all users. But because the audit trail history contains sensitive information, IT users, such as administrators, may not be able to view audit trails.

Users generally find that the increased process transparency enabled by SAP BusinessObjects Financial Information Management — combined with the ability to accelerate audit time frames — helps build trust and confidence in financial data and EPM reporting generated by all integrated applications.

SAP BusinessObjects Financial Information Management performs comprehensive validations before data is loaded to help ensure that error-prone financial data is loaded correctly the first time. The software automatically detects invalid mappings and missing dimensions and performs any additional validations that are defined. These comprehensive validations increase user trust and confidence in data by helping to eliminate errors and reduce data integrity risk.

Comprehensive validations

The application can support the connectivity needs of large multinational businesses with thousands of reporting entities — each with data scattered across dozens of different source systems — and can provide a full audit trail for each. The application comes with (and fully integrates with) SAP BusinessObjects Data Integrator software, which is a robust data integration tool, as described in Chapter 6. Users can integrate directly with heterogeneous application and database sources, such as their general ledger, and map data contained within them directly to their application. Because companies no longer need to use intermediate flat files or manually rekey data to "move" data, the software saves time, reduces integration costs, and helps reduce the potential for human error.

The application also supports best-practice implementations by leveraging predefined templates for integration and SAP BusinessObjects Rapid Marts packages. These packages provide powerful and flexible

Best-practice implementations

data integration content to speed implementation, lower costs, and facilitate compliance. The content enables users to leverage SAP's domain knowledge, best practices, and prebuilt data models, as well as transformation logic and data extraction expertise for both SAP and non-SAP data sources, including Oracle applications. They also can view transformations and applied rules, as well as gain complete visibility into data lineage; for example, users can trace data back to its source even when integrating third-party data using connectors. As a result, even when data comes from sources outside the SAP software landscape, users can see precisely what has been integrated.

When SAP BusinessObjects Financial Information Management is deployed as part of a larger EPM strategy, it can help users maximize productivity, achieve transparency, minimize the cost of compliance, increase overall confidence in financial results, and focus on strategic EPM activities instead of data management.

Next, we'll look at the SAP BusinessObjects Intercompany Reconciliation solution.

SAP BusinessObjects Intercompany

Improve the speed and accuracy of your closing prices

The SAP BusinessObjects Intercompany application enables business units to reconcile intercompany balances in real time and allows corporations to close faster. It is the first intercompany application to work independently of a consolidation system. SAP BusinessObjects Intercompany provides the tools for business units to debate and reconcile balances directly with one another, eliminating extra work and delays at the corporate and divisional levels. This removes intercompany reconciliation from the critical path, improving both the speed and accuracy of the closing process. Here are some key features and benefits of SAP BusinessObjects Intercompany reconciliation:

> **Intercompany reconciliation:** Resolve disputes at the peer-to-peer level, and shave days from the intercompany reconciliation process.

> **Faster reporting cycles:** Remove the intercompany reconciliation bottleneck within corporate finance by using tools to enable busi-

ness units to resolve differences earlier in the financial reporting process.

> **Greater productivity:** Increase productivity by freeing the finance department for more valuable activities, such as analyzing data and measuring and improving performance.

> **Rapid implementation:** Enjoy centralized deployment and ease of use and maintenance, which together drive down TCO and increase ROI.

SAP BusinessObjects Intercompany is a web-based, peer-to-peer communication channel between those reporting units posting intercompany balances and transactions against each other. This lateral flow of information and automatic matching ensures faster agreements, thus easing the burden on corporate finance and eliminating days from the time-consuming closing process.

Web-based, peer-to-peer

The application manages all data submitted to the central server, providing finance and other users with a real-time overview of the intercompany reconciliation process. These views also help the company adhere to deadlines, corporate policy, and timelines, regardless of a reporting unit's location or time zone.

Matching is automatic and can occur at the balance or invoice level, with the option to attach comments or other documents to facilitate more efficient communication. Matching is performed in either the local reporting or the transaction currency, with built-in support for multiple languages.

SAP BusinessObjects Intercompany offers highly sophisticated status tracking, email summaries, alerts on significant events, and a complete audit trail. It also provides a comprehensive set of reconciliation reports that enable individual reporting units as well as corporate headquarters to fully automate and follow their global intercompany process.

The application allows corporate or divisional headquarters to monitor the collaborative matching process continuously, using standardized exchange rates, materiality levels, and dedicated reconciliation views. This enables at-a-glance status checks of the global reconciliation

Freezing function

process. A "freezing" function prevents users from making additional changes after a cycle has ended.

A centralized deployment fosters rapid implementation and ease of use and maintenance. When combined with a highly intuitive user experience, this centralized approach drives down TCO to further increase user acceptance and ROI. End users of SAP BusinessObjects Intercompany can make balance adjustments that can be stored and used to create journals to update source systems. This ensures consistency among source, reconciliation, and consolidation systems.

The software provides centrally managed and easily configured access rights and is compatible with existing security infrastructure investments such as firewalls, public key infrastructures, Secure Sockets Layer (SSL), and virtual private networks (VPNs). It also leverages Microsoft .NET and relational database management system (RDBMS) support for Oracle and Microsoft SQL Server for improved scalability and performance.

SAP Intercompany is a powerful tool that can be used by any commercial user to help shave a dramatic amount of time from the close process. Next, we'll take a look at SAP BusinessObjects Profitability and Cost Management.

SAP BusinessObjects Profitability and Cost Management

Identify causes for underperformance

Users can gain a deep understanding of the levers affecting organizational costs and profitability with the SAP BusinessObjects Profitability and Cost Management application. They can identify underlying causes of underperformance, test potential impacts of changes, and take action to reduce costs and optimize profitability of products, customers, and channels. Some key features and benefits of SAP BusinessObjects Profitability and Cost Management include the following:

> **Activity-based costing:** Make informed management decisions that optimize customer and product profitability, reduce the cost to provide services, and optimize the cost of key processes.

> **Shared-services costing and cross-charging:** Align resources and capacities with demand, reduce delivery costs, and gain process transparency.

> **On-demand, what-if scenario analysis:** Model costs at any level in the organization, down to highly granular transaction data.

> **Driver-based and activity-based budgeting:** Accurately cross-charge IT and other shared services with predefined dimensions and reiterative reallocation functionality.

> **Increased visibility:** View the true drivers impacting costs and profitability, including IT shared services, via a user-friendly interface.

> **Lower costs and higher profits:** Optimize costs and profitability thanks to a detailed understanding of multidimensional drivers such as products, services, customers, and channels.

> **Organizational alignment:** Match operational capacity and support functions with demand for flawless execution of strategy.

> **Incisive decision-making:** Make better decisions due to rapid identification of underlying causes of changes in organizational cost and profitability, with the ability to test the impact of potential adjustments.

The SAP BusinessObjects Profitability and Cost Management application supports value stream performance management using lean accounting principles for enterprise-wide managerial and financial reporting. The application can help a lean enterprise produce financial statements written in plain English that provide accurate information on value stream costs. In addition to improving overall decision making, the software helps managers focus on improving cash flow, reducing inventory, and building only to actual demand.

Organizations can implement and use SAP BusinessObjects Profitability and Cost Management at any time during a lean transformation — even prior to their organizational changes. The application integrates easily with Microsoft Office and other third-party reporting and analysis tools and is designed to work across multiple enterprise resource planning (ERP) solutions and data sources.

The application enables visibility into the drivers of cost and profitability with activity-centric, multidimensional modeling and analysis functionality. Modelers across the enterprise can build even complex activity-based costing models with an intuitive, user-friendly interface and predefined dimensions. (Activity-based costing assigns costs to products or services based on the corporate resources used to produce them.)

Activity-centric, multidimensional modeling

SAP BusinessObjects Profitability and Cost Management is a web-based and scalable application designed to meet business requirements ranging from single-site implementations to global deployments. In addition, the application is flexible enough to meet the complexity of any organization's analytical requirements.

SAP BusinessObjects Profitability and Cost Management helps identify areas for cost improvements and facilitates proactive actions to rectify problems. Corporations can improve organizational understanding of how customers contribute to fixed costs — and make more precise decisions on how to grow the business, re-engineer products, or re-educate customers on purchasing activities.

The application enables activity-centric performance management in a single application, with functionality that goes beyond costing and profitability reporting. It facilitates services costing and cross-charging, along with driver-based and activity-based planning and budgeting, enabling users to cross-charge IT and other shared services accurately with predefined dimensions and reiterative reallocation functionality.

SAP BusinessObjects Profitability and Cost Management gives organizations the freedom to choose one or a combination of the most appropriate activity-based costing assignment methodologies for each responsibility center and activity: time-split, time-capture, and time-driven. Business users can drill down to the most granular level to analyze the profitability of individual customer accounts, sales order lines, or SKUs. They can use multidimensional analysis to look beyond user-level data for visibility into what products are being purchased, which are the most profitable, which delivery channels are being used, and the costs of each transaction delivered through each channel. Cost and profitability information can be presented to managers and users through fully configurable web books and reports, either in the form of an executive dashboard or in more detailed grids and charts, as shown in the executive profitability dashboard in Figure 7.5.

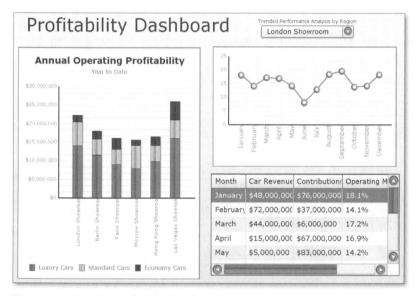

Figure 7.5 Executive Profitability Dashboard

Business users can drill down into customer data to measure profitability more accurately, instead of being limited to information from sources such as general ledger line-item entries. This helps users identify how different customer behavior influences cost and profitability. By gaining a better understanding of how resources are consumed, the enterprise can assign costs based on the consumption of resources — instead of on outdated and perhaps unreliable estimates.

Assign costs based on the consumption of resources

SAP BusinessObjects Profitability and Cost Management is built with predefined dimensionality specifically optimized for activity-based costing, which translates into fast, efficient, multidimensional model building for users across the organization. Business users can build models with multiple versions, periods, and currencies, with up to five core cost-object dimensions and attributes for unlimited grouping and alternate hierarchies.

Point-and-click model building interface

Users can take advantage of specific revenue and services dimensions that provide the suppliers of shared services within organizations — such as IT, legal, and HR — with the ability to cross-charge internal business users accurately for consumption of services. The specific revenue and services dimensions also enable better-informed strategic discussions concerning services demand, forecasts, and plans. In addition, a flexible rules engine and point-and-click assignment functionality across multiple dimensions provide modelers with an intuitive user interface to build models rapidly and maintain them with relative ease. The application has sophisticated cell-level security features and user-friendly model-control functionality to manage access and version control. Figure 7.6 shows an example of the point-and-click model-building interface.

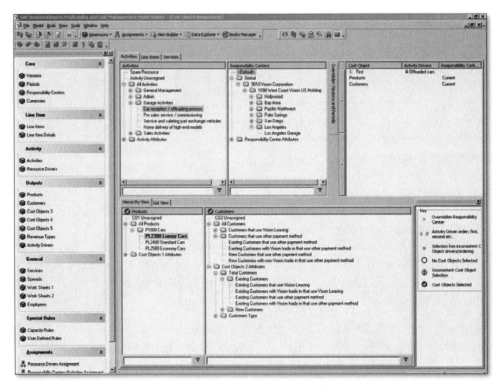

Figure 7.6 Point-and-Click Model Building Interface

The application enables users to optimize nonsystem data collection and reporting for local and remote users with unique web-based forms and integrated work-management functionality. They can speed remote deployment, minimize training, accelerate user adoption, and increase productivity through web-based data entry and reporting with context-aware views. In this way, a single report is automatically tailored to the exact needs of each user.

Remote users can input data and view reports in their local currency and language, enabling cross-border deployments. The application features security and audit-trail functionality to facilitate compliance and data and system safety. Centralized model administration and maintenance over the Web eliminate the need for local models distributed throughout the organization. There is also a user-configurable timestamped and date-stamped audit trail.

SAP BusinessObjects Profitability and Cost Management enables users to take a dual approach to analyzing transactional data, using both multidimensional and relational activity-based costing approaches for transaction-level models. The application uses a relational data structure to crunch high volumes of numbers, with a multidimensional structure to calculate unit rates accurately. The multidimensional environment gives analysts visibility into individual records with a standard, role-based, user-friendly interface. Figure 7.7 illustrates the high-volume transaction-costing model.

Mulitdimensional and relational activity-based costing

Users can slice and dice data and analyze results, create charts, and drill down from summary views to detailed cost data. They can link to related budgeting and metrics models to view performance achievement with drill-through, in-system dials, and gauges. They can perform on-demand queries and what-if analysis on trusted, web-accessible data, testing the financial impact of assumptions before committing to them. And users can maintain data in a central repository for greater efficiency and control over business information. See Figure 7.8 for an example of the what-if scenario analysis.

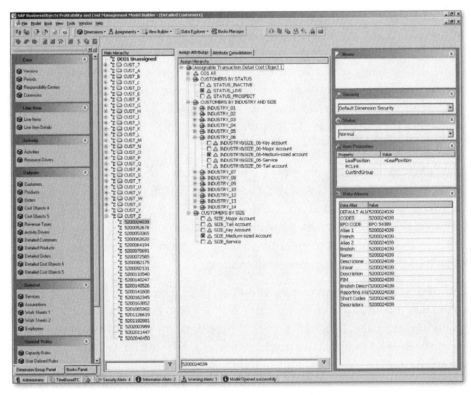

Figure 7.7 High Volume Transaction-Costing Model

As we have seen, SAP BusinessObjects Profitability and Cost Management can perform accurate analysis across multiple dimensions to gain visibility into enterprise costs and access the information that users need to make decisive business decisions.

Next, let's look at SAP BusinessObjects Spend Performance Management.

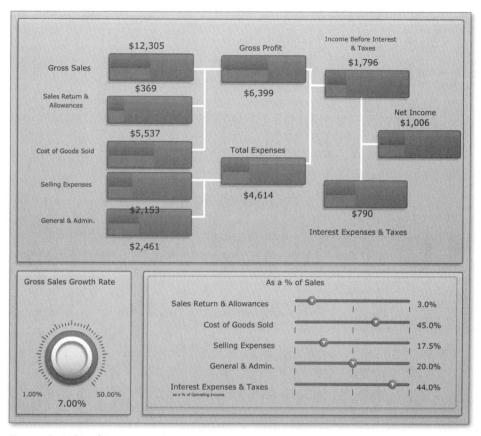

Figure 7.8 What-If Scenario Analysis

SAP BusinessObjects Spend Performance Management

The SAP BusinessObjects Spend Performance Management application provides full visibility into direct and indirect spend, helping users to proactively identify cost-savings opportunities and supplier risk. As a result, users are better positioned to reduce cost and ensure supply continuity, thereby increasing spend under management. Some key features and benefits of SAP BusinessObjects Spend Performance Management include the following:

Reduce cost and ensure supply continuity

> **Savings identification:** Present savings potential and supplier rationalization opportunities.

> **Collaborative performance management:** Capture performance goals, contributing factors, and snapshots of savings opportunities.

> **Proactive risk identification:** Identify supplier risks and prioritize alternate supplier strategies.

> **Spend and supplier data validation and enrichment:** Link spend data across business data views; normalize, validate, and enrich supplier data; assign classification structures.

> **Business process support:** Support supplier risk analysis processes with workflows, metadata, and industry expertise; provide detailed procurement analytics by leveraging data from back-office systems as well as real-time feeds from news, credit ratings, and financial indicators.

> **Increased understanding:** Gain full spend visibility by automating data capture from disparate systems and improving data accuracy.

> **Faster reactions:** Rapidly identify savings opportunities by finding savings potential and supplier rationalization opportunities.

> **Reduce supplier risks:** Reduce risks by pinpointing single-supplier dependencies and analyzing supplier risk factors.

> **Higher performance:** Increase spend under management by setting up performance goals on critical success factors and collaborating to act on insights.

The SAP BusinessObjects Spend Performance Management application can help organizations discover significant savings opportunities through an intuitive user interface that brings together accurate measures for spending, supplier or buyer volume, supplier risk factors, budgets, plans, and prices across multiple dimensions. They can use the application to establish key performance measures, identify hidden negotiating power, and launch procurement initiatives that meet strategic goals. Such goals include reducing costs, finding compliance leakage, and identifying sole-sourced suppliers or suppliers at financial, operational, or legal risk.

Deriving insights on savings opportunities and compliance leakage based on aggregated and enriched spend data is essential for procurement category managers, finance analysts, or LOB managers. To make the most of supplier relationships and contract opportunities, business users must be able to identify fragmented contracts, distributed supply bases, or multiple contracts with single suppliers on an ongoing basis. They need a way to easily analyze the distribution of company spend and market factors that may affect that spend in the future. And they need to spend less time uncovering these opportunities manually.

Identify fragmented contracts, distributed supply bases, and duplicate contracts

With SAP BusinessObjects Spend Performance Management, procurement business users can find and act on potential savings as well as proactively monitor contract compliance. The software provides continuous spend analysis across such key dimensions as supplier, category of purchased goods and services, geographic area, business unit, spend type, and contract usage. This helps companies identify opportunities for savings and supply base rationalization.

Integration with the SAP E-Sourcing application or other Web services–enabled sourcing solutions provides business users with one-click functionality to launch sourcing initiatives from an identified opportunity. Contextual information related to the opportunity — such as historical spend volume, suppliers, item or service descriptions, price, or quantity — automatically carries over to the sourcing initiative, eliminating the need for complex spreadsheets to design a sourcing project.

SAP e-Sourcing integration

The application integrates with existing ERP software. Taking an integrated and self-service approach to data management, the software includes tools to link spend data sources to extract relevant business data and context for spend analysis. It facilitates the data extraction process by supporting ETL processes for data from various SAP and non-SAP sources.

After spend data has been extracted, the software enables users to normalize supplier data, address any issues of inconsistency, help ensure the validity of the supplier you are doing business with, and remove duplicate information. To leverage total spend with the parent supplier, business users can organize supplier information according to corporate parent-child relationships.

Normalized data is classified to assign a standard classification structure for goods and services. These classifications can include the United Nations Standard Products and Services Code (UN SPSC), eCl@ss, the North American Industry Classification System, and Standard Industrial Classification codes. Classifying spend data to a taxonomy that benefits sourcing teams can gives users a critical negotiation platform to work from.

Identifying supplier risks

An effective procurement organization must be able to proactively identify supplier risks and effectively manage strategic supplier relationships. Large enterprises with a globally distributed supply base need to ensure that their supply chain is not disrupted by suppliers getting into difficulties or even going bankrupt, especially in today's volatile economy. SAP BusinessObjects Spend Performance Management helps users proactively identify supplier risks as well as prioritize these risks by spend volume and affected buying centers. Supplier risk factors may include sole-sourced suppliers, supplier concentration, supplier quality, compliance with corporate initiatives to use minority suppliers, and accounting for market risks and opportunities. In addition, a company's exposure to supplier risk cannot be adequately determined solely from the data contained in its internal systems.

Users can use SAP BusinessObjects Spend Performance Management to incorporate external information into their risk evaluation. For example, companies can include externally driven news feeds; financial, operational, and legal risk factors; and credit-scoring data from their respective data enrichment service. The application can help procurement decide whether to incorporate a master supplier agreement with volume discounts or identify alternate sources to mitigate supplier risks. Correlating a supplier risk factor with spend volume, for example, can help users prioritize their actions. The application provides configurable risk hierarchies that let users get up and running quickly.

The final SAP BusinessObjects solution that we'll cover here is SAP BusinessObjects Supply Chain Performance Management.

SAP BusinessObjects Supply Chain Performance Management

The SAP BusinessObjects Supply Chain Performance Management solution helps companies measurably improve supply chain effectiveness, for more responsive supply chain networks and improved cost control. By focusing on the right process metrics, companies can identify and diagnose bottlenecks and uncover opportunities to take informed action toward improved supply chain performance. Some key features and benefits of SAP BusinessObjects Supply Chain Performance Management include the following:

> **Business content**: Comply with leading frameworks such as the Supply Chain Operational Reference (SCOR) model.
> **Data extraction and transformation:** Access data and gain insight more quickly thanks to preintegration with transactional systems and precalculation of metrics.
> **Analysis and reporting:** Produce more useful reports with semantically consistent navigation across information.
> **Impact analysis:** Qualify relationships between supply chain metrics.
> **Metrics management:** React quickly to changing market conditions by readily defining or refining metrics and threshold values.
> **Deeper insight:** See more clearly into operational and related financial performance while complying with performance management standards, thanks to standards-based support for end-to-end processes.
> **Improved performance:** Get relevant and timely information with automated data collection derived from actual business processes.
> **Deeper understanding:** Understand operational drivers, opportunity discovery, and timely awareness of deviations from performance targets thanks to proactive diagnostics.

Lower costs and improve return on working capital

The SAP BusinessObjects Supply Chain Performance Management application helps users measurably improve the effectiveness of supply chain operations and better deliver on corporate mandates such as lowering costs and improving return on working capital. In addition to providing a more accurate measure of whether an organization is meeting its supply chain goals, the application can warn users of potential bottlenecks and identify new opportunities. Functions for root-cause diagnostics let business users take measured responses where needed.

Relying on embedded data-integration functionality, a calculation engine, and an intuitive user experience, the application is preconfigured and preintegrated to work effectively within any enterprise. It is built from a business perspective, and the software contains data models and metadata based on leading industry standards. It can automate data collection from multiple sources and proactively diagnose potential problems.

SAP BusinessObjects Supply Chain Performance Management provides companies with much-needed visibility into supply chain processes such as order-to-cash. Executives stay clearly informed about performance metrics such as shipment reliability, perfect-order fulfillment, or supply chain cost. Furthermore, users get to understand the underlying factors such as production cycle times, order backlogs, or warehouse cost, and even correlations and mutual impacts of one on the other. Figure 7.9 provides an example of a supply chain scorecard screen.

In today's IT-heavy supply chain networks, there is no shortage of data points. In any given situation, however, only a few numbers are truly important. Unable to identify the right key performance indicators (KPIs), managers may focus only on improving the measures under their immediate control, which is an approach that fosters silo thinking and frequently sacrifices overall supply chain network effectiveness for departmental efficiency. For example, isolated focus on capacity use may result in excess inventories. Likewise, merely reinforcing departmental efficiencies, such as reducing departmental cost, may simply shift costs across departments.

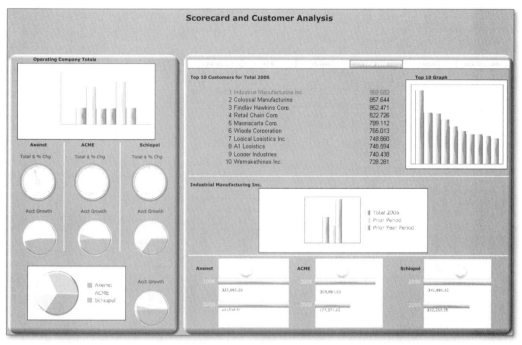

Figure 7.9 Supply Chain Scorecard

With the right metrics architecture, an organization can break down functional silos and align stakeholders behind common goals, such as improving cash-to-cash cycle time, reducing total supply chain cost, or delivering on perfect-order goals. SAP BusinessObjects Supply Chain Performance Management helps users identify and monitor the metrics that really matter for their organization. At the enterprise level, these might be perfect-order fulfillment rate, forecast accuracy, or supply chain cost. At the department level, such metrics might include on-time delivery by suppliers, plant use, or order cycle time. Figure 7.10 shows a metrics hierarchy sample.

The prebuilt metrics architecture within the application is based on the Supply Chain Operational Reference (SCOR) model and other industry standards frameworks, yet is flexible enough to meet any organization's particular requirements. Metrics are defined, documented, and associated with specific individuals within the supply chain network. This fosters accountability, which is a key premise for strategy-aligned

Accountability

supply chain execution. In the end, the right metrics drive individual behavior, and behavior drives enterprise performance.

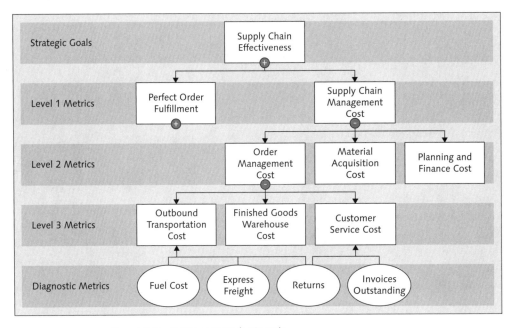

Figure 7.10   Metrics Hierarchy Sample

Business users can define new metrics, adjust threshold values, and customize dashboard views without using IT resources. If the impact of fuel costs on transportation costs declines with the introduction of hybrid vehicles, for example, the application can immediately reflect those changes. Business users can change relationships and definitions for KPIs and immediately see the results of those changes. It is also possible to change scorecard contexts as the supply chain strategy evolves — for example, moving from a geographical orientation to a category orientation. As business requirements and metrics architectures evolve, the data structures built into the application assure information integrity, without project rework.

Case Studies

SAP BusinessObjects Financial Consolidation

A large company manufactures windshields, back windows, side glass, and sunroofs for almost all of the world's major car companies as well as the replacement market. With revenues of $2.5 billion, manufacturing operations in 15 countries, and 3 affiliate companies, this organization has achieved a dominant position in the highly competitive automotive supply market. Recently, however, the company faced challenges stemming from inefficient financial consolidation and reporting processes. Financial managers were finding it increasingly difficult to deal with multiple currencies, accounting standards, reporting guidelines, and compliance regulations.

Consolidation was a particular concern. The process consisted of amalgamating subconsolidations submitted via spreadsheets from many different business units and regions. When the financial staff tried to integrate and standardize the figures, they had trouble applying consistent rules across the overall consolidation process. Although financial information was collected monthly, it was treated somewhat differently each time.

Not surprisingly, few executives or managers trusted the accuracy of the financial information, which meant that supplying consistent data for management presentations was problematic.

To resolve these issues, the IT organization concluded that the company needed to make several key improvements. The first step was creating a common database of financial information. A second goal was creating a standardized approach for the treatment of financial data. With different accounting policies and reporting cultures in the company's many regions and business units, the company needed to harmonize both the data and the processes used to collect and share it. A third objective was to increase the flexibility and accuracy of consolidation and reporting activities.

After an in-depth evaluation of competitive products, the organization chose SAP BusinessObjects Financial Consolidation to help streamline and enhance the financial closing and reporting processes. The application is used by the head-office finance team for financial consolidation and reporting and by one finance person per region. The company now leverages the software to track performance versus budget and performance versus prior year — both with full monthly consolidation that includes reports on profit and loss, balance sheet, and cash flow.

The organization implemented the consolidation software in less than 90 days. The IT team brought the project in on time and within budget by deploying the application with very few changes to its standard configuration settings. End users were pleased that the software accommodated familiar data entry processes with virtually no disruption to their work patterns.

Shortly after deployment, financial leaders noted significant improvements in many aspects of the consolidation process — particularly a newfound ability to standardize financial data across the enterprise. As part of the effort to provide better financial data to senior managers, the IT organization is using the consolidation software to sharpen cash flow calculations.

SAP BusinessObjects Profitability and Cost Management

A healthcare conglomerate provides services to more than 6.5 million people. In addition to managed care, the company provides administrative services such as claims processing and call center management, as well as pharmacy benefit management services. As the company's service portfolio became more complex, cost allocation became more difficult. The company relied on a laborious, spreadsheet-based process that allocated costs to each regional office or user. The process was prone to errors; worse, it couldn't be completed until two months after a quarterly closing. To get a better picture of the cost of doing business, financial leaders needed to understand the variables associated with providing a specific service to a specific user.

To gain a more accurate picture of costs — and provide the data needed to optimize prices — the organization implemented the SAP BusinessObjects Profitability and Cost Management application. The company chose the application because of its versatility, ease of use, and ability to accommodate preexisting business activity definitions. Shortly after implementation, the organization used the software to evaluate its claims processing activities. By breaking claims processing down into a series of steps such as receiving, processing, auditing, and reworking — and then allocating a portion of overall corporate costs to each step — the company uncovered a wide range of variables. The company reduced the cost to process a claim by 10%. The savings stemmed from making greater use of automated claims processing services and subsequent staff reassignments.

Accurate cost data helps the company renegotiate contracts, price new services, and create more accurate requests for proposal. The company can now give detailed explanations about why certain services have relatively high or low prices, and can also suggest ways for customers to cut costs. For example, when customers use electronic claims submission or automatic claims adjudication instead of manual processing, prices can be adjusted accordingly. Equally important, precise cost information helps the company assess the profitability of each customer so that prices can be realigned and margins improved. This improved insight is being used by the company's pharmacy benefit management program business, which has experienced a 20% growth in revenues.

Activity-based costing also helps the company improve auditing and reporting. Preparation time for quarterly reports has decreased from months to weeks, and the annual budget has been improved through the use of more accurate cost forecasts.

Summary

SAP BusinessObjects EPM solutions help organizations capitalize on the value of their existing data. They allow companies to better understand their strategies across the enterprise and understand how to reduce cost and increase working capital. The solutions help to increase profitability by gaining insight into the best and worst products, customers and channels. These applications empower end users to close the books faster and more accurately as well as create what-if scenarios and understand the impact of plan changes.

In the next chapter, we'll take a look at the fourth component of the SAP BusinessObjects solutions, governance, risk, and compliance (GRC) solutions.

SAP BusinessObjects Governance, Risk, and Compliance Solutions

The SAP BusinessObjects governance, risk, and compliance (GRC) solutions close the gap between strategy and execution, and establish a clear path to long-term value by enabling a preventative, real-time approach to GRC across heterogeneous environments. The solutions provide complete insight into risk and compliance initiatives and enable greater efficiency and improved flexibility. SAP BusinessObjects GRC solutions enable complete insight by providing a common approach to risk and compliance initiatives and continuously monitoring them to help users understand business conditions, manage risks, and improve decisions. In simple terms, SAP BusinessObjects GRC solutions provide companies with the ability to manage performance across the enterprise by using risk-balanced strategy management and by embedding risk-based controls in business process areas ranging from financials, to human resources, to supplier controls, to trade management.

SAP BusinessObjects GRC solutions are designed to efficiently support the documentation and implementation of automated controls for any framework. Automation of manual risk and compliance activities, compliance rationalization, and prepopulated line-of-business (LOB) and industry-specific content reduces costs and uses resources more effectively. This leads to a much more efficient compliance environment. Let's start off by taking a look at one of the most important solutions in today's marketplace, SAP BusinessObjects Risk Management.

SAP BusinessObjects Risk Management

The SAP BusinessObjects Risk Management application enables risk-adjusted management of enterprise performance to optimize efficiency, increase effectiveness, and maximize visibility across risk initiatives. Business owners can make risk-intelligent decisions, drawing from proven best-practice risk responses. Analytic dashboards provide cross-enterprise transparency to deliver stronger corporate governance. Some key features and benefits of SAP BusinessObjects Risk Management include the following:

> **Automated key risk indicator (KRI) monitoring combined with automated workflow:** Reassess risks and align strategy as changes occur.

> **Alignment of key risk and performance indicators across all business functions:** Enable earlier risk identification and dynamic risk mitigation.

> **Cross-platform, cross-vendor features:** Have an enterprise-wide picture of risk exposure and strategy execution.

> **Integrated survey features:** Accelerate input collection and collaboration.

> **Forward-looking, predictive indicators and easier KRI setup:** Enable continuous risk monitoring.

> **Predefined KRIs:** Speed implementation of relevant risk content.

> **User-friendly KRI templates:** Speed the process of measuring, organizing, and reporting on risks.

> **Optimized efficiencies:** Automate manual and fragmented risk and control activities across lines of business to optimize efficiency across the entire risk management effort.

> **Increased effectiveness:** Increase the effectiveness of risk management efforts with continuous monitoring, proactive identification, and quick response.

> **Maximized visibility:** Increase visibility for all stakeholders with a platform that aligns and integrates the management of risks and controls across all functions and processes.

The risk environment faced by most organizations is complex, including both internal and external risks from a wide range of sources. These risk sources include financial management and treasury operations, economics, operational issues, legal and regulatory concerns, and geopolitical factors. Many of these risks are interrelated, producing compounded consequences that are often difficult to spot, prepare for, or understand.

To begin addressing the challenges presented by interdependent risks, an enterprise needs a comprehensive solution that leverages powerful tools, processes, and techniques to effectively manage multiple and complex risks. Enterprise risk management (ERM) evaluates risks across the organization and across all sources. Risk assessment is embedded into major business processes, such as strategy development, performance management, and business planning. And relationships between risks are more clearly understood and monitored.

Enterprise risk management (ERM)

The impact of inadequate risk management on an enterprise can be understood by looking at three factors. First is the inability to proactively identify and mitigate risks before they become loss events and negatively impact performance. A risk manager may identify a risk and see that an acceptable risk threshold has been crossed during an annual risk assessment, but unless a system is in place to track risks in real time, the risk manager will have no idea when that threshold was crossed and for how long the risk exposure has existed. The threshold could have been crossed yesterday, with minimal impact to date, or six months prior to detection, with catastrophic consequences already underway.

Impact of inadequate risk management

The next factor is the lack of context regarding risk data. A company may have information about a specific risk to the business but lack the context in which to analyze that information to see how it affects the execution of a process or strategy or processes across other business units. Companies often find they have very little ability to analyze the impact of risks on a specific business process, let alone see how the risks across business units affect each other. The organization may have little or no knowledge regarding the sources of risks, with substantial loss event potential.

A third key factor is the inefficiency and high cost of traditional approaches to risk management. Many enterprises rely on manual processes and spreadsheets to monitor risks. Relying on spreadsheets and manual procedures is not only time consuming and resource intensive but also vulnerable to multiple inaccuracies and errors. Add to this the typically fragmented approach to risk management. Individual business units identify and monitor their risks independently, often duplicating tasks, using different methods, and lacking any coordination across the enterprise.

A poor understanding of and visibility into risks can result in multiple risks turning into loss events at one time — leading to an even greater impact.

Ex Example

Imagine a new competitor entering the marketplace at the same time a key supplier is experiencing operational problems. It is critical for the organization to get an enterprise-wide view of the full range of external and internal risks to performance and to understand the relationship between them.

To protect the value of their brands, organizations need to develop the ability to "see around corners." That is, by developing a proactive risk management strategy and implementing strong preventive controls against "hot issues" such as data privacy leaks, consumer privacy leaks, environmental accidents, financial fraud, and so on, an enterprise is in a better position to protect its reputation and sustain a positive brand image. Risk management programs, in conjunction with social and economic development initiatives, ultimately help to build up the corporate profile and improve the organization's reputation.

Another critical component of enterprise risk management is the ability to identify and manage all of the "enterprise" risks that could impact an organization. A common assumption is that most risks are financial risks. Many organizations focus a large percentage of their risk management efforts on financial controls. However, nonfinancial risks actually make up the overwhelming portion of risks to organizations. Nonfinancial sources of risk with the potential for severe business impact include the following:

> Operational

> Environmental and health

> Financial

> Legal and compliance

> Strategic

> Political and geographical

To understand how risks can impact each other, consider the following example.

Ex Example

An event occurs, such as a faulty product causes damage at a customer's facility or home, that raises questions about the safety of a company's goods or products. At about the same time, the company suffers a cancellation of a major customer contract. First, the company needs to launch expensive and resource-intensive legal and public relations efforts. These responses may or may not successfully mitigate the potential damage to the business. Either way, these actions require focus and energy from senior executives across an organization. At a minimum, these activities take executives away from their other day-to-day responsibilities, putting company performance in jeopardy. In the extreme, this type of crisis can force wholesale changes or delays in key strategic initiatives such as new product launches, business alliances, or other ventures.

The SAP BusinessObjects Risk Management application enables risk-adjusted management of enterprise performance to optimize efficiency, increase effectiveness, and maximize visibility across risk initiatives. It provides executives with the tools needed to make risk-intelligent decisions across their areas of responsibility, drawing from proven best-practice risk responses. The application provides all risk management stakeholders (including risk managers, line-of-business [LOB] managers, and corporate executives) with a single platform to automate risk management processes across disparate systems within their enterprise. This is no simple task, as the spectrum of sources of GRC information includes systems across functions, geographies, and even external sources such as supplier and partner data.

Complete visibility into internal and external risks

SAP BusinessObjects Risk Management is architected with an open framework to facilitate access to all relevant information. As a result, risk managers can eliminate much of the time spent collecting and organizing data and instead become strategic advisors to the business units. LOB managers have more complete visibility into both internal and external risks, enabling them to have a better understanding of all risks to their own business performance as well as the impact of risks they manage in other parts of the enterprise. Finally, executives have access to contextual risk information, so they can truly incorporate risk intelligence into both day-to-day and long-term decision making and strategic planning.

With this approach to ERM, companies are able to achieve agreement on top risks and accessible thresholds. The application includes tools to identify all key risks across the enterprise, perform qualitative and quantitative analysis, and build proactive monitoring into existing business processes and strategies.

SAP BusinessObjects Risk Management provides strong support in each of the major process areas required for a complete and comprehensive ERM solution. As you can see in Figure 8.1, there are five major ERM process areas:

> Risk planning
> Risk identification
> Risk analysis

> Risk response and mitigation

> Risk monitoring

SAP BusinessObjects Risk Management automates the overall ERM effort and supports key capabilities in each process area to maximize effectiveness and efficiency.

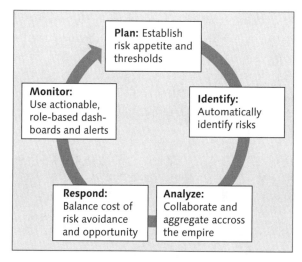

Figure 8.1 Five Major ERM Process Areas

The risk planning process involves defining the context within which business risks are to be managed. This includes setting risk threshold levels and identifying the business activities to be assessed. After the enterprise has set its strategic objectives, the ERM team must align the objectives to organizational entities. SAP BusinessObjects Risk Management facilitates this effort by providing an intuitive method of assigning business objectives to organizations, defining organizational structure for risk reporting, setting up risk appetites and threshold levels, and assigning specific risk manager responsibilities.

Risk planning

The next part of the risk planning process is to define a risk classification system. Here the application provides features to set up activity categories, risk and opportunity categories, and impact and benefit categories. In addition, the application includes user-friendly key risk indicator (KRI) templates to speed the process. This classification

Risk classification system

system is often overlooked but is critical in that it establishes a structure around which risks can be measured, organized, and reported on. The last step in the risk planning process is to define and identify all risk-relevant business activities. SAP BusinessObjects Risk Management helps in this step with tools to ease the mapping of risk activities to processes, products and services, and assets.

Risk identification   Risk identification is the next major ERM process area. The output of this step is to capture the events that can have a negative or positive impact on business objectives. The first step is to identify risks and opportunities. SAP BusinessObjects Risk Management includes survey features that accelerate input collection and foster collaboration. This is critical because successful ERM requires common understanding and consensus on the top risks.

KRIs   Next, for each risk or opportunity, drivers and impacts are defined, and then KRIs are established. The application allows for forward-looking and predictive indicators and supports flexible methods for setting up KRIs for continuous risk monitoring in operational systems. In addition, SAP BusinessObjects Risk Management flags KRIs that need to be manually updated.

Document risk interrelationships   The final step is to document risk interrelationships, including defining how risks influence one another and consolidating risks that are similar. Another feature provided by SAP BusinessObjects Risk Management is the overall process automation included in the application that helps to make risk association and consolidation a much more efficient process and much less prone to errors.

SAP BusinessObjects Risk Management includes a wide selection of predefined KRIs, defined by overall category and by industry, to help speed implementation of company-relevant risk content.

Risk analysis   The third major ERM process area is risk analysis. This step involves assessing and evaluating risks for prioritization and developing effective response strategies. The automated risk analysis feature provided by SAP BusinessObjects Risk Management is one of the most valuable components of the application.

Most companies today have no way to proactively and automatically identify and analyze risks. Their processes are mostly manual, with few analysis tools. SAP BusinessObjects Risk Management incorporates several best practices whereby risk managers start with a qualitative analysis and then add quantitative measures. Risk managers can build increasing sophistication into the risk analysis by looking at business scenarios to determine risk exposure and additional risk drivers. What-if risk analysis and Monte Carlo simulations can also be performed using historical as well as estimated or third-party data.

After risks have been analyzed, they need to be presented in a visual manner for easier prioritization. SAP BusinessObjects Risk Management leverages numerous features, including risk heat maps, dashboards, and tools, to configure the output and embed it in presentations. Risk prioritization helps allocate working capital efficiently by determining which risks to respond to and how.

Risk prioritization

The application integrates embedded SAP BusinessObjects Xcelsius Enterprise software and SAP Crystal Reports software to extend powerful reporting and visualization features that provide users with the tools to effectively communicate information across the enterprise.

The fourth major process area is risk response. In this step, the objective is to evaluate the analyzed risks and select the risks (and opportunities) that should be "treated" by balancing the costs of implementing each option against the benefits to be derived. The recovery risk responses are developed here. SAP BusinessObjects Risk Management provides the repository that enables added context to help increase the overall risk intelligence level. This helps the risk manager identify alternative responses. These approaches help determine the type of response necessary and whether it is a response to a risk or the addition of a new control to help mitigate that risk. The responses are categorized in accordance with best-practice frameworks, such as COSO II and AS/NZ 3460. Risk managers can assign ownership for risk responses and also share responses across risks.

Risk response

The final major process area in ERM is risk monitoring. The objective here is to monitor the effectiveness and completeness of the response actions, take corrective action, and communicate the status of the

Risk monitoring

risks to key stakeholders. In this area, SAP BusinessObjects Risk Management enables some very powerful capabilities.

SAP has made significant investments in developing risk monitoring software to incorporate key differentiating features. Continuous monitoring of KRIs allows risk owners to recommend and take action before risks occur.

KRIs are embedded in operational business processes so that the investment in and analytical strength of both SAP Business Suite software and non-SAP and legacy systems can be fully leveraged. Risk exposure information is automatically updated, triggering corresponding impacts to strategic objectives. The result is that, in real time, LOB managers and corporate executives have extensive visibility into risks affecting key performance indicators (KPIs). Managers and executives can respond prior to negative business impact. When risk increases, users can capture incidents along with the loss information, allowing for more informed and more productive decision making.

Now that we have a good understanding of what SAP BusinessObjects Risk Management provides to organizations, let's take a look at SAP BusinessObjects Access Control.

SAP BusinessObjects Access Control

Segregation of duties

The SAP BusinessObjects Access Control application enables business managers, IT security, and auditors to collaborate in controlling access and preventing fraud across the enterprise. The application helps streamline processes and establish controls to maintain segregation of duties (SoD), minimize critical access risk, and assign compliant user access, while minimizing audit time and audit-related costs. Key features and benefits of SAP BusinessObjects Access Control include the following:

> **SoD rules library:** Leverage best practices and SAP expertise of business processes.

> **Automated workflows:** Increase efficiency and collaboration between IT and business owners.

> **What-if simulations:** Define compliant roles proactively using preventive simulations.

> **Reporting:** Improve visibility of user provisioning, potential and actual risk, policy reporting, and superuser access.

> **Reduced risk of fraud:** Reduce fraud risk by supporting the creation of compliant business processes.

> **Ensuring compliance:** Reduce SoD violations and critical access risk across SAP and non-SAP software through visibility of the current risk situation based on real-time data.

> **Faster response:** Minimize time to comply with regulatory requirements by automating the detection of access risk.

> **Better auditing:** Minimize audit time and audit-related costs through automated audit trails, real-time detection controls, and transaction monitoring.

> **Increased clarity:** Improve visibility of current risk situation through real-time reporting.

The regulatory environment for public and nonprofit organizations has become increasingly complex. Companies must address not only horizontal mandates in such areas as financial reporting, security, privacy, records retention, import–export regulations, environmental standards, occupational safety, and credit risk exposure but also vertical mandates for their industry-specific areas. The growing number of regulatory requirements often results in a fragmented approach across the enterprise in which each department or business unit is independently tasked with implementing policies, identifying and measuring risks, and supporting regulatory mandates.

The SAP BusinessObjects Access Control application helps organizations overcome these challenges so that they can confidently control access and prevent fraud. The application enables business managers, IT security, and auditors to do the following:

Control access and prevent fraud

> Reduce SoD violations and critical access risk across the enterprise

> Streamline compliance processes

> Deliver real-time oversight of the current risk situation

The application delivers risk analysis and remediation functionality that enables businesses to analyze critical access risk rapidly and identify SoD conflicts based on real-time data. It identifies potential access risks using a robust database of SoD rules that are based on best practices. The rule set leverages SAP expertise in business processes and the company's years of experience assisting customers with SoD implementations.

Rules for the most common business functions and associated risks are included, which are requisite for identifying SoD violations and critical access risks. The rules database is compatible with SAP and non-SAP software, including Oracle, PeopleSoft, and JD Edwards products, as well as legacy software and applications not classified as enterprise resource planning (ERP) software. This comprehensive integration enables the mapping of functions and associated risk across all these software solutions to establish a consistent policy and prevent duplication of effort.

Sorting SoD violations

Upon identifying SoD violations and critical access risks, business managers can then review issues found during the initial risk analysis. Robust reporting functionality in SAP BusinessObjects Access Control allows business managers to sort the SoD violations by role, by business process, and by user, and to review the root cause of the violation. The software also indicates the severity level of any violation. With this level of detailed reporting, stakeholders are able to resolve issues found during the analysis and prevent risk.

SAP BusinessObjects Access Control reduces SoD violations and critical access risks across the enterprise, which allows companies to streamline compliance with regulatory requirements. In addition to helping eliminate existing access risks, the application helps you prevent the addition of new risks by supporting compliant business processes during, for example, role creation and role provisioning. The software leverages prepackaged rule sets that were developed by SAP over a period of 12 years based on best practices.

Ex Example

> If employees are authorized both to create new vendors and to make payments to those vendors, that opens up the possibility of fraud because the employees can pay money into accounts that they themselves have configured. Authorization for this combination of business functions represents an SoD violation. To prevent the risk, the manager must decide how to mitigate the violation. One way is to rescind employees' authorization to perform one of the business functions. If both functions are required, the manager can choose an appropriate mitigating control and assign a monitor to oversee that the mitigating control is carried out. After the initial cleanup, managers can conduct regular risk analyses of user access requests and role definitions to sustain SoD control and prevent critical access risks on an ongoing basis.

The application also helps organizations introduce continuous access management. The solution automates all aspects of access management, including enterprise role management, compliant user provisioning, and emergency privilege management to increase efficiency and reduce the resources and time required for compliance.

Continuous access management

As a single authoritative source for enterprise role definition, SAP BusinessObjects Access Control enforces best-practice methodologies while eliminating offline, manual processes such as updating Excel sheets — actions that can escape automated, software-supported SoD rules, as illustrated in Figure 8.2. Its approval workflow can serve as a record for documentation and audit purposes. With this centralized tool, technical and business owners are able to use the same, consistent terms to document role definitions. Business users are empowered with automated change management, single-click automatic role creation, and role comparison features. By automating enterprise role management, businesses can reduce the cost of role maintenance, eliminate manual errors, and enforce best practices.

Eliminating offline, manual processes

SAP BusinessObjects Access Control enables fully automated and compliant user provisioning throughout the employee lifecycle to prevent SoD violations. Employees can request access using a structured dialog of self-service workflows that specify business processes and roles, reducing the IT resources required. Managers receive an email notification of an employee's request. The application automatically tests for SoD issues, removes SoD or critical access risks, and implements mitigating controls prior to approval. With this functionality, the application prevents SoD violations from being introduced into the production environment. Additionally, its dynamic workflow provides end-to-end automation for user provisioning in multiple applications. The application also offers expanded automated provisioning through integration with standards-based identity management software. Requests can be automatically integrated with user identity information from a Lightweight Directory Access Protocol (LDAP) directory or other HR databases so that managers can approve requests via email.

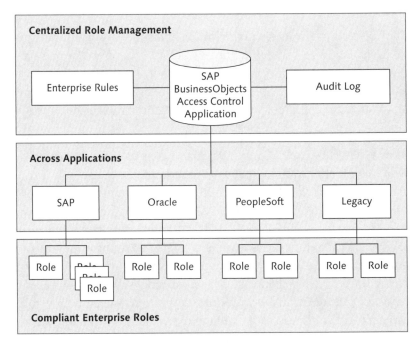

Figure 8.2 Centralized Role Management

Efficient internal audit

In addition, SAP BusinessObjects Access Control creates a more efficient internal audit process with business-friendly reporting and features such as audit logs for detailed tracking, customizable reporting, and process-efficiency statistics. Instead of trying to find forms, email messages, and relevant files, change logs are readily available electronically, which minimizes audit time and audit-related costs.

The access control application enables internal and external auditors to complete comprehensive and efficient testing to make sure all access is properly authorized and that controls are in place and regularly tested to mitigate all SoD risks. The automation built into the application simplifies the investigation process and delivers standard, audit-ready reporting to confirm that all access to systems was properly authorized, including user access approval as well as role approval. Instead of trying to find manual forms, spreadsheets, and files, approval workflows and a role-change history automatically provide an audit trail. Notifications of emergency privilege usage and detailed activity logs are also available for auditors to track this type of usage.

SAP BusinessObjects Access Control is a powerful robust component of the SAP BusinessObjects GRC set of solutions that should be of interest to any company looking to institute controls and rigor in the organization. Next, we'll look at SAP BusinessObjects Process Control.

SAP BusinessObjects Process Control

The SAP BusinessObjects Process Control application supports control monitoring across policies and regulatory requirements. The automated rules framework, with more than 120 delivered rules, enables quick deployment. The application offers cross-system visibility and a unified repository of compliance information for efficient initiative management. Automated workflows and notifications promote enterprise-wide accountability and confidence in decision making. Some key features and benefits of the SAP BusinessObjects Process Control application are the following:

> **Continuous visibility:** Deliver actionable intelligence across regulations and policies.

> **Comprehensive reports and dashboards:** Monitor control effectiveness across systems.

> **Unified repository:** Force cross-function accountability and standardization.

> **Complete compliance solution:** Align activities and manage processes.

> **Delivered and configurable rules:** Enable fast deployment across complex environments.

> **Automated workflows and notifications:** Shorten audit cycles, and reduce compliance expense.

> **Single system of record:** Help ensure audit integrity of compliance activities.

> **Continuous cross-system monitoring:** Reduce fraud and compliance exposure.

> **Remediation plans:** Speed responses to deficiencies in the control environment.

> **Simplified interface:** See a single view of multiple compliance initiatives.

> **Improved visibility:** Provide transparency across SAP and non-SAP software systems and increased agility and speed of response.

> **Greater cost savings:** Increase cross-function accountability and standardization.

> **Improved processes:** Lower operating costs via streamlined processes and lower fraud-related costs and exposure.

> **Simple implementation:** Use faster and simpler deployment.

> **Improved audits:** Employ shorter audit cycles and reduced staff needs.

> **Higher level of trust:** Enjoy greater executive confidence in operations and reporting results.

In today's business environment, companies must continuously monitor massive amounts of information across many different systems and business operations to meet the demands of compliance and risk management. Current methods and processes are often highly manual, time-consuming, and unreliable, and they rarely provide cross-system visibility or analysis. The result is a fragmented view of what is happening across an organization and a limited ability to spot irregularities in a timely manner and react effectively. Further, multiple systems cause confusion. The sheer expense of maintaining multiple point software solutions increases the cost of compliance and risk management significantly.

The SAP BusinessObjects Process Control application enables users to manage a wide range of compliance and business policy initiatives in one system, with different access, reporting, and configuration options for each one. At the same time, all initiatives can share common services such as the same workflow and planning/scheduling functions. For example, a customer might choose to use corrective and preventive action (CAPA) features for FDA or other operational compliance but opt not to use the sign-off functionality. Then, for financial compliance, the customer could turn on the sign-off and aggregation of deficiencies features, but choose to disable CAPA. This can all be done using SAP BusinessObjects Process Control.

Managing compliance and business policies in one system

SAP BusinessObjects Process Control works across non-SAP software systems by using new cross-system technology. The application now extends continuous monitoring to non-SAP environments with cross-platform process controls. These controls operate within the application to provide cross-system, unified reporting for enterprise controls. This functionality applies to a growing list of non-SAP environments, including Oracle, PeopleSoft, JD Edwards, Lawson, and Baan, as well as legacy and custom applications. The cross-platform controls allow for continuous monitoring of non-SAP enterprise resource planning (ERP), financial, and other system-based process controls, working to deter fraud and irregularities.

Continuous monitoring

Cross-platform controls are preconfigured with rules optimized for the individual ERP systems, based on best business practices. The multi-application query tool provides the ability to author custom controls. This tool acts as a broker and invokes the query in the target application (non-SAP) and sends the results back to SAP BusinessObjects Process Control.

SAP BusinessObjects Process Control includes a wide range of both predefined and customizable reports that enable an enterprise-wide view of control status. SAP Crystal Reports software and Xcelsius software are included with SAP BusinessObjects Process Control to provide more than 40 reports and dashboards. This facilitates creation of customized reports and deployment of advanced features such as combined graphics and text reporting.

Comprehensive perspective

Having all of these reports readily available gives control managers a comprehensive perspective across systems and across the organization and helps ensure transparency. This is essential for effective continuous monitoring, risk and alert assessment, and decision making, as shown in the sample dashboard in Figure 8.3.

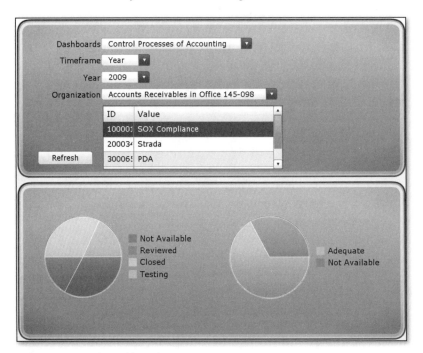

Figure 8.3 Sample Dashboard

Companies can manage all of their external compliance initiatives and internal policies within a single solution, enabling consistency and unification across the organization. The application uses centralized data catalogs and provides user activity traceability for compliance control and visibility. This increases standardization as well as cross-function accountability via certification and sign-off integration into process workflows.

SAP BusinessObjects Process Control integrates fully with the SAP BusinessObjects Risk Management application and exists on a unified SAP NetWeaver technology platform. All information on remediation plans, rules, and control history is maintained in a single location, allowing for optimized workflows across multiple compliance initiatives. Because of this common location, available across the organization, information can be accessed, shared, and reused much more efficiently, greatly reducing the effort required in developing remediation plans and producing specific documentation.

SAP BusinessObjects Process Control is a complete compliance solution, delivering functionality for continuous monitoring and process management from end to end, all within one application. Workflows are developed across systems and organizational functions to align activities and create efficiency and collaboration. The application's ability to integrate with other SAP and non-SAP software systems enables a full, continuous monitoring or remediation effort that can be managed holistically. Controls and rules are maintained in a single location and can be viewed and managed together, reducing the risk of duplication, or conflicting remediation efforts and alerts.

The application accelerates implementation with key delivered business content that allows for quick creation of new rules. Companies can leverage more than 200 rules — included with the application — along with industry-standard content to dramatically speed definition and implementation of new rules.

An automated rules framework is also provided that enables business users to create unlimited tests to monitor critical setups and transactions for violations and unacceptable risks. The delivered content can be plugged in "as is" or modified to address specific monitoring requirements across different landscapes. In addition, all of the content and activity reporting is stored in centralized data catalogs for user activity traceability, compliance control, and overall transparency. Figure 8.4 shows a sample automated rule.

Automated task rules framework

Job Name :DEMO_Z_SDCMM_01C2_A

Result

Rule:	DEMO_Z_SDCMM_01C2_A	Organization:	MO UH6
Rule Description:	DEMO_Z_SDCMM_01C2_A	Organization Level System Parameter:	MO OLSP 1 - name
Execution Date:	13.01.2009	Process:	MO Process 1.1
Execution Time:	04:45:51	Subprocess:	MO SubProcess 1.1.1
Overall Status:	Low	Control:	MO Control 1.1.1.1
Total Exceptions:	12	Target Connector:	VFG
High:	0	Year:	2009
Medium:	0	Timeframe:	Custom Year
Low:	12	Variant:	Not Applicable
From Date:	01.01.2009	Frequency:	Custom Annualy
To Date:	31.12.2009	Currency:	NA
Script Type:	GRC Configurable	Significant Amount:	Not Applicable
Script Category:	Change Log Check	Total Number of Records Analyzed:	12

Details

Print Version Export ▴

Sequence Number	Delivery type	Description	Delivery credit grp	GI credit group	Deficiency Type	Deficient Field Description	Old Va
3	PB	PB DELV. type	Z3	Z1	Low	Delivery credit group	
4	PB	PB DELV. type	Z3	Z1	Low	Goods issue credit group	
5	RL	Returns (pur.ord.)	Z1	01	Low	Delivery credit group	
6	RL	Returns (pur.ord.)	Z1	01	Low	Goods issue credit group	
7	HTP	Deliv.for post.chge	Z1	03	Low	Delivery credit group	
8	HTP	Deliv.for post.chge	Z1	03	Low	Goods issue credit group	
9	WID	WMS Inbound Delivery			Low	Delivery credit group	Z2
10	WID	WMS Inbound Delivery			Low	Goods issue credit group	02
11	ZBV	Cash Sale (ECM1)	01	Z3	Low	Delivery credit group	
12	ZBV	Cash Sale (ECM1)	01	Z3	Low	Goods issue credit group	

Figure 8.4 Sample Automated Rule

SAP BusinessObjects Process Control is designed for building new automated control tests in a straightforward, repeatable manner. The architecture involves a number of building blocks that together greatly ease the process of defining and implementing new rules, as shown in Figure 8.5.

Shorten audit cycles and reduce overall compliance expense

Additional significant features offered by SAP BusinessObjects Process Control are automated workflows and notifications. Automated workflows help control owners and decision makers understand control readings and alerts so they can react efficiently and effectively. This shortens audit cycles and reduces overall compliance expense by automating the certification and sign-off process and also by helping ensure that all appropriate stakeholders are involved in the relevant business processes. The workflows also include automated notifications to minimize manual intervention. As the key processes are defined and rules are established, critical owners, organizations, or stakeholders are flagged for notification on key events. In the end, this helps to optimize compliance activities by notifying the critical process participants in a timely manner when action is required on their part.

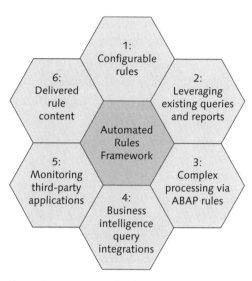

Figure 8.5   Automated Rules Framework

Next, let's look at SAP BusinessObjects Global Trade Services.

SAP BusinessObjects Global Trade Services

The SAP BusinessObjects Global Trade Services application helps reduce the cost and risk of international trade by automating compliance with global regulations, accelerating trade activity, and minimizing duties and landed cost. Companies can streamline complex import and export processes, automate compliance checks, and expedite customs clearance. The software is also certified for electronic communication with customs systems around the globe. Some key features and benefits of SAP BusinessObjects Global Trade Services include the following:

> **Export and import management:** Classify products, comply with regulations, manage embargo checks and export and import licenses, calculate duties, generate documentation, handle customs warehousing procedures, track inventory, streamline electronic communications, and manage letters of credit.

> **Support for specialized customs procedures:** Carry out complex tasks, such as managing customs warehouses and inward and outward processing relief.

> **Trade preference management:** Manage and request vendor declarations, determine product eligibility for preferential treatment, and issue certificates of origin.

> **Restitution management:** Handle export licenses, securities, and restitution procedures; calculate restitution amounts; and gain insight into restitution-related activities.

> **International trade improvements:** Automate global trade compliance with high-integrity compliance checks, support for e-filing, and a centralized view of activities.

> **Improved trade performance:** Accelerate trade with timely insights into filing status and integrated processes that reduce lead times.

> **Improved compliance:** Minimize costs by staying compliant with global regulations and agreements, reducing duties and landed cost, and lowering inventory carrying costs.

Economic globalization

Economic globalization continues to be a major business reality as enterprises increasingly source, manufacture, and distribute goods on a worldwide basis. Long ocean voyages, fluctuating transportation costs, cross-border regulations, and extensive filing and documentation requirements combine to make global trade inherently risky and volatile. At the same time, a growing body of new regulations, e-filing mandates, free trade agreements, and customer requirements steadily adds to the complexity of international trade.

To understand the demanding challenges associated with international trade, consider the scope and complexity of a typical cross-border shipment. Such a shipment involves multiple parties (such as suppliers, shippers, government agencies, and brokers), numerous trade and industry-specific documents, various country-specific laws and regulations, and a vast number of trade agreements.

The tasks required to complete this type of transaction — not to mention the knowledge, experience, and collaboration requirements — can quickly become overwhelming and expose organizations to error, delay, and inefficiency. If not managed properly, international trade can drive significantly increased costs and put a company's operations at tremendous risk.

Largely due to the greater volume and complexity of global trade, companies must now comply with a steady increase in the quantity and variety of regulations. Countries are looking to protect their own interests and maintain control over the materials that flow across their borders. With the continuing threat of global terrorism added to the list of concerns, export and import processes are under closer scrutiny than ever before.

The ways in which companies interact with customs authorities is also changing dramatically. Historically, paper forms and manual processes have dominated international trade. However, governments around the world are now upgrading and standardizing their IT systems, introducing new e-filing procedures, and requiring the trade community to automate its processes and communicate customs documents electronically. For an enterprise to operate globally, it needs to interact simultaneously with numerous e-filing mandates and formats worldwide.

Trade liberalization around the world is accelerating as bilateral and regional free trade agreements continue to be initiated and completed. For many companies, participating in preferential trade programs, such as the North American Free Trade Agreement (NAFTA) and European Union (EU) trade agreements, is essential to gaining and maintaining a competitive edge. However, demonstrating the eligibility of products for reduced or zero tariffs is often an expensive task.

Free trade agreements

The SAP BusinessObjects Global Trade Services application provides enterprises with a single, comprehensive solution for global trade management. The application helps companies secure and streamline complex import and export processes by providing support in these five major areas of trade:

> **Export management:** Automating and streamlining complex export processes, enables faster delivery to customers by minimizing delays at national borders. It also supports compliance with relevant regulations and mitigates the financial risk of global transactions.

> **Import management:** Expediting customs clearance for import shipments reduces costly buffer stock and enables just-in-time inventory management. The application allows business users to readily classify products, calculate duties, streamline electronic communication with customs authorities, comply with import requirements, and efficiently manage letters of credit.

> **Special customs procedures:** Using comprehensive duty-optimization software enables significant cost reductions by supporting such processes as customs warehousing, processing under customs control, and inward and outward processing relief.

> **Trade preference management:** Fully leveraging international trade agreements enables companies to solicit vendor declarations, determine the eligibility of products for preferential treatment, and issue certificates of origin to customers.

> **Excise movement and control system (EMCS):** Electronically communicating information with authorities (and thereby doing away with cumbersome, paper-based processes) enables companies to suspend taxes on the movements of excisable goods and comply with the European Union EMCS requirements.

A centralized view of trade operations across the entire enterprise allows a broad understanding of the overall trade ecosystem, resulting in fewer errors and more efficient and informed trade operations. In addition, the comprehensive automated compliance check functionality speeds the compliance process. To further facilitate efficient compliance with e-filing mandates worldwide, the application is certified for numerous import and export customs systems:

> U.S. Customs Service's Automated Broker Interface (ABI)

> Germany's Automated Tariff and Local Customs Processing System (ATLAS)

> France's Dédouanement en Ligne par Traitement Automatisé (DELTA D)

> Belgium's Paperless Douane en Accijnzen (PLDA)

> Netherlands' Sagitta system

Corporations can accelerate trade by gaining timely insights into filing status, import and export processes, and potential compliance violations. The application includes an extensive array of certified electronic customs communication interfaces, as well as a comprehensive inventory of global trade forms. It also helps reduce lead time and expedite customs clearance by integrating the logistics process from start to finish and enabling the integration of logistics with other business functions, including sales, purchasing, HR, and transportation. Through its exception-based management functionality, the software increases productivity by alerting users of any transaction that fails to meet global trade compliance regulations and requires action.

SAP BusinessObjects Global Trade Services helps reduce cost, time, and resource requirements across the range of international trade functions. By maintaining electronic communication with countries and trade authorities around the globe, the application allows corporations to cost-effectively stay current with a growing and frequently changing body of global trade regulations and agreements. Integrated trade preference management — including support for trade agreements and preferential origin determination — means the application can monitor the entire product catalog and trigger alerts when opportunities arise to reduce duties and lower landed cost. By automating customs processes, the application also lets users track inward processing relief (IPR) and outward processing relief and (OPR) and manage customs bonded warehousing more cost effectively.

Integrated trade preference management

SAP BusinessObjects Global Trade Services is fully operational in heterogeneous environments of both SAP and non-SAP software systems. Through the service-oriented architecture (SOA) supported by SAP NetWeaver, organizations can deploy specialized business processes that operate with their existing systems and software. Now, we'll move on to taking a look at SAP Environment, Health, and Safety Management.

SAP Environment, Health, and Safety Management

The SAP Environment, Health, and Safety Management (SAP EHS Management) application can help organizations achieve comprehensive

SAP EHS Management

and sustainable regulatory compliance in the areas of health, safety, and the environment as well as in chemical and product stewardship. By leveraging an existing SAP software environment, it helps customers integrate compliance and safety activities with current business processes and improve sustainability performance. Some key features and benefits available in the application include the following:

> **Health and safety:** Help ensure safety in the workplace and comply with health and safety regulations that affect workers.

> **Environmental performance:** Run operations, factories, and plants in a sustainable way and comply with regulations affecting air, water, and land.

> **Product safety and stewardship:** Support the safe handling and disposal of regulated products and full compliance with regulations; meet local, national, and global regulations regarding chemical substances.

> **Sustainability initiatives:** Enhance sustainability by supporting the integration of corporate policies and EHS compliance activities into related business processes.

> **Improved risk mitigation:** Improve risk mitigation by identifying and addressing business risks that derive from EHS failure and non-compliance.

> **Increased integration with EHS processes:** Improve EHS performance and reduce compliance and operating costs with integrated EHS processes applied across the enterprise.

> **Enhanced transparency:** Get transparent EHS performance through a reliable foundation for auditing, documenting, and communicating relevant EHS information.

> **Increased compliance:** Achieve compliant operations for most business processes and regions.

Traditionally, the effectiveness of an organization has been measured solely on the basis of financial results. This is no longer the case. Along with profitability, company stakeholders have increased concerns about protecting corporate reputation and brand value, reducing operational risk, and improving sustainability performance.

They now demand that organizations meet guidelines for corporate responsibility while minimizing the cost of managing compliance.

Global companies face a growing number of national and international rules and regulations that are becoming more and more complex, resulting in higher compliance costs and greater business risks. Manual approaches to compliance, for example, simply cannot keep pace with the sheer volume of global and local regulations. And where compliance solutions exist, they are often designed to address specific regulations at the plant or local level — without integration into business operations and without the ability to meet the larger needs of the organization at the enterprise level. Overall, a persistent lack of IT integration and poor visibility into business operations make the cost of achieving safety and compliance prohibitive.

Manual approaches are no longer an option

SAP EHS Management is a comprehensive integrated application that helps companies implement their EHS strategies to govern and execute their EHS compliance and risk management initiatives on a local and global level. With its broad range of functionalities and global scalability, SAP EHS Management helps companies overcome the challenges of disconnected systems, regions, and departments. Because SAP EHS Management offers an integrated set of functions — rather than disconnected IT tool sets — customers can avoid the limitations inherent in silo-based EHS software deployments. The application provides support for executives to handle regulatory compliance, take an integrated approach to operational risk management, and address the needs of their corporate sustainability initiatives.

SAP EHS Management works with a customers' existing SAP software landscape, integrating their compliance needs into the way they do business. Unlike applications that focus narrowly on specific regulations, SAP EHS Management supports an end-to-end EHS compliance management process. Because it is an integrated part of the SAP ERP application, it supports operational transparency. And as part of SAP BusinessObjects GRC solutions, it helps companies monitor and promote ethical business conduct, which can help them establish a strong reputation for corporate accountability and responsibility.

Health and safety, environmental performance, and product safety and stewardship

SAP EHS Management provides comprehensive support for an organization to perform processes across the three fundamental pillars of EHS compliance management: health and safety, environmental performance, and product safety and stewardship (Figure 8.6).

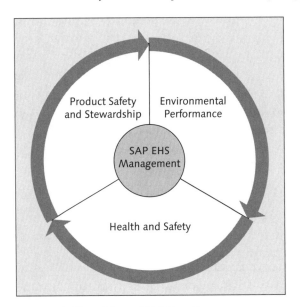

Figure 8.6 Three Pillars of EHS Compliance

SAP EHS Management helps customers streamline EHS operations across their company and supporting processes for risk assessment, incident management, and health surveillance. For example, drawing on information supplied by the asset lifecycle management functions in SAP ERP, business users can arrange, follow up, and assess plant maintenance tasks. And tight integration with HR and other business processes allows SAP EHS Management to track the healthcare of employees and monitor results and diagnoses.

SAP EHS Management is a comprehensive offering that helps organizations run operations, factories, and plants in an environmentally responsible manner and comply with regulations affecting air, water, and land. Organizations can monitor facility emissions and simultaneously maintain emissions accounting so that the business can leverage maximum benefits in the carbon trading and tax arenas. The software also supports full permit management of air, water, and waste emissions, helping businesses to fulfill regulatory obligations — whether local, national, or international.

The application further augments corporation's environmental compliance functionality and saves time and resources by automatically generating product safety documentation, bills of material, and safety data sheets. In addition, it allows users to fully integrate their waste management processes with their other business software to better track activities related to materials, compliance, manifests, transportation, and disposal.

SAP EHS Management takes a uniform and integrated approach to complying with the mandates that regulate the registration, evaluation, authorization and restriction of chemicals (REACH). By enabling collaboration among corporate supply chain partners, the application allows business users to track and document substances used in their products. They can quickly classify reportable and non-reportable substances; automate preregistration and registration processes for the European Chemicals Agency; and provide comprehensive substance inventory support, usage and exposure management, and volume tracking.

Registration, evaluation, authorization, and restriction of chemicals (REACH)

The application supports companies in meeting regulatory mandates such as the restriction of hazardous substances directive (RoHS) or the waste in electrical and electronic equipment directive (WEEE). The ability to manage regulatory content with an application fully integrated across the supply chain helps users streamline the collection, organization, and dissemination of data. It also helps them automate processes to support compliance activities across their supply chain.

Registration of hazardous substances and waste in electrical and electronic equipment directives

SAP EHS Management helps customers meet global, federal, and regional standards for product safety and hazardous substance management with functions, such as automatic composition calculation and safety data sheet authoring, management, and shipping. It also helps them manage the logistics related to such materials with global label management and generation of inventory reports for hazardous substances, such as the labeling and reports required to comply with the U.S. Superfund Amendments and Reauthorization Act (SARA). In

U.S Superfund and Reauthorization Act

addition, it supports the purchasing process for hazardous materials while helping customers meet the mandates posed by global and local regulations such as section 12(b) of the Toxic Substances Control Act.

SAP EHS Management supports customers in conducting efficient comprehensive EHS risk management across global business processes and helps them streamline compliance processes toward reducing the costs of managing EHS risks.

Next, let's move on to the most recent addition to the SAP Business-Objects GRC solutions, Sustainability Performance Management.

SAP BusinessObjects Sustainability Performance Management

The SAP BusinessObjects Sustainability Performance Management application establishes a foundation for reporting and performance management. It helps customers communicate sustainability performance, set goals, manage risks, and monitor activities while reducing data collection and reporting time and costs. Some of the key features and benefits of SAP BusinessObjects Sustainability Performance Management include the following:

> **Defining reporting frameworks:** Manage multiple sustainability frameworks and KPIs while optimizing opportunities for reuse.

> **Data collection:** Automatically gather quantitative and qualitative sustainability performance data from people and systems.

> **Performance management:** Align sustainability KPIs to corporate objectives and risks; turn sustainability data into actionable information to improve financial and sustainability performance; and set goals to motivate improvement.

> **Integration:** Leverage existing data and management processes by integrating with other SAP applications.

> **Lowered cost:** Reduce the cost of measuring sustainability performance.

> **Actionable insights:** Turn strategy and data into actionable insights where sustainability performance improvements also improve profitability.

> **Higher transparency:** Improve enterprise transparency and performance by making key drivers visible.

> **Improved sustainability:** Provide sustainability results to the right levels in the organization so information is actionable.

> **Improved risk management:** Manage and mitigate stakeholder risk.

> **Integrate sustainability:** Incorporate sustainability into existing management systems and processes through strategic planning, initiative creation, risk management, and process streamlining.

Sustainability is a rising priority on the CEO agenda as management, investors, customers, and employees all try to understand the social and environmental implications of the company's financial and operational decisions. This is especially critical for companies in highly regulated and brand-conscious industries.

A growing priority

Leading companies realize sustainability is not about "going green" for the sake of going green. To be feasible, sustainability practices and processes must work in concert with core business goals and strategies to improve enterprise profitability. In the end, companies need to protect their brand, manage risk, and find opportunities to improve returns.

Sustainability practices must connect to core business goals and strategies

The SAP BusinessObjects Sustainability Performance Management application helps organizations track and communicate sustainability performance, set goals and objectives, manage risks, and monitor activities while reducing the time and cost spent collecting data and compiling disclosures and reports.

The software helps organizations tailor their sustainability strategy to their respective industry and business context. This includes modeling and managing multiple concurrent sustainability frameworks, including internal, management-focused frameworks as well as external, disclosure-focused frameworks.

Business users can focus on the metrics that will have the greatest impacts for their stakeholders by leveraging a central KPI library that includes metrics based on the Global Reporting Initiative (GRI) standard. The KPI library also enables business users to create and update their own sustainability KPIs that may be composed of other standards, multiple tiers of subindicators, and calculations. All these KPIs are stored in a searchable and filterable central library that allows users to share and reuse their work.

SAP BusinessObjects Sustainability Performance Management guides KPI data collection activities for both automated and manual sources. Workflow, data requests, validation, and approval processes facilitate manual qualitative and quantitative data collection. Users can perform automated KPI data collection from source systems, and adjustments can be performed centrally at period close to help deal with missing and anomalous data. Audit trail functionality maintains a searchable record of every action taken to provide transparency and enforce high-integrity reporting.

Analytic functionality; enables users to aggregate results and examine performance across multiple dimensions. Planning workbooks enable companies to set targets or benchmarks for different organizations and sustainability indicators. Dashboards and scorecards provide clear and insightful graphical displays that help business users get the most out of their data. Interactive briefing books make available organized compilations of reports, dashboards, and scorecards to communicate performance to stakeholders.

The application can operate as a standalone application to facilitate sustainability and performance management activities. It also integrates with other applications to leverage existing investments:

> Synchronizes with key master data in SAP Business Suite software related to organizations and materials

> Incorporates data from operational systems, including the SAP ERP, SAP Recycling Administration, and SAP EHS Management applications and the SAP Carbon Impact OnDemand solution

> Applies additional management frameworks and tools to sustainability, such as the SAP BusinessObjects Strategy Management, SAP

BusinessObjects Process Control, and SAP BusinessObjects Risk Management applications

SAP BusinessObjects Sustainability Performance Management gives companies the ability to streamline and reduce the cost of monitoring sustainability performance, while aligning sustainability performance to corporate strategies, risks, and process improvements — all on a single platform.

Case Studies

SAP BusinessObjects Access Control

One of the world's largest global technology distributors, with $22.95 billion in sales and approximately 12,000 employees in 310 locations worldwide, is located in the United States. As a distributor, the company operates in an industry famous for razor thin margins and is constantly looking for new ways to improve efficiency as part of its operational excellence initiative. With increasing amounts of regulatory compliance required for all public companies, the company saw this as an area to explore automated solutions to help improve process efficiency. This company began by focusing on processes related to the SoD requirement, under which no one individual could control all of the steps in financial transactions, and maintaining records of proof required to be available through audit trails and documentation.

Previously, this organization had developed multiple disparate spreadsheets and databases throughout the company to address and track information and processes related to compliance. However, using these tools and having IT maintain them was time consuming, especially for a globally growing company that services more than 70 countries. The company determined that redesigning the processes and automating them could help meet the operational excellence goals and reduce administrative time in managing multiple spreadsheets and databases.

In 2009, this organization standardized on SAP applications for its financials and on Tivoli Identity Manager and Tivoli Access Manager from IBM for centralized user management and application access control. Because the systems users fell squarely under the SoD require-ments, the company looked for a compliance automation solution that would integrate readily with SAP software. The SAP BusinessObjects Access Control application was selected because of its integrated func-tionality for assigning roles, provisioning users (assigning them access privileges and corresponding system resources), and delivering an evidentiary trail.

SAP BusinessObjects Access Control integrates inherently with the financials functionality of SAP software, but integration with the IBM Tivoli software was equally important. The organization had to bring in a systems integrator to help build the necessary components in Tivoli. To accommodate the adapter, SAP simultaneously developed new functionality, which is now standard in SAP BusinessObjects Access Control. The two developments were coordinated by the sys-tem integrator, which served as a single point of contact for the cus-tomer. This integration, which was completed on schedule in 2009, enabled full lifecycle management of user IDs, close control over user access, and highly automated processes for complying with regula-tory requirements and the distributor's own internal policies.

By automating the processes to manage access to its systems and to provide evidentiary trails, the distributor now has an integrated solu-tion for scalable access control. This solution enabled the organization to avoid increases in administration and audit costs relative to previ-ous systems and processes.

SAP BusinessObjects Global Trade Services

A company manufactures heavy-duty diesel engines for a wide vari-ety of off-highway applications. The company is a major exporter to nations all over the world, and it also imports many parts. Even though international trade is such a big part of the organization's business, the company used to rely on manual processes for comply-ing with the U.S. government's import/export regulations. Screening and licensing processes were labor-intensive and time-consuming. Noncompliance could result in audits, fines, and penalties.

To avoid these costs and risks, the company needed tools to automate its compliance processes and make them systematic. The organization got the chance when it became independent from its previous parent, adopted SAP software to run its overall business, and included the ideally suited SAP BusinessObjects Global Trade Services application in the portfolio.

The company found that the application had all of the necessary exports-related functionality, but for imports, it needed careful configuration to include the unique needs of its third-party broker. The project went very smoothly, and the company met all schedule and budget goals. One reason for this success is that the firm assembled representatives from all affected departments who collaborated to optimize the new processes.

The organization went live with its new exports-related processes first, which enjoyed immediate and widespread acceptance. When it followed several months later with the new imports-related processes, however, the results were very interesting. SAP BusinessObjects Global Trade Services raised many warning flags that at first glance seemed unwarranted, prompting some to blame it for inhibiting the flow of business. Upon close inspection, however, the company learned that the warnings were actually alerting the company to paperwork problems that would arise later, when the finance group would find them costly and time-consuming to fix. Soon everyone appreciated the value of these early warnings and fully embraced the application for imports as well.

SAP BusinessObjects Global Trade Services has fully automated export administration regulations and International Traffic in Arms Regulations license determination, as well as embargo and sanctioned party list screening. The application automatically downloads the most current version of these lists from the Internet every day, avoiding errors due to out-of-date information. Because of the broker-specific configuration, the company also automated communications with its imports broker.

Summary

The combined set of applications in this chapter; make up the SAP GRC solutions. They are very powerful and designed to meet the challenges of today's marketplace. The solutions provide the capability to create a unified GRC environment across both SAP and non-SAP systems. This enables users to create a preventative, real-time approach to their systems. Additionally, they can predict and manage the risks in their respective applications and business domains.

In the next chapter; we'll take a look at some of the SAP Business-Objects tools that are designed specifically for small and midsized organizations.

9

Solutions for Small Businesses and Midsize Companies

While all previously mentioned solutions best apply to larger enterprise customers, in this chapter, we'll introduce the SAP solutions that have specifically been designed for small and midsize companies.

The definition of SMB (small and medium businesses) varies from one country to another. However, if your company's revenue is around $500M or less, chances are that you fall in this category. Again, your mileage may vary here, some include in this segment companies up to 1,000 employees depending on market and revenue.

Unique BI Needs of Small Businesses and Midsize Companies

Whatever the definition, we're talking about companies that share a common set of challenges when it comes to BI and IT:

> Limited resources for the acquisition and maintenance of IT solutions. SMBs have to focus resources and budget on growth; they

have to tackle smaller incremental IT projects for which they get quick ROIs along the way.

> On the same idea, SMBs — more than larger companies — need solutions that are easy to use and don't require massive rollout plans or training.

> From a technical architecture standpoint, smaller companies don't have the same level of complexity as larger corporations. This results in different needs regarding software solutions integration.

> Smaller companies often run without the help of BI and because of this, face the problems of multiple version of the truth, lack of facts, and analysis tools beyond the spreadsheet. Starting from scratch, they need BI solutions that focus on the key areas of the business that can provide an immediate competitive advantage.

As an SMB, if you look at your own business, you'll certainly find more of those characteristics that you feel make your business different from the Fortune 500s and prompt for specific BI solutions.

To fulfill those unique needs of SMBs, SAP offers a specific line of BI products discussed here.

SAP Crystal Reports

SAP Crystal Reports is one of the best choices for SMBs when it comes to creating highly formatted reports such as listings, statements, or other legal documents that need to be published or distributed to report consumers.

SAP Crystal Reports was discussed in Chapter 5, which you can refer to for all of the details about the tool's positioning and its capabilities.

Although SAP Crystal Reports was presented earlier as part of the SAP BusinessObjects Enterprise solution, it also comes in a number of other packages that make sense for SMBs.

Did You Know?

Crystal Reports is the reporting solution embedded by Microsoft in Visual Studio.

SAP Crystal Reports now comes in a single edition that is equivalent to the previous Developer Edition. It gives you the desktop design environment to build reports against a number of data sources and then export them in a number of formats, including PDF and HTML.

Table 9.1 provides a list of export formats supported by SAP Crystal Reports 2008.

Page-Based Formats (these formats preserve the layout)
PDF
Crystal Reports (RPT)
HTML 3.2 and HTML 4.0
MHTML
Microsoft Excel (97-2003)
Microsoft Word (97-2003)
Microsoft Word (97-2003) – Editable
Rich Text Format (RTF)
Data-Based Formats (these formats export the raw data)
Microsoft Excel (97-2003) – Data only
ODBC
Record Style
Comma-Separated Values (CSV)
Tab Separated Text (TTX)
Text
XML

Table 9.1 SAP Crystal Reports Available Export Formats

Note

> For more information and details about the SAP Crystal Reports export formats, look into the product help. Press [F1] while in the export dialog box.

SAP Crystal Reports can be a good starting point

If you currently have a handful of advanced users that know the data structure well and need to design reports such as invoices, balance sheets, legal documents, inventory listings, or any other document of that sort, then SAP Crystal Reports is your starting point.

A standalone SAP Crystal Report designer lives on the computer of the power user who has to refresh the data and then publish or send the report in the previously mentioned formats to the rest of the company. No security is associated with the document, so anyone accessing it may read the content.

Much has changed in SAP Crystal Reports

There are numerous versions of Crystal Reports, not only due to new releases but also because there are many packages that adjust to final customers and OEM needs. You may have come across Crystal Reports in the past and believe it's not the right tool for your needs; however,, we encourage you to take a look at the current offering just to confirm what the newest versions and packages have to offer.

You should probably start in the SAP Crystal Reports section of the SAP website, where you can read a detailed white paper comparing the features of the different releases.

You can also download a trial version of the software directly from the SAP website. You may also purchase SAP Crystal Reports directly from the site. At the time of printing, SAP Crystal Reports was starting just under $400.

Sample reports and database

After you download and install SAP Crystal Reports, the starting page allows you to download sample reports and databases. This is very useful to get you started with the product. Browsing through the sample reports gives you a good idea of the formatting capabilities, and you can export to a number of formats, email the reports, and see how this all ties together.

Tip

The SAP Crystal Reports sample package comes with a Microsoft Access database named xtreme.mdb so you can learn from the samples and with a local data source.

The reporting samples are organized along two axes:

> Business samples to demonstrate what kind of common business reports can be easily created with the tool

> Feature samples to demonstrate some of the key features of SAP Crystal Reports and how to implement them in a report

Here are a couple examples of the samples that you can download from SAP:

> **General Business**

- Employee Profile.rpt
- Inventory CrossTab.rpt
- Order Packing List.rpt
- Order Processing Efficiency Dashboard.rpt
- Product Catalog.rpt
- Sales With Geographic Map.rpt
- World Sales Report.rpt

> **Financial**

- Combination Balance Sheet and Income Statement.rpt
- Consolidated Income Statement.rpt
- Current Period and YTD Cash Flow.rpt
- Rolling Quarter Income Statement.rpt
- Sorted Variance Analysis Report.rpt

> **Features**

- Custom Functions.rpt
- Hierarchical Grouping.rpt
- Record Selection on DateRange.rpt

– Alerting.rpt

– OLAP Cube Report.rpt

 Best Practices Included

Besides the samples, a series of financial tutorials come in the form of PDF documents. They guide you through creating some common reports such as balance sheet and income statement, consolidated income statement, full year budget report, rolling quarter income summary, variance analysis report, statement of cash flow, and more. Not only do they help you ramp up with the product, but they also reflect the best practices in the domain.

After starting with the reporting tools, most companies will feel the need to aggregate the data in the form of KPIs and create dashboards with them. So let's now take a look at SAP Crystal Dashboard Design.

SAP Crystal Dashboard Design

Interactive business dashboards

Formerly known as Xcelsius Engage, the SAP Crystal Dashboard Design is the perfect tool to create stunning interactive visualizations. It is primarily a dashboard and decision-making tool directed to decision makers who need interactive business dashboards with the ability to perform what-if analyses.

Figure 9.1 provides an example of an SAP Crystal Dashboard Design dashboard.

If your company relies on Excel data and tentatively on Excel charts to aggregate and present the KPIs, then this tool would be useful and relevant to you. Although there are other options, the most straightforward use is to leverage data from an existing Excel spreadsheet, drag and drop your preferred visualizations on a canvas, and link with the data.

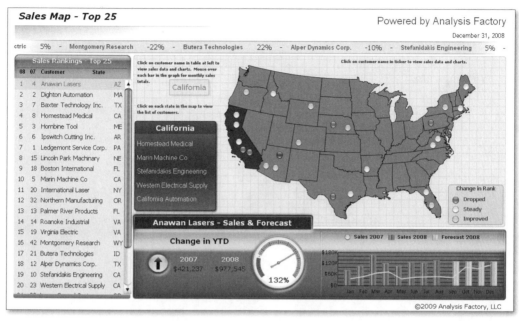

Figure 9.1 Example of an SAP Crystal Dashboard Design Dashboard

 Tip

Although you'll be presented with an empty spreadsheet upon opening SAP Crystal Dashboard Design, don't copy and paste all your exiting data manually. Use the IMPORT function that you find in the DATA menu of the application.

Although the tool is largely used in large companies in its enterprise version, the lighter versions give the smaller businesses access to the same powerful capabilities.

A Personal Edition is also available, but SAP recommends that SMBs use the departmental edition because it provides the following useful additional options:

> Live data connectivity to multiple data sources
> Connectivity to Adobe LiveCycle Data Services ES and Microsoft SQL Server Reporting Services

> Integration with Microsoft and IBM portal

> Integration with SAP Crystal Reports Server

Grow your reporting tools With the integration capabilities offered in this edition, you'll have the opportunity to grow your reporting tools into a full BI solution.

Data sources that are supported by the departmental edition of SAP Crystal Dashboard Design include the following:

> SAP Crystal Reports via SAP BusinessObjects Live Office

> Microsoft Excel 2003/2007

> XML-compliant databases

> Microsoft SQL Server Reporting Services 2003

> SOAP-based Web services

> Adobe LiveCycle Data Services

> Flash variables

> ODBC data source via SAP Crystal Reports Server Web Service Design Tool

Download and online purchase available As is true with SAP Crystal Reports, SAP Crystal Dashboard Design can be downloaded from the SAP website as a trial version so you can familiarize yourself with its capabilities.

SAP Crystal Reports Dashboard Design Package

As you look into your options and needs, don't overlook that SAP Crystal Reports and SAP Crystal Dashboard Design can be purchased as a bundle named SAP Crystal Reports Dashboard Design Package.

Through the package, you benefit from the individual tool's capabilities as described in the previous sections but also from the combination of both formats into a single SAP Crystal Report.

So you can now produce a formatted report that includes nice and interactive data visualizations as shown in Figure 9.2.

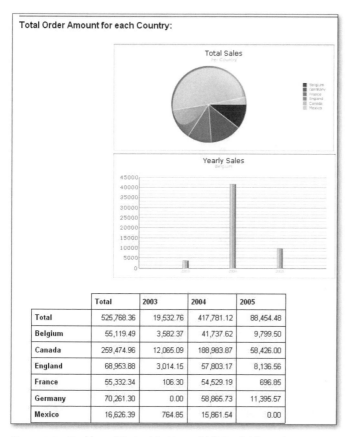

Total Order Amount for each Country:

	Total	2003	2004	2005
Total	525,768.36	19,532.76	417,781.12	88,454.48
Belgium	55,119.49	3,582.37	41,737.62	9,799.50
Canada	259,474.96	12,065.09	188,983.87	58,426.00
England	68,953.88	3,014.15	57,803.17	8,136.56
France	55,332.34	106.30	54,529.19	696.85
Germany	70,261.30	0.00	58,865.73	11,395.57
Mexico	16,626.39	764.85	15,861.54	0.00

Figure 9.2   Dashboard Embedded in an SAP Crystal Report

SAP Crystal Reports Server

While the previously mentioned versions of SAP Crystal Reports offer the full design capabilities and a nice range of distribution options, refreshing and publishing reports remains a manual process. There are ways to distribute reports, for example, saving them as PDFs on a shared drive, sending to an email distribution list, and so on. You can also save them in an HTML format or publish on your intranet.

Security is also a concern, especially for SMBs. As reports proliferate with more confidential data and loosely secured distribution channels, you may want to look for managed publication. The SAP Crystal

The need for security

Reports Server was specifically designed for SMBs that need to add advanced publication and security capabilities to their SAP Crystal Reports. The platform provides the following capabilities:

> Securely access reports and dashboards on a single server
> Personalize reports using data-driven publications
> Refresh reports in Excel, and PowerPoint documents
> Integrate reporting into Microsoft SharePoint
> Lower operating costs with virtualization-friendly licensing and auditing
> Integrate reporting with custom Java or .NET applications

So let's look at a situation where our fictitious employee, John from the finance department, has access to the sales database and produces a summary report of sales per customer per region.

The sample sales report that John can pull is shown in Figure 9.3.

Each week, John refreshes the report, exports it to a PDF, and sends it via email to the managers throughout the country.

John knows the program well and takes advantage of the bookmarks with the sections so each country manager can quickly scroll to his own country. However, this process is still manual.

Ongoing, time-consuming process

John not only needs to arrange backup when he's out, but the country managers have also started to ask for more frequent updates so they have a better control on their business. Moreover, the company wants to distribute this report more widely but is concerned with the confidentiality of the data because this report consolidates all sales for the company.

Now John's company decides to leverage the SAP Crystal Reports Server. Country managers and their organization get security profiles defined in the system.

Grouping and Sorting

Country	Region	Customer Name	Last Year's Sales
Belgium			**200,000.00**
	Brussels	Belgium Bike Co.	200,000.00
Canada			**166,031.37**
	BC	Pedal Pusher Bikes Inc.	39,277.38
	BC	Crazy Wheels	38,280.53
	BC	Cycles and Sports	38,199.10
	BC	Biking's It Industries	30,348.92
	BC	Bikes for Tykes	1,800.00
	MB	Dag City Cycle	1,276.74
	NS	Halifax Cycle Centre	1,489.05
	ON	Cycle Fever	6,629.10
	ON	Don't Tread On Me	5,879.70
	PQ	Wheels 'n' Deals	2,850.85
England			**578,229.17**
	Avon	McDonald Klein Sports	3,618.00
	Berkshire	Life Cycle Centre	8,819.55
	Cambridgeshire	Hit the Dirt	4,637.00
	Co Durham	Donview Bike Co.	35.00
	Devon	Exeter Cycle Source	1,030.08
	Dorset	Source One Cycle	1,119.50
	Greater London	BBS Pty	500,000.00
	Greater London	Picadilly Cycle	5,321.25
	Greater Manchester	Great Outdoors	3,024.85
	Hampshire	Wheel to Wheel	5,912.70
	Kent	Sunrise Cycle	1,690.05
	Nottinghamshire	Tom's Bikes	36,330.00
	West Midlands	Westerly Sports	47.00
	West Yorkshire	LifeCycle	6,644.19
France			**717,529.32**
	Alsace	Sports Alsace	52,787.50
	Alsace	Mulhouse Vélos	5,359.70
	Aquitaine	Lourdes Sports	53,370.14
	Aquitaine	Bordeaux Sports	533.75

Figure 9.3 Sample Sales Report

John can now schedule the report to run every 24 hours. A security profile gets applied, so each manager only sees the data related to his country.

The resulting report is converted to a PDF by the system and sent in an email attachment as the preferred distribution channel for the country managers. Additionally, reports get published to the secured

Reports available as PDFs

portal so there is one trusted place to get the latest version as well as the historical data.

 Tip

> If you are interested in a real-life scenario of deploying SAP Crystal Reports along with the SAP Crystal Reports Server, the SAP website has a variety of webcasts posted that features the experiences of customers. Just navigate to the SAP Crystal Reports Server section of the website, and check the resources.

Although SAP Crystal Reports Server is a good step toward a global BI deployment, for SMBs, SAP proposes its most advanced solutions under the Edge brand.

SAP BusinessObjects Edge Business Intelligence (BI)

SAP BusinessObjects Edge BI is the most comprehensive offering for SMBs that see the need for a full-featured BI solution. The implementation of SAP BusinessObjects Edge BI does require some level of IT support.

The most comprehensive BI solution for SMBs

This first product from the SAP BusinessObjects Edge series focuses on BI and at this time comes in three packages:

> The standard package provides reporting capabilities and advanced visualization.

> The version with data integration includes the standard version plus the capabilities to merge data from different sources and even build a Data Mart.

> The version with data management includes the previously mentioned versions plus the ability to do data cleansing.

Table 9.2 shows a summary features comparison for each of the versions.

Feature	Standard Package	Data Integration Version	Data Management Version
Operational reporting	✓	✓	✓
Ad hoc query and analysis	✓	✓	✓
Dashboards	✓	✓	✓
Microsoft Office integration	✓	✓	✓
Security	✓	✓	✓
Scheduling	✓	✓	✓
Auditing	✓	✓	✓
Mobile	✓	✓	✓
Data integration		✓	✓
Data quality			✓
Rapid Marts		✓	✓
SAP BusinessObjects Explorer	✓	✓	✓

Table 9.2 SAP BusinessObjects Edge BI Features Comparison Chart

Let's look at those three versions in a little bit more detail.

SAP BusinessObjects Edge BI Standard Package

Although midsize companies may initially look into dedicated reporting or dashboarding products, there are multiple reasons why SAP BusinessObjects Edge BI should be considered instead. First of all, these products are based on the SAP BusinessObjects Enterprise platform, which is a guarantee of leading-edge BI capabilities and robustness.

As importantly, SAP BusinessObjects Edge BI delivers end-to-end integration of all the best-of-breed BI tools you'll ever need to run your midsize business:

SAP BusinessObjects Edge provides a BI platform

> SAP BusinessObjects Web Intelligence
> SAP BusinessObjects Xcelsius Enterprise
> SAP Crystal Reports
> SAP BusinessObjects Voyager
> SAP BusinessObjects Live Office
> SAP BusinessObjects Explorer

 Did You Know?

Products within the SAP BusinessObjects Edge family carry the same feature sets as their counterparts from the large enterprise segment. The differences are mainly in the deployment area where SAP BusinessObjects Edge requires less effort, and SAP BusinessObjects Enterprise offers more options and scalability.

All those products already described in previous chapters of this book rely on the BI platform, which provides all of the underlying services to enable a seamless and secured rollout of BI capabilities in your SMB. Here is a list of the main services provided by the platform:

> **Users and rights management:** Allow administrators to centrally manage user access and security of the BI content.
> **BI content management:** Store all the BI content in the platform, and publish, share, secure, and organize.
> **BI portal and third-party portals integration kits:** Allow integration with your existing landscape or use the provided portal.
> **Search:** Powerfully search across the BI content and any other file uploaded to the BI platform.
> **Scheduling:** Refresh and publish reports and dashboards automatically. Distribute securely.
> **Auditing**: Ensure compliance with regulations and corporate governance. Understand the use of the BI platform, and plan growth.
> **SDK and Web services:** Integrate BI with other applications in your landscape.

A web tool, the Central Management Console (CMC), helps administrators manage all the servers and content within a unique intuitive interface. Figure 9.4 shows the main screen displaying all possible administration options in the CMC.

The Central Management Console is used to administrate the system

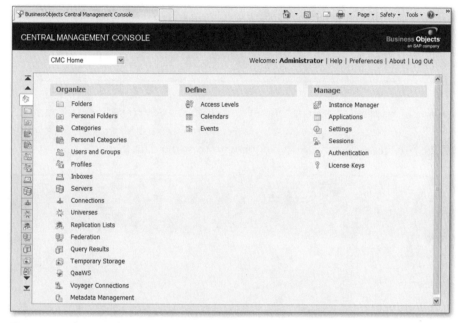

Figure 9.4 The Central Management Console

SAP BusinessObjects Edge BI with Data Integration

Data Integrator tool

In addition to the previously mentioned platform, reporting, and dashboarding capabilities, customers opting for SAP BusinessObjects Edge BI with data integration get the capabilities of SAP Business-Objects Data Services discussed earlier in Chapter 6. Refer to Chapter 6 for more details on this product.

It's generally a good idea, even for smaller businesses, to leverage data integration because you can't have good BI without a solid data foundation. As soon as your business started to grow, you probably found yourself with a proliferation of data silos created through the various ERP (enterprise resources planning) tools, Excel spreadsheets, and other data storage.

You could, for example, have all of the data related to product shipping entered into an Access database from a homegrown shipping system in your warehouse. On the other side, your customer's database is in a SQL Server database used by your CRM system. Lastly, like quite a few businesses, all your finance data is maintained in Excel. Reporting off those three systems independently will not give you the business insight you were hoping for while deploying BI. A large part of the success for BI relies on the work done at the data level.

Single version of the truth   The proliferation of sources quickly creates discrepancies in your data and hurts the golden "single version of the truth" that allows knowledge workers in your company to trust the data they use.

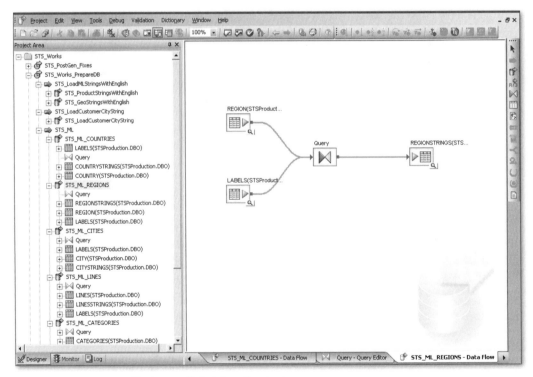

Figure 9.5   Data Integration tool

A great advantage of the data integration tool that comes with the SAP BusinessObjects Edge BI software, as shown in Figure 9.5, is the ease of use and very graphical interface to create data flows. So you can focus on fulfilling the business needs, rather than learning how to use a complex tool.

Let's now look at the third package of the offering: SAP BusinessObjects Edge BI with data management.

SAP BusinessObjects Edge BI with Data Management

Although it sounds obvious, the following truth is unfortunately often overlooked, even in larger companies: The quality of your BI and thus your decisions is directly related to the quality of your data.

As you start to have more customers, providers, employees, invoices, and so on, the quality of your data is going to suffer, and you may either start making decisions on poor data or spend a lot of effort manually editing addresses, removing duplicates, and so on.

The importance of data quality

 Tip

> Many SAP BusinessObjects Explorer users find it useful to manually identify data quality issues. Because SAP BusinessObjects Explorer allows fast parsing and drilling into very large data sets and presents the results along with facets, it's easy to visually identify, for example, if you have multiple similar names for the same customer.

With the addition of data management, SAP BusinessObjects Edge BI helps you automate the discovery and correction of data quality issues. For example, the software is capable of checking the integrity of addresses for more than 190 countries; it can also help you check and synchronize data from different sources. Again, please take a look at Section 3.6, SAP BusinessObjects Enterprise Information Management, to learn more about the data quality capabilities of the product because those offerings are similar.

Conclusion on SAP BusinessObjects Edge BI

So we've now discussed the three options available to you with SAP BusinessObjects Edge BI: the standard package, the data integration

Data integration and quality

version, and the data management version. Per experience, most businesses tend to rush to dashboarding/reporting without much thought about the data integration and quality part of the equation. In terms of strategy, we recommend that you take a dual approach. Companies need to showcase BI to prove the value and get the projects going, while data integration projects may need a little more time but will provide even greater value.

> **Ex** Example
>
> In customer management databases, you'll often come across a few data quality issues. Misspelled customer names, type mismatches in email addresses, and incorrect formatting of mailing addresses are very common. These errors cause duplicates in your reports or the inability to properly aggregate your KPIs because the system sees two records where there should be one. Using data quality tools helps you resolve the inconsistencies and base your decisions on more accurate facts.

You may have initially started to look for a simple dashboarding solution, decided to read this book to see what SAP has to offer, and now find yourself thinking about data integration and probably a little overwhelmed. This is where the Rapid Marts and QuickStart packs come into play as we'll discover next.

SAP BusinessObjects Rapid Marts

SAP Business-Objects Rapid Marts and QuickStart packs

If you are running ERP or CRM from SAP, PeopleSoft, Oracle, or Siebel, the SAP BusinessObjects Rapid Marts deliver a packaged data integration solution and prebuilt reports to get you quickly up and running with BI on top of your ERP system. You can then leverage this foundation and amend/modify whatever is delivered with the package to adjust it to your needs or use the content as an example to develop additional BI content.

While SAP BusinessObjects Rapid Marts are focused on bootstrapping companies with creating data marts or a data warehouse from their ERP, QuickStart packages bring a complementary business angle to the mix. QuickStart packages are designed by functional experts and help you benefit from industry best practices and achieve fast ROI right from the start.

 Note

> Because QuickStart packages change rapidly, we won't go into the details of what they are. If interested, a good first stop is to search for QuickStart at *www.sap.com*.

SAP BusinessObjects Edge Planning and Consolidation

A recurring problem in all businesses, but often more prevalent in smaller companies, is the challenge of financial planning. It usually starts with Excel spreadsheets, sometimes also with unstructured data, and, as the business grows, quickly becomes a bigger problem that may affect the company's ability to grow.

Typically, financial planning data resides in multiple systems scattered across the company, spreadsheets get sent by email, and multiple versions of the same information get created to a point where a coherent vision of the planning along with consolidation becomes a time-consuming and error-prone manual effort.

Scattered data makes financial planning a challenge

As we saw earlier, SMBs operate on low IT budgets and often believe that advanced systems are out of their reach. The SAP BusinessObjects Edge Planning and Consolidation application offers an integrated way to solve this problem by providing end-to-end planning, budgeting, and consolidation suite that includes collaborative workflows. As part of the SAP BusinessObjects Edge family, this offering was specially designed and priced to enable smaller companies to access the technology they need.

SAP Business-Objects Edge Planning and Consolidation is specially designed and priced for SMBs

Compliance

> SAP BusinessObjects Edge Planning and Consolidation automatically generates a full audit trail of the financial consolidation process, making it easy to validate the compliance with regulatory and financial standards.

SAP BusinessObjects Edge Planning and Consolidation offers the following benefits to users:

> The solution is fully integrated into the familiar Microsoft Office applications. This makes it easy for users already used to the Office applications to get started. Because most of these users already operate in Excel, additional training needs are limited, and both cost of ownership and time to value are reduced.

> The intelligent panes display context-sensitive information, and options not only make the interface easier to read but also guide users into what to do. This helps users understand the next step in the process, guarantees that best practices are applied, and reduces training needs.

> Integrated business process workflows guide users step by step into performing the most common financial processes, such as budgeting. Processes are customizable directly by users to fit specific needs. The same processes are automatically audited to ensure proper usage and compliance.

> Unlike the spreadsheets sent by email and scattered across the company, all the data is kept in a central and secured repository. This allows for efficient collaboration in the planning process, as well as a complete, trusted picture of the business performance.

> The solution includes full reporting capabilities. Reports can be created in familiar office applications such as Excel or PowerPoint depending on needs. They offer contextual filters that allow users to quickly modify the view or filter data. Templates are provided for common reporting needs and can always be enriched with additional analytics.

Let's now look at the next solution from the SAP BusinessObjects Edge family: Strategy Management.

SAP BusinessObjects Edge Strategy Management

In an ever-changing business environment, companies need to quickly adapt. The time is long gone when companies could make multiyears plans and take time to implement and execute them. Today, mid- to long-term strategies obviously still exist, but two factors have substantially changed:

> The strategy needs to be tuned and refined along the way based on the economic context, competitor moves, or innovation.

> The strategy, or refined versions of it, needs to be implemented quickly and efficiently despite complex and distributed organizations.

Here again, SMBs — actually more specifically medium businesses — face the same challenges as the larger companies but amplified by an even faster pace of business and no room for failure because small failures look big in a small business.

SAP BusinessObjects Edge Strategy Management again provides the benefits of the enterprise version packaged in a format that best suits smaller companies. It provides both the tools and a structure to guide each level in the organization through defining a strategy and implementing it down to the operations.

The solution covers the following areas of the business:

> **Setting goals:** The application allows for high-level goals and objectives to be set collaboratively.

> **Create initiatives:** Within SAP BusinessObjects Edge Strategy Management, initiatives are defined in direct relation with the higher goals set in the tool. This creates a clear understanding of how the initiatives tie into the big picture and takes care of priority management. The performance against the goals can then be measured through KPIs defined along with the initiatives.

> **Communicate:** The application allows for the rollout of the strategy across the company, at all levels in the organization.

The interface of the tool is simply organized and presented around tabs:

Mid- to long-term strategies

SAP Business-Objects Edge Strategy Management

❯ The HOME tab presents a summary dashboard that can include highlights of the user's initiatives and performance. Users can personalize the summary to track objectives and metrics that are important to them. Additionally, they can add bookmarks of their interest or subscribe to alerts tied to their mission or metrics.

❯ The STRATEGY tab presents the set strategy in the form of a goal diagram. There are multiple predefined diagrams that follow the best practices in the industry for presenting strategies. Additionally "pathways" diagrams are an innovative way of presenting the evolution of the execution versus the planned strategy.

 About Pathways Charts

> Pathways charts are graphic representations of the various components of your strategy and plot the emphasis of each component in time. Pathways charts are especially useful to represent launch plans and other communication campaigns.

❯ The INITIATIVES tab is the place for operational managers to break the strategy down into executable actions. The application links initiatives to the larger goal. So on one hand, employees can immediately relate initiatives to the goals and understand the strategy, while on the other hand, performance indicators for the initiatives are aggregated to reflect the progression on the goals. Besides the list view, initiatives and associated performance can be displayed in other formats such as the fishbone chart. Managers with the appropriate authorizations can take action and modify the initiatives and resources allocations as needed to tune the execution of the strategy. Teams are automatically notified of changes.

❯ The SCORECARD tab allows for a quick and efficient overview of the progress of initiatives against KPIs. The user can drill from the initial aggregated dashboard to details to identify the reason for the indicator's status.

❯ The OPERATIONAL REVIEWS tab provides everything required and guides the user through preparing and executing an operational review. A PDF version of the operational review is generated and stored in the system where other users can view it or download it for broader distribution.

SAP BusinessObjects OnDemand

SAP BusinessObjects OnDemand along with SAP StreamWork was covered in Chapter 5 so we won't go into detail here. Refer to Chapter 5 for more information on these products.

The existing SAP Crystal Reports website that's accessed though *www.crystalreports.com/share/* has an appealing offer for SMBs but is in the process of being replaced by the new SAP BusinessObjects OnDemand at *www.ondemand.com/businessintelligence/*.

 Tip

> Customers can still use the legacy *www.crystalreports.com* site without disruption. At a later stage, they will be offered a migration tool to help them move their content to the new site. They can also use their existing login to connect to the new SAP BusinessObjects OnDemand platform.

The SAP BusinessObjects OnDemand offering is available right away without the need to install a server or a desktop piece of software, which makes it a good option for simple collaboration in an SMB with limited IT support.

At the time of printing, SAP BusinessObjects OnDemand offers you an easy way to start exploring data from Excel but also upload your reports created with SAP Crystal Reports to distribute and securely share them. Although not as advanced as SAP Crystal Reports Server, some publication can be achieved using the Desktop Publisher tool, a free download from the site.

Desktop Publisher tool

Case Studies

SAP Crystal Reports and SAP Business-Objects Xcelsius Enterprise

This company is a small European designer and manufacturer of customer aluminum frames with less than 100 employees. They were using an homegrown timesheet application derived from the previous paper-based process. Their challenge was a poor visibility into resources allocation leading them to inefficiencies and delivery delays. By introducing business intelligence tools, they could get immediate visibility into their resources allocations per project and track absences in a way that allowed them to increase by 15% the number of orders they could manage without increasing the resources. Additionally they detected and fixed some labor laws compliance issues.

Business Challenge

This small family-owned business puts the majority of its investments into machinery and workers to keep the business growing. IT systems are minimal. But with growth came more orders and workers with challenges for the managers to keep track of shifts, absences, and overall resources allocations.

For example, a worker could be assigned to a project for which the material was delayed. Or a worker could be on sick leave but still be assigned to a shift for the next day.

The company strongly felt it could output more projects with the same workforce if it could have an overview of the business and could react faster to changes.

Solution Deployment

With the help of a part-time IT contractor, the company implemented SAP Crystal Reports and SAP BusinessObjects Xcelsius Enterprise on just two computers. So as soon as the daily timesheets were in the database, the company could right away produce a resources allocation dashboard and make adjustments for the next day.

Value Achieved

This allowed the company to take in 15% more projects in the first year.

Expanding on this, the company started to use SAP Crystal Reports to output timesheets to distribute to workers, whereas previously this was based on a print-screen of the displayed timesheet. This provided employees transparency and confirmation that their time was properly logged in the system.

Eventually, the company started to expand aggregations and calculations and run more analysis on the business to discover some compliance issues with the labor laws that could be adjusted.

Looking Ahead

The company now produces more dashboards and reports, from pay stubs to professional-looking project quotes.

SAP BusinessObjects Edge BI with Data Management

This small business based in the United States has a little over 500 employees and distributes IT equipment and software. Their existing solution was based on Microsoft Office, mainly Excel.

The main challenge with this setup was the quality of the data which led to un-trusted reporting and ultimately improper decisions being made. The benefits were immediate with over 180 hours per week saved in the operational reporting process, allowing resources to focus on value added tasks.

Business Challenge

This business has to adapt quickly to customer demand while keeping an eye on suppliers, purchasing, and stock to safeguard the margins. The environment is complex due to the number of references. When based on Excel, the numerous spreadsheets were shared and modified constantly, with no tracking. Data was untrusted, and long to reconcile and verify. A product manager could spend up to three hours to compile a report while having limited trust in the result.

The Solution

Operating on limited IT resources and unable to afford a bigger IT department, the company decided to leverage SAP BusinessObjects Edge BI with data management. The platform was easy enough to implement, and the entire strategy was designed around SAP Business-Objects Web Intelligence with self-service in mind. The demand for reports is high, and the company wanted the users to be self-sufficient so IT could focus on the infrastructure. The data integration tools pull data from the various legacy systems so they remained untouched. A data warehouse was created from these systems with a step of data cleansing to ensure the best quality.

Universes were designed, giving the product managers the power to create their own queries. The operational reports were completely automated via scheduling, and every morning they delivered the status of stocks, orders, and supplies broken down by business line.

Value Achieved

The company now has a much better insight in the business and can already detect margin problems that were promptly fixed. Employee satisfaction has increased because product managers can now spend more time analyzing the data, talking to customers, and putting together new offerings rather than compiling data in Excel. It is estimated that a total of 180+ hours per week is saved, which translates into over $1 million per year on nonvalue-added work hours

Looking Ahead

Now that the company has been very successful with SAP Business-Objects Web Intelligence, the managers are looking into building some SAP BusinessObjects Xcelsius Enterprise dashboards to keep track of aggregated KPIs. They believe it could help them detect problems and make adjustments earlier and consequently increase their competitive advantage.

Summary

In this chapter, we presented the SAP BusinessObjects Edge BI series along with a couple of other options for SMBs.

It is important to remember that SAP BusinessObjects Edge BI is also a safe and ready for growth investment because growing companies can upgrade at a later time to the SAP BusinessObjects Enterprise version seamlessly, building up on their investments in training and BI assets.

In the next section, we'll discuss how the portfolio of solutions can be best leveraged depending on whether you already have investments in SAP, have investments in Business Objects or are completely new to the BI and EPM solutions.

PART III
SAP BusinessObjects Solutions for Non-SAP Customers

10

Customers with Previous Investments in SAP BusinessObjects

In this chapter, we'll discuss the reasons why customers who already had an investment in the Business Objects solutions should consider this investment safe and continue to rely on the SAP BusinessObjects solutions for their business moving forward.

One of the key strengths of Business Objects prior to being acquired by SAP was that it was agnostic to the underlying IT systems already in place. At the time of the acquisition, SAP committed to keep Business Objects products agnostic and so far, both the roadmaps and recently released products have delivered on this commitment.

Investment Protection

While new solutions and new capabilities in existing products are being released, a special effort is made to make sure that SAP Business-Objects remains the best possible solution for customers running SAP systems. SAP obviously wants its solutions to be the best possible stack.

However, customers that were running previous versions of SAP BusinessObjects with or without SAP systems can see for themselves that new products and features remain mostly independent to the underlying systems and data sources. Additionally, updated support for non-SAP systems is being added with each new release and service pack.

Solutions that integrate well with non-SAP systems

While some believe that innovation investments in the SAP BusinessObjects solutions were mostly used toward innovating for SAP customers, the newly released SAP BusinessObjects 4.0 actually includes a variety of innovations agnostic to the underlying systems. Let's review a couple examples:

> The concept of semantic layer (universes) remains central to the SAP BusinessObjects solution and pervasive to all sources of data. Moreover, a new generation of the semantic layer appears — clearly setting the direction for the future.

> The SAP BusinessObjects Enterprise platform hasn't been retired to the profit of SAP NetWeaver as some might have expected in the early stages of the acquisition. The platform also gets a significant number of new capabilities to improve its deployability and cost of ownership.

> SAP BEx clients are being gradually replaced by SAP BusinessObjects Web Intelligence and SAP BusinessObjects Analysis. The latter is a replacement for the OLAP analysis tool SAP BusinessObjects Voyager, augmented with some BEx capabilities.

> A full set of new monitoring capabilities is being added to benefit customers that don't use SAP Solution Manager.

> SAP continues to support and further develop integration with the Oracle E-Business Suite as well as PeopleSoft, making the SAP BusinessObjects solution a natural choice for customers with a significant Oracle investment.

> **Ex** **Example**
>
> Existing SAP BusinessObjects deployments needed an integration kit to connect to Oracle or PeopleSoft systems. In the new 4.0 version, the integration is built into the BI platform.

The same story holds true for information management products, such as SAP BusinessObjects Metadata Management and SAP Business-Objects Data Services.

While support for SAP NetWeaver BW was added in 2009 to SAP BusinessObjects Metadata Management, the tool provides metadata integration from all SAP BusinessObjects products and the major database vendors, as well as more than 50 additional metadata sources provided through a partner.

The SAP BusinessObjects Rapid Marts, already presented in this book include all the best practices and technology to efficiently implement data marts on top of PeopleSoft, Oracle, and Siebel enterprise applications.

As you can see through these examples, products in the EIM area are not only available to customers without SAP systems but also totally relevant in Oracle environments.

On the EPM side, SAP has been working since the acquisition of Business Objects to deliver integration with SAP ERP and the SAP NetWeaver platform, but at the same time, remain open to non-SAP platforms. Major investments are actually being made in harmonizing all of the products that compose the EPM suite, making sure that they properly leverage the BI platform as well as share common user experiences and visualizations.

Upgrade Considerations

If you already have an investment in previous versions of SAP BusinessObjects such as XI, XI R2, or even still on BusinessObjects 6.5, your investment is fully protected. You can upgrade to any of the newer versions of SAP BusinessObjects because no product was changed to become SAP-specific.

 Tip

> Companies still on BusinessObjects 6.5 or Crystal Enterprise 10 need to stage their upgrade through SAP BusinessObjects XI R2 or SAP Business-Objects XI 3.1 before upgrading to SAP BusinessObjects 4.0.

Check supported platforms

While considering the newer SAP BusinessObjects 4.0, you'll have to pay attention to the list of supported platforms and compatibility with your existing infrastructure because the support for some of your components may be planned for a later version of this staged release. Again, this is best practice and normal for an upgrade to a new major release.

If you were on the 6.5 version and migrated to XI R2, then you probably experienced some challenges in the process. This process was a real migration in the sense that the SAP BusinessObjects Enterprise platform had been completely redesigned to provide for future capabilities and enhanced scalability.

XI R2, XI 3.x, and 4.0 operate with the same architecture

SAP BusinessObjects Enterprise XI R2, XI 3.x, and the new 4.0 operate with the same architecture. This means that we're now talking about an upgrade, no longer a migration, and consequently a lot less effort and costs to move from your existing platform to a newer one.

 Definition

> For the SAP BusinessObjects portfolio, we usually talk about a *migration* when some architecture redesign implies a significant transformation of the features, security model, BI content, and so on.
>
> An *upgrade* occurs when new capabilities are added without disruption. In an upgrade scenario, the content is expected to be 100% reusable. In the 4.0 upgrade, there are exceptions to this rule due to retired products.

Upgrade Management tool

The recommended approach for an upgrade to the new 4.0 is a side-by-side system upgrade, which means the 4.0 system is installed alongside the existing system, and existing BI content is brought over into the new system using the new Upgrade Management tool shown in Figure 10.1.

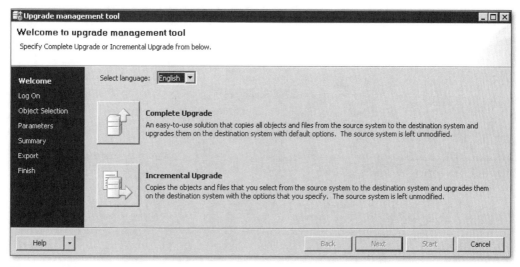

Figure 10.1 The Upgrade Management Tool

Although SAP BusinessObjects 4.0 is still very fresh at the time of this writing, this should allow for a much smoother and less costly upgrade than what you may have experienced in the past. Globally, SAP put a lot of effort into this release to make sure it would be less costly to implement and maintain than previous versions.

In the same way, you'll note that 4.0 comes with a new Information Design tool shown in Figure 10.2. This is the tool used to develop the new version of the universes.

Information Design tool

However, 4.0 also ships with the existing Universe Designer, so, you can continue to work with your existing universes.

Again the idea here is to allow for an incremental and safer upgrade where you can first upgrade the platform and system, while leaving the BI applications untouched for business continuity. Then, in a second stage, you can start to explore the new capabilities, use the new tools, and convert some of your BI content.

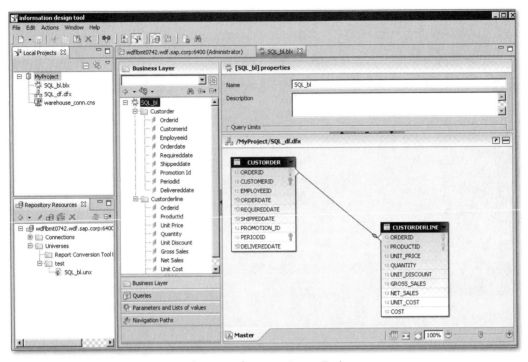

Figure 10.2 The New Information Design Tool

Upgrade points Although the upgrade should be pretty easy, here are a couple high points you want to pay attention to while planning your project:

> SAP BusinessObjects 4.0 servers are 64 bits only, so you'll need to make sure that the hardware and operating systems provisioned for the system are 64 bits.

> Desktop Intelligence (DeskI) was completely retired and removed from 4.0. DeskI reports will not convert 100% to WebI (now SAP BusinessObjects Interactive Analysis), so, you need to plan accordingly. Look at what reports are obsolete, what reports will automatically convert to WebI, and what reports may need manual redesign. Don't overlook that some reports may actually be replaced by SAP Crystal Reports rather than SAP BusinessObjects Interactive Analysis. You'll find very experienced partners on the market prepared to help you quickly and smoothly through that process.

The initial version of SAP BusinessObjects Analysis (the OLAP analysis client) only supports SAP NetWeaver BW and Microsoft Analysis Services. Although SAP provides migration from SAP BusinessObjects Voyager workspaces to SAP BusinessObjects Advanced Analysis, the migration won't be perfect and requires a good planning and phased approach.

Beyond the security of their investments, and the pertinence of upgrading to the new 4.0 release, customers with an existing investment in SAP BusinessObjects solutions will also get the advantage of being offered a broader portfolio of solutions as you'll see in the next section.

Access to a Complete Portfolio of Solutions

As noted in the previous section, companies with an existing investment in SAP BusinessObjects products may continue to operate newer and future versions of SAP BusinessObjects Enterprise in non-SAP environments.

Moreover, the integration of Business Objects into SAP gives former Business Objects customer access to a much broader range of solutions from a single vendor.

On the BI side, the most obvious example is SAP BusinessObjects Explorer Accelerated, which is the version of SAP BusinessObjects Explorer associated with the in-memory SAP NetWeaver BWA engine for fast response times. In its latest release, this technology is capable of accelerating non-SAP data.

 Tip

SAP BusinessObjects Explorer is now available on data sources other than SAP NetWeaver BW. As such, it became a viable solution for companies with non-SAP systems.

As discussed in Chapter 5, the new SAP BusinessObjects Advanced Analysis OLAP client is also issued from the convergence of SAP

Convergence of SAP BusinessObjects Voyager and SAP BusinessObjects BEx

BusinessObjects Voyager and SAP BEx Analyzer, taking the best of both technologies to propose an improved tool. On the EPM side, the SAP BusinessObjects portfolio was also largely enriched with SAP technology so companies now have full coverage of their needs while there were gaps in the Business Objects offering as a standalone company. Figure 10.3 represents the logical view of the portfolio and the way it now covers the full circle from strategy to optimization.

The coverage now includes the following:

> **Strategy management:** Allows companies to set their high-level objectives, map their strategy to the objective, and manage their performance down to the operational metrics.

> **Business planning:** Streamlines and aligns the budget-planning process across the organization. Reduces risks typically associated with using spreadsheets while keeping users in the familiar Microsoft Office environment. Produces an audit trail for regulatory compliance.

> **Financial consolidation:** Improves time to consolidate and close the books while ensuring trust and compliance. Additionally, intercompany reconciliation enables business units to reconcile intercompany balances in real time and directly with each other.

> **XBRL publishing:** Simplifies and accelerates the preparation of XBRL documents to communicate financial and business data across organizations.

> **Profitability and Cost management:** Provides a series of tools to understand the profitability drivers and optimize resources. Identifies the cost-saving options based on your growth strategy. Optimizes profitability across dimensions such as product, customer, and channel.

> **Spend performance management:** Understands company-wide spending patterns, rationalizes products and vendors, maximizes cost savings and reduces supplier risk.

> **Supply chain performance management:** Monitors the delivery reliability, understands factors that influence the full cycle, and improves supply chain effectiveness by focusing on actionable, operational process metrics that impact supply chain performance.

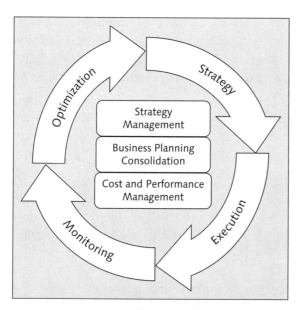

Figure 10.3   The EPM Portfolio, from Strategy to Optimization

Thanks to SAP, the SAP BusinessObjects portfolio also includes GRC applications, as shown in the following list. Once again, although those applications can be integrated with the rest of the SAP offering, they are also available for companies that don't use SAP as their ERP.

> **SAP BusinessObjects Risk and Compliance Management**: Maximizes corporate performance through balancing risks and rewards for maximum return. Identifies key risks and creates mitigation strategies; builds monitoring for existing business processes.

> **SAP BusinessObjects Access Control and SAP BusinessObjects Process control**: Ensures regulation compliance through SoD checks. Streamlines and simplifies the process for authorizing system access while enabling full transparency. Detects possibly fraudulent events such as billing with no associated shipping. Raises exceptions.

> **SAP BusinessObjects Global Trade Services:** Lowers the cost and risk of international trade. Streamlines import/export license management and embargo checks, and ensures trade compliance, expedited cross-border transactions, and optimum use of trade agreements.

> **SAP BusinessObjects Environment, Health, and Safety Management:** Manages and controls compliance with environment, health, and safety regulations across the world. Implements standard processes to reduce the cost of compliance and guarantee transparency.

> **SAP BusinessObjects Sustainability Performance Management:** Sets objectives and tracks your performance against sustainability goals. Reports and communicates efficiently against your sustainability KPIs.

Figure 10.4 shows how those solutions rely on a common semantic built from the existing corporate systems and integrate with each other to form a comprehensive risk and compliance management platform.

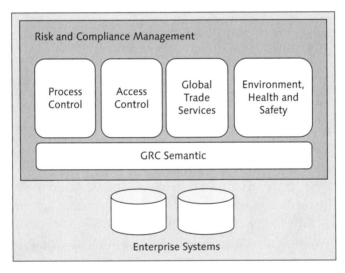

Figure 10.4 The Complete GRC Solution

Get More Value from SAP Enterprise-Ready Standards

For years, SAP has been associated with high product quality and very tight lifecycle management. The reason is simple: From the beginning, SAP has been in the business of mission-critical software where production downtimes can quickly turn into big losses.

For this reason, SAP developed a very rigorous series of software development practices, product quality standards, and a highly controlled rollout process with the objective of offering a seamless lifecycle management for its customers.

SAP often talks about the concept of timeless software, which means the continuous delivery of software upgrades and additional capabilities without disruption to the existing system.

Timeless software

While the Business Objects company was constantly improving in the enterprise readiness aspect of the software, the acquisition by SAP enables synergies that allow for a much faster integration of the SAP best practices in that domain.

Enterprise readiness

Some of those improvements will only be visible to customers with other SAP software because they are linked to product integration, for example, the integration with SAP Solution Manager. But the majority of the improvements required by SAP standards and best practices actually benefit all customers whether they are within a SAP landscape or not. This should be evident in such domains as accessibility, languages standards, overall quality, and much more.

 Did You Know?

SAP has developed a strict accessibility compliance plan through its Accessibility Compliance Center. The SAP Accessibility Standard is leveraged by new developments and based on the section 508 requirements, Web Content Accessibility Guidelines 1.0 Priority 1 checkpoints and WCAG 2.0 level AA success criteria.

There isn't a lot of visibility on the changes SAP made internally to the engineering process for SAP BusinessObjects products, but we know, for example, that the product development lifecycle was redesigned to leverage the best practices developed by SAP while keeping the innovation and agility of Business Objects.

Some other changes are more visible, such as the maintenance model on SAP BusinessObjects products, which was changed to adhere to SAP's standards with the following rules:

> Seven years of mainstream maintenance

> Two years of priority-one support

Mainstream maintenance begins with the release-to-customer date for the major release and covers any subsequent minor releases in the release family that might be shipped. Each release in a release family has a mainstream maintenance period of at least two years after the start of restricted shipment for that release. As soon as a new release enters unrestricted shipment, the previous release is maintained for at least one more year. The last release closes the nine-year maintenance cycle for this release family. This maintenance cycle is illustrated in Figure 10.5.

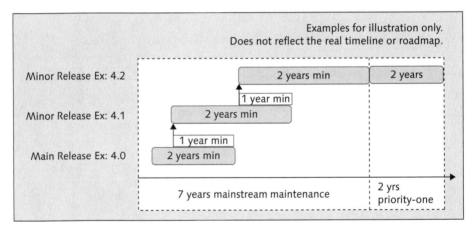

Figure 10.5 New Maintenance Model for SAP BusinessObjects Solutions

Ramp up phase

SAP BusinessObjects products now have a ramp up phase. SAP BusinessObjects Explorer was the first product to use the ramp up process while 4.0 is the first release of the BI platform to leverage ramp up.

Leveraging the latest technology while controlling the risks

The ramp up is a controlled release that provides an opportunity for a few selected customers to implement the new capabilities in production with full support from SAP and gives SAP an opportunity to fine-tune the release before general availability.

 Did You Know?

Ramp up is not to be confused with beta. SAP ramp up releases are full featured and production-ready quality.

Supportability standards are also being added to SAP BusinessObjects products, for example, the ability to perform end-to-end root-cause analysis or the integration with performance monitoring tools, such as CA Wily Introscope.

Clearly, many of the improvements, directly visible or not, also benefit customers that decided not to use SAP for their ERP or their data warehouse.

Case Study

This company is a large international consumer goods distributor making over $7 billion in revenue. They are currently running a shared services environment on SAP BusinessObjects 3.0. As the SAP and BusinessObjcts worlds come together, they are facing challenges with setting up a common BI center of excellence. The expected benefits of a joint BI center of excellence would be a better ROI on the investments as well as increased user satisfaction.

Business Challenge

Up to 2009, the company operated both SAP NetWeaver BW and SAP BusinessObjects in silos. SAP BusinessObjects XI 3.0 was leveraging exclusively relational data sources from Oracle and IBM. At the same time, SAP NetWeaver BW was serving financial departments with SAP Business Explorer (SAP BEx) reporting. Both solutions were supported by their own center of excellence. After the Business Objects acquisition, the company moved forward with a strategy to leverage the SAP BusinessObjects platform for SAP NetWeaver BW data as well as merge the centers of excellence under one BI group. However, beyond some technology challenges, the company quickly identified quite a gap in best practices and methodologies that created challenges with achieving its one-BI strategy.

The Solution

By looking into the SAP BusinessObjects roadmap and working directly with SAP, the company knew that some integration in the products, but most importantly in the processes and practices, was coming down the road. Keeping the SAP BusinessObjects toolset agnostic to the data source was a must for the company because only financials were on SAP NetWeaver BW, and the company expected it to remain this way moving forward. This meant that 70% to 80% of BI was going to stay on Oracle and IBM. After evaluating the capabilities of the new SAP BusinessObjects 4.0, the company was convinced that its investment in SAP BusinessObjects XI 3.0 was safe, and the company was ready to look into a future upgrade project. The following points were specifically appealing:

> Unified SAP maintenance model and support practices allowing the company to bring its BI teams under one single center of excellence.

> The integration with SAP Solution Manager allows the one-BI strategy by leveraging SAP's best practices and methodologies in availability and root-cause analysis. This also helps the teams to start speaking the same language and have common maintenance practices.

> The release of SAP BusinessObjects Analysis, which was tested and got lots of traction from the business, will eventually lead to phasing out BEx Analyzer, allowing the SAP BusinessObjects BI suite to be the only frontend to deploy.

> Multisource directly built into the new semantic layer will allow for significant reduction in maintenance costs on the relational reporting. Instead of merging data sources in each report, they will be merged directly at the universe level. Because of heterogeneous Oracle and IBM systems, merging the data is a common practice in the business.

> Life cycle management was one of the top challenges because of SAP content on the SAP Change and Transport System (CTS) and SAP BusinessObjects content on LifeCycle Management, while the use case needs both. With the new integration capabilities, they will be able to control all BI content directly from the LifeCycle Management tool.

All of these perspectives were based on working on the roadmap and some experiments with the software. It was not deployed in production yet. However, the perspectives reassured the company on its choice for the SAP BusinessObjects solutions

Perspectives

Because the solution is not in place yet, no ROI or value could be measured. However, it is already clear that the new solutions will support the one-BI strategy with the perspective that the SAP BusinessObjects tools will become the universal frontend to all sources of data, which are SAP, Oracle, IBM, or others. Along with the adoption of the SAP best practices and tools for the platform maintenance, this opens the way to significant savings and ROI on BI across the company.

Summary

As we saw in this chapter, companies that currently use products from the SAP BusinessObjects portfolio can be reassured that their investment is safe and that SAP is committed to keeping the right balance between a best-of-breed integration with other SAP products and keeping the solutions available and innovative to non-SAP customers. Additionally, the integration of Business Objects into SAP allowed for the rationalization of the product portfolio as well as improvements in the mission-critical readiness of the BI products.

Now, let's move to the next chapter that looks at the benefits to customers who are new to the SAP BusinessObjects solutions.

Customers New to SAP BusinessObjects Solutions

In this chapter, we'll look at some of the reasons companies without any investment in SAP or SAP BusinessObjects should consider implementing those solutions and where to start.

We'll look at why SAP BusinessObjects solutions are a safe and sound choice for any company willing to develop their BI, IM, or PM footprint. Then, we'll move on to talk about where to start and how to be successful.

The Safe Choice

Business Objects solutions were already a very sound technology choice as most of them are leaders in their domains and benefit from a constant stream of innovations. Now integrated within SAP, those solutions are backed up by one of the largest and strongest players in the software industry.

If you are new to SAP BusinessObjects solutions and need more details on the offering and technology, you can review any of the chapters in Section II of this book.

 Tip

> If you are completely new to the SAP BusinessObjects BI solutions, make sure you pay attention to Section 5.2.1, The Semantic Layer, in Chapter 5. This is a founding principle of the solution.

Now, there are many choices for BI solutions in the market. So why consider SAP BusinessObjects?

While features and capabilities of the software are important, remember that this comparison is not the most crucial factor of the decision for a vendor versus another.

Comparing vendors feature to feature is almost irrelevant in today's competitive landscape

All players competing with SAP on BI, information management (IM), or performance management (PM) have a solid set of features, and this probably won't be the most discriminating factor for your software choice. It's virtually irrelevant to compare software feature to feature because software vendors compete on a strategy and vision, not on features.

So as you look at the business problem you're trying to fix or the competitive advantage you're trying to get, you should start with understanding which solutions the vendors have to offer and how well the solutions and strategy presented to you resonate with your own strategy and requirements.

This is even more true in a solution replacement scenario, where you must deal with users who are very familiar with a specific tool and immediately want to compare the old software with the new.

By now, you should understand that gains in productivity, costs, and competitive advantage are best realized if you introduce a "solution" which is also likely to mean some changes in processes and work habits.

Ex Example

Although it's now commonly accepted that a corporate address book is more efficient in software than in hard copy, you can't imagine how many feature-to-feature comparisons the business could come up with that were favorable to the printed version. There are always ways to resist change and make something new look bad.

There's no way we could make a definite software recommendation in this book. We all understand that each situation is different, and you'll have to define your project and look at various solutions to make your own choice. However, let's look at some of the core strengths of the SAP BusinessObjects offering:

> First, SAP is a very solid company. When you invest in a software solution, you don't want to see the vendor disappear overnight. SAP has been around for about 35 years and provides solutions to more than 97,000 customers in more than 120 countries. Financial results are strong; the company is recognized by the market and analysts as a key player and leader in the industry. So buying a solution from SAP guarantees that you'll get upgrades and support for the years to come.

> SAP also has the claimed ambition to help companies become best-run businesses. SAP also makes it fully part of its strategy and communication that this is for any size business. So beyond the words, it's interesting to look at the intention. SAP is talking about a customer-centric approach where it intends to help businesses run better. This ties back to the features versus strategy discussion. SAP focuses on helping the business rather than being a tool provider. Choosing SAP means that you're choosing a partner that doesn't want to sell tools and then walk away, but instead provides solutions and expertise to help you be more efficient in your business.

> SAP was in the past identified as a vendor dedicated to large enterprise customers. As we saw in Chapter 9, this perception is outdated as SAP expands its offerings with quite a few solutions dedicated to small and medium businesses (SMBs). Are you concerned that smaller businesses are going to be ignored by such a large software vendor? Don't be. SAP understands the incredible market

SAP Business-Objects offerings strengths

SAP offers specific solutions for SMBs

opportunity of this segment and has organized specific product lines and dedicated distribution channels.

> By choosing SAP, you have access to a significant pool of service resources, directly from SAP or from its large ecosystem. This allows a business to find external help for pretty much anything SAP-related, from the definition of the solution, to the architecture, development, support, and training. Some partners are focused on large enterprises while others specialize in smaller businesses.

 Did You Know?

SAP has thousands of partners across the world and is very committed to this ecosystem. SAP considers partners as extending the reach of its solution and enabling customers far beyond their own capacity. When selecting partners, make sure they are skilled with the SAP BusinessObjects portfolio.

Now that we looked at SAP as a company and its strategy, let's quickly go over a few points that we already covered in detail earlier:

> SAP has an extensive portfolio of products that are well integrated and interact together, so almost any kind of business solution can be designed from these elements. Each investment is like a building block on which additional solutions can be developed as new needs emerge.

> Customers that already invested in SAP solutions benefit from continuous improvements in the SAP BusinessObjects portfolio for best-of-breed integration with SAP solutions. Products such as SAP BusinessObjects Explorer Accelerated or the new SAP BusinessObjects Analysis demonstrate the success of SAP's strategy for converging the best of SAP and Business Objects technologies. For customers with SAP systems, the choice looks obvious.

Native support for non-SAP systems

> Customers that made a different choice for their ERP systems and data warehouse need not forget that the SAP BusinessObjects portfolio was designed with the idea that users should be able to access all data in whatever system the data lives in. The initial idea that is still supported today by SAP's strategy was that IT systems are heterogeneous by nature. By strategic decision or for historical

reasons, companies almost never run a unique software stack. Hardware systems, operating systems, application servers, database servers, and other components coexist. With their extensive list of supported platforms, the SAP BusinessObjects solutions can pretty much work with any existing system.

Overall, SAP BusinessObjects solutions in BI, IM, or PM offer all the guarantees to make it a safe choice both from the standpoint of the company's robustness and the technology portfolio. Now let's review some implementation considerations.

SAP Business-Objects is a sound choice both from a company and technology standpoint

Blueprint for Adopting SAP BusinessObjects Solutions

As we saw in Section II of this book, the SAP BusinessObjects portfolio is organized in four product lines: business intelligence (BI), enterprise information management (EIM), enterprise performance management (EPM), and governance, risk and compliance (GRC). Figure 11.1 shows a graphical representation of the portfolio.

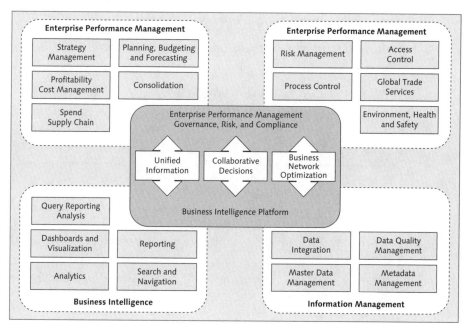

Figure 11.1 SAP BusinessObjects Portfolio

Where You Should Start

While the portfolio is designed to be coherent, inter-operate, and address the business needs end-to-end, it's actually articulated around fairly independent components technology-wise. This means there is no unique way for implementing the solutions and no specific sequence that a company must follow in adopting the solutions; you get to decide where you want to start depending on your immediate business needs and investment priorities.

In almost all cases, you need the BI platform

On the BI side, however, in most situations, you'll need to implement the SAP BusinessObjects BI platform to support the deployment of the BI clients, such as SAP BusinessObjects Web Intelligence, SAP BusinessObjects Analysis, or SAP BusinessObjects Explorer.

How to Start

Don't start looking at the products quite yet; just keep in mind that an entire portfolio of solutions is there to answer almost any kind of need. It's best to start by understanding what problem you are trying to solve or which part of your business you want to make more efficient. Ask yourself these questions:

> Are you spending too much time closing the books?
> Do you face inaccurate and long budgeting cycles?
> Are you having data quality problems?
> Is the business screaming for better analysis capabilities?

 Tip

Clearly articulating the challenge you need to overcome or the efficiency you want to gain is the number one step to success.

After that, well... call SAP. You have a business problem to solve, and SAP has years of experience solving similar problems and obviously wants your business. Why not leverage the experts and let them guide you through the next steps?

If you're not quite ready yet and prefer to do a little bit of homework first, try to qualify your project a little more:

> Don't try to solve everything at once. Look at one problem or opportunity at a time. If you don't break problems down in smaller pieces, you may end up with a project that has so many dependencies, it never completes.

> Collect high-level requirements from the business. Is this a need for a new system or a replacement for an existing system?

After you have a more precise idea of what you are trying to achieve, you can start looking at the SAP BusinessObjects portfolio for what category your project is likely to fall in. Don't overlook the fact that larger projects may require solutions across the portfolio.

Projects require products from across the portfolio

Documenting and finding information about the solutions on your own is pretty easy. There are other books like this one, and the SAP website provides some insight into the solutions, with sometimes recorded demos and customer testimonials. SAP has a very active community of users on SCN (SAP Community Network). Users and administrators share their experience through blogs, white papers, and forums.

User groups and conferences such as SAP SAPPHIRE or SAP TechEd are also very good places to hear more about the solutions and trigger ideas.

Leverage user groups, SAP SAPPHIRE, and other events to learn about the solutions and best practices, and to collect ideas

 Did You Know?

SAP and ASUG still run a SAP BusinessObjects User Conference in the United States in the fall that is fully dedicated to the SAP BusinessObjects portfolio.

Doing your homework will give you the overall understanding of the solutions and the insight to support your discussions with your implementation partner. Let's see in the following section the reasons why you should look at getting help with implementing your solution.

Implementing BI

Now let's focus for a moment on BI, for two reasons: For a large part, readers of SAP BusinessObjects topics have BI in mind and, from our experience, quite a few things are often overlooked in BI projects.

BI projects are... projects. With the exception of very small implementations, you won't be successful unless you properly define your requirements, architecture, rollout plan, and so on. Too many projects fail because BI, or most often in this case "reporting," is considered the last bit of a solution and not given the proper attention.

Solid system architecture

Whereas SAP BusinessObjects solutions designed for SMBs are straightforward to implement with limited IT, the SAP BusinessObjects Enterprise solutions require the proper skills. The BI solutions are meant to be very user friendly and could give the wrong impression that anyone can deploy them with a few mouse clicks. For a successful enterprise deployment that provides the availability and performance expected by users, you'll need a solid system architecture. If no BI platform skills are available, you should get help from SAP field services or another qualified partner.

 Tip

As always, the most important step for the success of your project is the upfront design and architecture. Improper design or overlooks at this stage will be very costly down the road. Building the BI applications (universes, reports, dashboards) is more forgiving. So make sure you invest in a highly experienced, probably also more costly, partner for the design phase.

BI projects often drive an IM project

You should expect that a BI project will often drive an IM project because BI systems are not meant to access transactional data (exceptions apply). BI is best performed against a specially designed database schema found in data warehouses or data marts. So the data you need in your reports, dashboards, and analysis will have to be loaded from the transactional systems to the data warehouse. Additionally, a BI project is often the opportunity to discover that the quality of data is not ideal. Redundancies in the CRM system, improper address formats, and duplicate emails are very common and will limit the BI capabilities. So again, a data quality project may need to spawn off the BI project.

Start from the user requirements and work your way back to the data. A project that would look at reporting off an existing database structure is most often set for failure. Users generally don't get what they needed in the first place because of the data limitations or data quality we've discussed earlier. Such projects also often lead to severe performance problems. When a database schema or an OLAP cube is not designed to serve the purpose, it's usually not efficient. Starting from the data instead of starting from the user end is by far the main reason for failing BI projects. Figure 11.2 shows the recommended design flow.

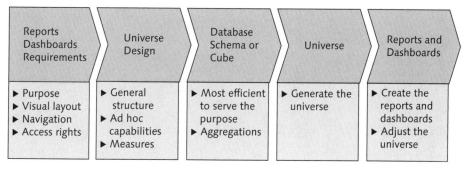

Figure 11.2 Typical BI Design Flow

Summary

In this chapter, we discussed why SAP's strategy, reliability, and technology make the choice of SAP BusinessObjects solutions sound and safe.

Additionally, we reviewed the flexibility of implementing the portfolio in no specific order and a few insights about preparing to talk with SAP when it's time to chose a tool.

Lastly, we discussed in a little more detail the specifics of BI projects that often are the most challenging to implement when best practices are overlooked. BI projects do require specific skills!

Let's move on to the next chapter, where we'll discuss the roadmap and future of SAP BusinessObjects solutions.

PART IV
The Future of SAP BusinessObjects Solutions

SAP BusinessObjects Product Directions and Roadmap

In this chapter, you'll develop some insight into the plans and directions for SAP BusinessObjects, so you can double-check and confirm your choice. We'll discuss some of the publicly available information that you may have missed, but we believe is important and relevant while making the choice of SAP as a partner.

SAP SAPPHIRE is one of the major events for SAP and probably the major one when it comes to understanding strategic directions across all product lines, and provides great insight into the directions SAP is taking. Let's have a look at some of the strategic directions that were announced and discussed in the last SAPPHIRE event.

In Memory

In-memory analytics is probably the next big thing for the SAP BusinessObjects BI portfolio. We already have a glimpse of this today through the SAP BusinessObjects Explorer Accelerated release. The strategy of combining a powerful analytical tool with an in-memory

In-memory analytics

database has proven successful and may be the reason SAP is now going full speed in that direction.

In the current paradigm, the BI tools analyze the data stored in hard drives. This process is relatively slow, and the technology is hitting the limits of physics because hard drives are mechanical devices. The only way to speed up the process efficiently is to preaggregate data in batch mode so some degree of computation is already there when the user queries the data.

With the in-memory strategy, SAP intends to completely change the paradigm. In perspective of the trends on memory technology, SAP wants to store the entire data sets into memory where it can be processed much faster. Storing data in memory is not just a matter of copying the content of a traditional database into RAM. To make the process much more efficient in size and speed, the data is organized in a different way, which drastically reduces its memory footprint.

 RAM Is the New Disk

The Sgi ALTIX 4700 supercomputer produced by Silicon Graphics International can leverage up to 1,024 cores per node and up to 128TB of memory.

As stated by Vishal Sikka in his SAPPHIRE keynote, in their initial research, SAP could load the entire ERP system of one typical customer into less than 256GB of memory.

Now, with such a technology in place, we can look at drastic changes in the way we approach analytical applications: data can be accessed, computed, and analyzed in real time and at the speed of thoughts. From a business perspective, this could mean, for example, that you'd be able to evaluate the impact of a decision on the business in a matter of seconds.

High Performance Analytical Appliance

As announced, HANA (High Performance Analytical Appliance) is the next generation product that makes the promise of "real" real-time as SAP puts it, without disrupting the existing productive environments.

As it stands today, HANA will be an appliance that sources data from the existing storage layers, such as the SAP ERP data storage or SAP NetWeaver BW. HANA stores the data in a compressed format and puts a new analytical engine on top, which serves the data requested by the client applications.

HANA has the advantage of being nondisruptive to existing landscapes because it can be deployed in parallel to the existing systems. The existing data are left completely untouched, keeping the SAP ERP operations and existing SAP BusinessObjects BI systems safe while the value of in-memory computing ramps up on the side, as shown in Figure 12.1.

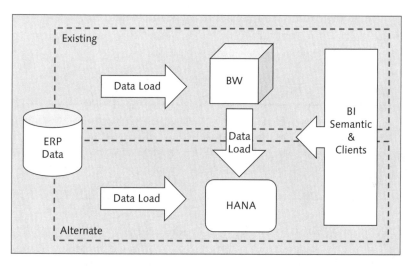

Figure 12.1   HANA Implementation

Extend the Reach

Another strategic direction that SAP is taking is based on reaching more users by making the products simple and intuitive to use, all while making them available on all devices, specifically mobile devices.

Readily available and intuitive

Looking at the easy-to-use objective, we can tap SAP BusinessObjects Explorer, detailed earlier in this book. With this newer BI client, SAP introduced a brand new paradigm for accessing data that was easier to access for casual users that were not familiar with traditional reporting tools. The point of entry into the data exploration workflow is based on a search concept that all users understand due to familiarity with Internet search engines.

Through the search engine, SAP BusinessObjects Explorer proposes a number of pertinent results. At the time of publication, SAP Business-Objects Explorer also proposes some visualizations and refining facets that guide the user through the exploration.

In the newly released SAP BusinessObjects BI 4.0, we also note the effort to harmonize the user experience across the tools and present a more modern interface that should appeal to a larger audience. This is again a proof-point that SAP is looking at making the tools easier to use and appealing to a wider audience of end users.

 Did You Know?

SAP BusinessObjects 4.0 comes with a major overhaul of the user experience for BI Launch Pad (previously InfoView), BI Workspace (previously SAP BusinessObjects Dashboard Builder) and SAP BusinessObjects Web Intelligence. Besides looking more modern, the new interface should allow end users to use more capabilities with less training.

But extending the user reach is also about going beyond the computer. Recent studies suggest that Internet traffic coming from SmartPhones doubled in 2009 and is likely to continue on this trend for the next couple of years. Figure 12.2 shows the trend as captured by Quant-cast, a provider of Internet audience measurement.

While it started from consumer applications, and for the most part from the iPhone applications, usage of mobile is quickly propagating the corporate world.

For SAP, addressing the demand for software that runs on handheld devices and tablet computers is vital to reaching its users now and tomorrow.

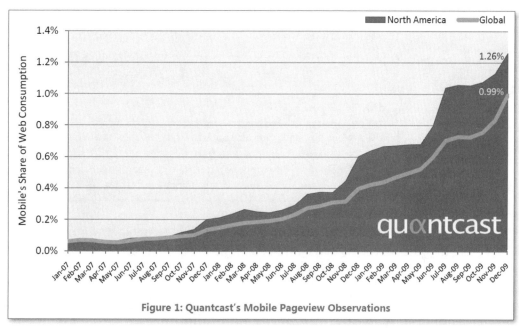

Figure 1: Quantcast's Mobile Pageview Observations

Figure 12.2 *Mobile Share of Web Consumption (Source: Quantcast 2009 Mobile Web Trends Report)*

In the SAP BusinessObjects portfolio, we currently find Mobile BI, which is a client to the SAP BusinessObjects BI platform and allows access and interactions with the reports. The prototype of SAP BusinessObjects Explorer for the iPhone leads the path to the development of BI on Apple devices, and specifically on the iPad.

 Test It Yourself

You can test drive SAP BusinessObjects Explorer for the iPhone, iPod Touch or iPad for free.

Just search for "SAP" in the App Store and download. The application comes with ready-to-use samples.

In the press release related to the acquisition of Sybase, SAP announces the intention to *accelerate the reach of SAP solutions across mobile platforms,* thus validating the strategy and roadmap toward mobile devices.

 Data Point

> While Sybase is commonly associated with databases, the company actually is a leader in mobile enterprise application platforms per Gartner's Magic Quadrant. The company's portfolio of solutions includes Sybase Unwired Platform, iAnywhere Mobile Office, and Afaria.

Moving forward, we can expect SAP's BI technology to become accessible to a wider range of users on a wider range of devices, making BI pervasive and embedded into environments familiar to the users.

Software as a Service and Cloud

Cloud-based, on-demand applications

The third trend we discuss here is Software as a Service (SaaS) and cloud computing. Although enterprise applications aren't going to disappear soon, there is an emergence of cloud-based, on-demand applications that was revealed through the success of SalesForce.com. Here, the strategy for SAP is not only to remain pertinent vis-à-vis the competition, but also reach more users through offering additional solutions tailored to a specific demand.

In that sense, SAP sees on-demand solutions as mostly complementary to on-premise software as opposed to a replacement. The idea is that lines of business have projects for which they need immediate implementations that can't be satisfied through the corporate channels. In this case, instead of having to cope with Excel spreadsheets, they may leverage the on-demand offering.

The current products from the SAP BusinessObjects portfolio are SAP BusinessObjects OnDemand, SAP StreamWork, and still crystalreports.com, which is being phased out. Following up with the strategy of on-demand complementing on-premise, the roadmap plans for both new products include integration with the corporate infrastructure.

Note

> As a matter of fact, SAP BusinessObjects BI OnDemand leverages all of the familiar content from the SAP BusinessObjects BI suite. You can leverage universes, SAP Crystal Reports, and BusinessObjects Web Intelligence reports created in the corporate BI environment.

Cloud-based SaaS is now fully part of the SAP strategy, not only in the SAP BusinessObjects portfolio but also with further investments in the SAP BusinessObjects OnDemand and SAP StreamWork solutions.

Social BI and Collaboration

More often than not, decisions are the fruit of a collaboration process that involves multiple actors analyzing the data and then presenting their findings and recommendations for a decision to be made.

Collaboration

BI was already part of that process, especially in the analysis phase. For most advanced businesses, this is also about publishing the reports and analysis into the BI platform repository, sharing with others, and most likely leveraging SAP BusinessObjects Live Office to embed the data into PowerPoint presentations or Excel spreadsheets. However, from a pure collaboration standpoint, the discussions and decisions based on the BI material is still happening outside of the tools.

An attempt was made to integrate the concept of *discussions* in the BI platform, however, the capabilities were limited, and the feature was not widely adopted by users.

With the newly released SAP StreamWork, SAP intends to close the gap on collaborative decision making, with the support of BI. Right now, SAP StreamWork is a powerful cloud-based decision-making tool that comes in handy for handling a number of collaborative activities such as making a decision, doing a sign off, preparing and having a meeting, and so on.

SAP StreamWork

> ▶ **Tip**
>
> If you are curious about SAP StreamWork, you can try it for free at *www.sapstreamwork.com*.

SAP StreamWork includes a number of tools now, but it didn't initially include anything from the enterprise BI infrastructure. However with the release of the SAP StreamWork Enterprise edition and the interoperability with other BI tools, SAP StreamWork is quickly becoming the tool of choice where material from multiple sources, BI included, can be collected and discussed as part of a decision-making process. Figure 12.3 shows SAP StreamWork collaboration based on an embedded Xcelsius dashboard.

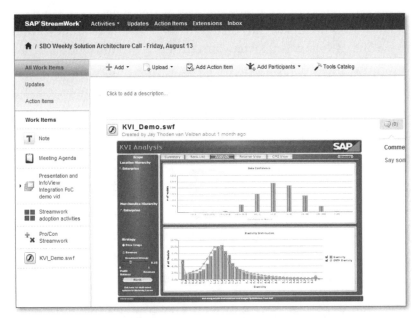

Figure 12.3 Collaborative Decision Making in SAP StreamWork

After the decision is made, the SAP StreamWork activity is closed but remains available with all its components for future reference.

On the social BI scene and since last year, SAP is investigating how to apply the SAP BusinessObjects Explorer paradigm to people's network. This led to the SAP BusinessObjects Social Network Analyzer prototype.

The objective of the SAP BusinessObjects Social Network Analyzer is to enable you to find the people that you need to collaborate with to achieve an objective. For example, you might need to find the people you need to invite to your SAP StreamWork decision-making activity discussed earlier. The SNA analyzes the data available for workers in your company, finds any kind of relationships — could be the reporting structure, a project organization, or otherwise a set of common skills — and then displays them in the form of a chart, as shown in Figure 12.4.

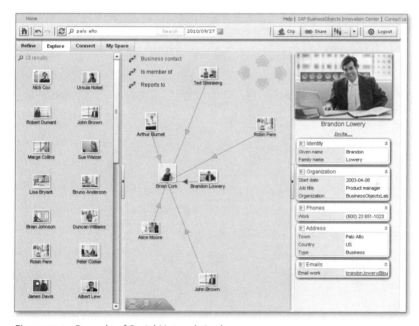

Figure 12.4 Example of Social Network Analyzer

The SAP BusinessObjects Social Analyzer is still a prototype at the moment, but it shows a completely new direction for BI that most of us had not thought of.

Summary

In this chapter, we discussed a couple of the strategy trends relevant to the SAP BusinessObjects portfolio. We saw SAP's intention to change the game through innovating in the in-memory domain. We also discussed the strategy to reach more users and globally more casual users of BI through expanding the offering into the space of mobile devices and SaaS.

Finally, we discussed how BI and collaboration are tightly woven together and the solutions SAP is putting together in order to create a more social and collaborative environment, enabling businesses to make faster and better decisions.

In the next chapter, we'll see how the innovation labs constantly search for new ways of leveraging the technologies.

SAP BusinessObjects Innovation Center

In this chapter, we'll take a look at the SAP BusinessObjects innovation center, which is one of the strategies Business Objects had put in place to innovate and develop the portfolio and that SAP kept after the acquisition.

Customer-Driven Innovation

For those readers who were familiar with Business Objects prior to the acquisition, the SAP BusinessObjects innovation center is the equivalent to what was once the BusinessObjects Labs, introduced to the market back in 2006.

The innovation center was created based on the concept that new ideas and innovations could be tested and validated with customers before they were either implemented or dropped.

New ideas tested and validated with customers

With the SAP BusinessObjects products growing in capabilities, interoperability, and user base, introducing innovation into the existing products becomes more challenging for the engineering teams.

Streamlined products need to remain extremely stable because they are used by a wide user base in business-critical applications. They also need to ensure an upgrade path and compatibility with the installed platforms. Lastly, a disruptive innovation could confuse end users and thus create training and rollout challenges.

One of the solutions retained by SAP to mitigate the challenge, while continuing to innovate at a fast pace, was the release of prototypes. Prototypes usually sit on top of the streamline products. Passionate users in search of solutions for specific problems can implement and test these prototypes.

Innovation Labs   In the process, users installing the prototypes have direct access to the engineering team to provide their feedback, suggestions, or even their own innovation ideas. The Innovation Center engineers follow up directly with the most involved customers who get a chance to directly influence the product strategy.

Prototypes that get enough attention and traction are proposed for integration in the existing products or for release as a completely new product. At that time, customers who participated in the prototyping phase get to confirm their feedback and requirements while the responsibility for the development is transferred from the Innovation Labs to the core engineering teams.

Let's review a few examples of how prototypes are handled:

> **New product offering:** SAP BusinessObjects Explorer was first released as a prototype. It was announced at the Business Objects Insight in November 2006: "The Labs team is now working on new 'data discovery' technologies, which provided sophisticated guided exploration for people who want to browse information to find answers to business questions." As a prototype, it was very well received by the market. It was productized as BusinessObjects Polestar back then, and then rebranded into SAP BusinessObjects Explorer. This is the example of a prototype that becomes a new product offering.

> **BI content search:** On the other hand, we have the example of a query as a Web service or the BI content search. Both of these in-

novations were also first released and tested by customers as prototypes. After the interest and design was validated by customers, the new capabilities found their way into the SAP BusinessObjects Enterprise XI solutions.

> **Monitoring add-on:** Lastly, let's mention the case of the Monitoring add-on for SAP BusinessObjects that was also productized and is coming to the market as part of the SAP BusinessObjects BI 4.0 release. If you looked at the prototype, you'd easily recognized the key concept of probes augmented with a number of capabilities and a full user interface in the Central Management Console.

Monitoring was first released as an add-on prototype

Now that you understand how the SAP BusinessObjects innovation center works, let's discuss how you can access those prototypes and contribute.

Get Involved

Getting involved is very easy. As a customer for the SAP BusinessObjects solutions, you'll find the value in discovering and understanding new capabilities that could help with your business moving forward. You'll also be able to directly exchange with the Innovation Labs engineers and influence some of the future directions and capabilities. If you ever wished the product could do something, it's your chance to propose the idea.

The SAP BusinessObjects innovation center website is hosted on the SAP Community Network (SCN) at the following address: *www.sdn. sap.com/irj/boc/innovation-center.*

SAP Community Network (SCN)

 Note

You may need to create an SDN (SAP Developer Network) account to access the downloads.

The innovation center currently has a number of interesting prototypes up for review:

Note

Most of these prototypes require some sort of integration with your current environment and thus some administration support. In addition, the prototypes are not supported products and not for productive use.

> The SAP BusinessObjects Explorer for iPhone and iPad brings the power and intuitive interface of SAP BusinessObjects Explorer to the Apple devices. You may try this prototype with your business data if you have an existing deployment of SAP BusinessObjects Explorer and some IT support. However, you may also download the application from the Apple Store and give it a try with a demo server from SAP.

> The *Carbon Exploration* prototype allows you to calculate your carbon footprint based on your lifestyle and hopefully identify opportunities for improvements. This is one of those cloud-based applications that you can try without IT requirements. It's even available as a Facebook application.

> We also discussed in previous chapters the convergence of on-demand and on-premise as complementary solutions. The *Business Intelligence in the Cloud* prototype allows you to export the data from a SAP BusinessObjects Web Intelligence ReportPart to your SAP BusinessObjects BI OnDemand account, thus creating a dataset for exploration and collaboration with users that may only be using the OnDemand solutions.

Co-innovate with customers

You can discover many other prototypes on the innovation center's website. Always remember that the intention is to co-innovate with customers, so make sure you share your feedback if you want those innovations to become products one day or you have additional ideas to submit.

Summary

In this chapter, we reviewed how SAP focuses on co-innovating along with their customers through the SAP BusinessObjects innovation center.

The collaboration with customers through an open dialog and the release of prototypes helps the company's innovation to stay focused on real market requirements and validates the interest before making significant changes to the products. It's also worth mentioning that the Academic Research Centers (ARC) recently joined the innovation center under the same umbrella.

Whereas the innovation center is focused on shorter-term innovation, the ARC creates partnerships with universities around the world to focus on longer-term challenges of two to five years.

Appendices

A Glossary

Access Control   This is a system which enables an authority to control access to transactions in a computer based information system.

ARC   Academic Research Centers are organizations that manage programs and facilities to promote research in universities. ARCs generally operate in partnership with R&D departments from industry leaders.

Beta program   In a beta program, a prerelease version of the software is provided to a select number of customers for them to test it and provide feedback on the new capabilities. Adjustments may be made to the software based on the feedback.

Block   In SAP BusinessObjects BI clients, a block is a component of the report meant to display data retrieved by the query. Blocks include tables, charts, and cross-tables. There can be multiple blocks of different types in a report, and they can be freely arranged on the canvas.

Break   A break in a report is a visual representation of the switch between one data value to the next one when data are grouped by value in a table. Breaks also provide context for the formulas so they can be evaluated in the context of the break.

Business planning   The business planning process converts the company strategy into quantified targets and associated resources investment.

Central Management Console (CMC)   The Central Management Console (CMC) is the web interface used to

perform administration tasks, such as user management, server management, audit, monitoring, and so on, on the SAP BusinessObjects BI platform.

CMC   See *Central Management Console*.

Continuous Monitoring   A combination of process and technology used to detect compliance and risk issues associated with an organization's financial and operational environment. Through the continuous monitoring of the operations and controls, weak and poorly designed and implemented controls can be corrected or replaced.

Crystal Report   A Crystal Report is the default output generated by the SAP Crystal Reports tool. The Crystal Report files bare the .rpt extension. Crystal Report is also often used to identify the SAP Crystal Reports business intelligence client.

Dashboard   Dashboards display the data of key performance indicators (KPIs) on a single page using visual representations such as gauges and charts. In the SAP BusinessObjects solutions context, dashboards are most often associated with the SAP BusinessObjects Dashboards (also known as Xcelsius) tool or the web portal pages created with BI Work Space (the successor of SAP BusinessObjects Dashboard Builder).

Data Integrator   A data integration and ETL tool in which transformations can be performed using the DI scripting language to access the data-handling functions to define inline complex transforms or building custom functions. It is commonly used to build data marts, ODS systems, and data warehouses.

Data lineage Data lineage is an important part of a business intelligence solution that allows report users to understand the origin and transformation of the data they're looking at. It also allows impact analysis on the business intelligence reports when the data structure or transformation processes are modified.

Data Services Designer A Graphical User Interface (GUI) development environment, in which users can define application logic to extract, transform, and load data from databases and data applications into a data warehouse. The tool can also be used to define logical paths for processing message-based queries and transactions from Web-based, front-office, and back-office applications. It is integrated with both Data Integrator and Data Services.

Data sets A data set is typically a collection of data fetched, used, or displayed by a business intelligence tool. In SAP BusinessObjects Web Intelligence, the term data set is often associated with the content of the microcube after the data is fetched from the data source.

Desktop Intelligence Desktop Intelligence or DeskI is the Windows-based business intelligence client available up to the SAP BusinessObjects XI 3.1 release. It was the first tool available from the former Business Objects company.

Dimension A dimension or dimension type object is an element of the SAP BusinessObjects universe that tracks the axis of the analysis. Typically, a dimension is a text-based object such

as country, employee, or product... or a date type object such as year, month, or a specific date. In the analysis, you want to identify some values for a dimension or a group of dimensions, for example, sales per year or revenue per country.

E-Sourcing Refers to using the Internet to assist in the purchase of goods and services needed by a business or organization.

Enterprise information management Enterprise information management (EIM) focuses on optimizing the use of the information collected through the various enterprise processes. In the SAP BusinessObjects solutions context, EIM groups the solutions used to create a coherent and clean data structure that will be leveraged by business intelligence clients. It can be extracting and loading a data warehouse, data cleansing, or creating a set of metadata.

Enterprise performance management Defines the set of processes and analytics used to define, support and control a goal-based strategy. In the SAP BusinessObjects solutions, this covers all solutions related to strategy planning, financial planning, consolidation, and cost management.

ERP Stands for Enterprise Resources Planning, which is an integrated information system designed to support and streamline processes across the company such as manufacturing, orders, accounts receivable and payable, general ledger, and purchasing. SAP ERP is part of the SAP Business Suite and includes the following solutions: Financials, Human Capital Management, Operations, and Corporate Services.

Facets   Facets offer a quick and intuitive way of refining the output of a search by suggesting to the user possible additional filters contextual to the information currently displayed. For example, in a search for "electronics," the system could present the TV, Cameras, and Computers facets as a way to refine the search to a subset of the category "electronics."

File Repository Server   The File Repository Server (FRS) is composed of two processes from the BI platform: the Input FRS and the Output FRS. The FRS reads and writes the content stored by the BI platform on the file system. By extension, the term FRS may be used to design the server components or sometimes the file system storage area they use.

Financial Consolidation   Refers to the aggregation of financial statements of a group of companies, divisions, or business units into a consolidated account.

Financial Information Management   Users manage the process of accessing, mapping, and loading information from source systems to the SAP BusinessObjects Enterprise Performance Management (EPM) solutions.

Flash   Adobe Flash is a multimedia platform used to develop interactive animations and videos for the Web. Flash files are displayed using the Adobe Flash player. SAP BusinessObjects Dashboard Design (formerly Xcelsius) leverages the Flash format to create and display highly visual and interactive dashboards.

Format formula   Formulas are expressions defined by the user and evaluated at the execution time. In the SAP BusinessObjects BI offering, formulas can be defined in all business intelligence clients as well as in the semantic layer (universe). Formulas can be numeric (calculations), or they can manipulate strings such as concatenation, Boolean conditions, and more. In the semantic layer, formulas may leverage the functions provided by the underlying database.

FRS   See *File Repository Server.*

GA   Stands for General Availability, which is the stage when a new software release becomes available to the public. In most cases, SAP software goes through a ramp up phase before GA where the software is in restricted shipment and only available to a select number of customers.

GAAP   Generally Accepted Accounting Principles is a term used to refer to the standard framework of guidelines for financial accounting used in any given jurisdiction which are generally known as Accounting Standards. It includes the standards, conventions, and rules that accountants follow in recording and summarizing transactions, and in the preparation of financial statements.

Global Trade Services   An SAP software application that automates global trade processes and enables users to manage large numbers of international business partners, and high volumes of documents while also helping companies to comply with constantly changing world wide legal regulations.

GRC   This is a term that SAP uses to refer to the SAP BusinessObjects set of solutions that are targeted toward the Governance, Risk, and Compliance solution marketplace.

Hosted   An IT environment or infrastructure is hosted when it is stored and managed by a third party, usually in a data center facility shared with other businesses. There are various combinations and degree of hosting, from the co-location of the infrastructure in a facility to the fully managed subscription-based cloud solutions.

IFRS   The International Financial Reporting Standards are principles based Standards, Interpretations, and the Framework adopted by the International Accounting Standards Board (IASB).

Information Design tool   The SAP Information Design tool first shipped with SAP BusinessObjects 4.0. It is the tool used to design the new dimensional semantic layer (universes). In previous versions, "classic" universes were designed with the Universe Designer, which also ships in 4.0.

Instance   See *Report Instance*.

Microcube   The microcube represents the data stored in a Desktop Intelligence or SAP BusinessObjects Web Intelligence report after the query is executed. The use of "cube" accounts for the fact that members of a hierarchy are retrieved in order to allow some degree of analysis and formula aggregation offline, when the report is disconnected from the data source.

Migration   In the SAP BusinessObjects context, a migration happens when a major architectural change is made in the products, requiring a significant transformation (migration) of the existing security model and BI applications to adopt the new release.

Monitoring   Ongoing check of the BI platform health and ability to serve requests from the users. Monitoring generally involves the definition

of thresholds for such indicators as CPU or memory consumption and an exception-based alerting process.

.PDF   File extension for the Portable Document Format created by Adobe. PDF files are generated by most business intelligence clients as a way to print or distribute content to users that do not have access to the tools.

PeopleSoft   A large ERP software application provider that was acquired by Oracle. It was well known for its Human Resources and Benefits modules.

PICK matrix   The PICK matrix in SAP StreamWork is a tool used to graphically represent and rank opportunities based on their difficulty of implementation versus their payoff.

Portlet   A web portlet is a small self-contained window within a web portal used to display specific information. In the SAP BusinessObjects solutions, portlets are used in BI Launch Pad (formerly SAP BusinessObjects Dashboard Builder).

Quality Management   The process of managing quality in systems, processes, and technology.

Ramp up   In SAP, the ramp up is a phase of the product lifecycle where the production-ready software gets shipped to a select number of customers in order to assess the quality and functionality of the new release in real production conditions. Ramp up customers benefit from being the first to access the new capabilities as well as getting strong support from SAP during their implementation.

Report instance   A report instance is a snapshot of the report at a certain time. Report instances are often created through report scheduling or report publishing. Instances are stored in the BI platform repository associated with the original report.

.RPT   File extension of the files generated and consumed by SAP Crystal Reports business intelligence client.

SaaS   See *Software as a Service.*

SAP BEx   For SAP Business Explorer, this is the reporting tool used to query and analyze SAP NetWeaver BW data. The SAP BusinessObjects solutions literature often refers to BEx queries as the object created with the BEx Designer and which can be used as a data source for SAP BusinessObjects BI tools. In most SAP NetWeaver BW users' minds, BEx is associated with the BEx Analyzer tool, which is the client used to interact with BEx queries.

SAP BusinessObjects Intercompany   This application enables business units to reconcile intercompany balances in real time via the Web and allows corporations to close their books faster.

SAP BusinessObjects Metadata Management   This collects and unifies metadata from disparate tools and sources into a single repository. IT managers and users can use the application to prevent unforeseen business impacts and provide impact analysis or data lineage for the enterprise.

SAP BusinessObjects Process Control   This application provides continuous control monitoring across policies and regulatory requirements.

SAP BusinessObjects Profitability and Cost Management   This is an application that is owned and managed by business users that give them the capability to accurately and effec-

tively measure product, customer, and channel profitability, and develop and dynamically test ways to improve each.

SAP BusinessObjects Rapid Marts   SAP BusinessObjects Rapid Marts are a set of prebuilt data models, transformation logic, and data extraction that allow quick implementation on the SAP, Siebel, Oracle, and PeopleSoft business applications.

SAP BusinessObjects Risk Management   This application provides risk-adjusted management of enterprise performance that can empower business users to optimize efficiency, increase effectiveness, and maximize visibility across risk initiatives.

SAP BusinessObjects 4.0   SAP BusinessObjects 4.0 is the latest release of the SAP BusinessObjects solutions. This name covers both the enterprise information management solutions and the business intelligence solutions.

SAP BusinessObjects Analysis software, edition for Microsoft Office   This is the client that enables multidimensional analyses of OLAP sources in Excel and the creation of interactive PowerPoint presentations from OLAP sources.

SAP BusinessObjects Analysis software, edition for OLAP   Web-based client for business analysts to run multidimensional analysis of OLAP sources and create workspaces for private or shared use.

SAP BusinessObjects BI 4.0   Names the subset of the SAP BusinessObjects 4.0 release related to the business intelligence solutions such as the BI platform and clients.

SAP BusinessObjects Business Intelligence platform   The business intelligence platform is a component of the SAP BusinessObjects BI solution that provides the architecture and services such as security, portal integration, sharing, scheduling, and all of the technical components to deploy a company-wide BI solution.

SAP BusinessObjects Dashboards   Provides secure, interactive visualizations with live, refreshable data from SAP BusinessObjects sources, Excel spreadsheets, or corporate databases.

SAP BusinessObjects Data Integrator   SAP BusinessObjects Data Integrator is the ETL (extract, transform, and load) tool from the solution that allows the creation of data warehouses from a variety of data sources. It provides superior integration with the business intelligence offering. It offers a subset of the SAP BusinessObjects Data Services offering.

SAP BusinessObjects Data Quality   This software, part of the EIM solutions, helps discover, fix, and prevent data quality issues such as incorrect address formats or duplicate entries. It offers a subset of the SAP BusinessObjects Data Services offering.

SAP BusinessObjects EIM 4.0   Names the subset of the SAP BusinessObjects 4.0 release related to the enterprise information management solutions such as SAP BusinessObjects Data Services.

SAP BusinessObjects Enterprise   SAP BusinessObjects Enterprise, also known as the enterprise platform was the name given the BI platform in releases prior to 4.0. See *SAP business intelligence platform* for details.

SAP BusinessObjects Explorer   BI client that offers users an intuitive path to quickly search and explore data for instant insight into your business. They can get quick, easy answers to on-the-fly questions without training or IT involvement by simply entering a few keywords to search for relevant information and then intuitively exploring large volumes of data.

SAP BusinessObjects Metadata Management   SAP BusinessObjects Metadata Management is about building and storing data about the data. For example, where does a piece of data come from? What does it represent? SAP BusinessObjects Metadata Management is key to the success of business intelligence because it provides the basis for data lineage and trust.

SAP BusinessObjects Spend Performance Management   This application enables business users to gain insight into savings opportunities and compliance by enabling access to aggregated and enriched spend data.

SAP BusinessObjects Strategy Management   This application empowers business users at all levels to rapidly align resources to execute on strategies, understand risk, and drive effectiveness. It allows users to clearly link strategic plans to initiatives, performance measures, and people.

SAP BusinessObjects Text Analysis   This software enables customers to unlock insights that are hidden in unstructured text sources such as blogs, Web sites, e-mails, support logs, research, and surveys. It allows those businesses to get an analytic view of customer's thoughts and feelings on the respective products and services.

SAP BusinessObjects Universal Data Cleanse This solution is an add-on to the SAP Data Quality Management software. It allows business users to be able to leverage an automated data standardization solution that helps to identify abnormalities that normal processing of the data may not capture.

SAP BusinessObjects Web Intelligence BI client that allows users self-service access to data, reporting, and analysis. SAP BusinessObjects Web Intelligence is an ad hoc query, reporting, and analysis tool designed to empower users with its intuitive interface that allows users to turn information into actionable insight and make better decisions in less time.

SAP BusinessObjects Xcelsius This application is a design and delivery tool that allow for the creation of highly interactive and intuitive visualizations that make it easier for business users to understand company performance. It has recently been re-branded to SAP Crystal Dashboard Design.

SAP Crystal Reports This BI client is a reporting tool that helps developers and IT professionals rapidly create flexible, feature-rich reports and tightly integrate them into Web and Windows applications.

SAP Environmental Health and Safety Management SAP EHS Management is a comprehensive, integrated application that enables companies to streamline and implement EHS strategies. It addresses regulatory compliance and helps customers to identify, manage, and mitigate EHS risks cost effectively by taking an integrated approach to all aspects of risk and compliance.

SAP NetWeaver BW SAP NetWeaver Business Warehouse is the data warehouse offering from SAP. Data coming from the SAP Business Suite or other business software is provisioned and preaggregated into SAP NetWeaver BW in order to enable reporting and analysis

SAP NetWeaver BWA SAP NetWeaver Business Warehouse Accelerated is an appliance based on the in-memory technology that allows indexing of the SAP NetWeaver BW data for instant query results.

SAP Sustainability Performance Management This application is used by organizations to track and communicate sustainability performance, set goals and objectives, manage risks, and monitor activities.

Section In a business intelligence report, a section visually groups data that have a value in common. For example, all orders in the same year are grouped into a year section. While breaks keep the data in the same table to display calculations results, sections break the data in multiple tables under section headers.

Scorecard A strategic management tool that tracks processes, activities, and financials via metrics to give an overview of how the business or organization is doing. The Balanced Scorecard is the most popular approach to using scorecards.

Semantic layer The semantic layer is an abstraction layer that isolates the end user from the complexity and technicality of the data source by creating an environment where queries can be generated through familiar business terms. Additionally, the semantic layer provides functions and calculations that allow some level of transformation to the data. The latest release provides on-the-fly aggregation of multiple data sources. The semantic layer is created with the Universe Designer or Information Design tool and is materialized in the universe files.

Siebel   A software application that focused on CRM (Customer Relationship Management) software. It was acquired by Oracle.

Software as a Service   Software as a Service (SaaS) also known as Software OnDemand is an application that is deployed in the Internet, outside of the corporate firewall. It is fully hosted and maintained by the vendor and is licensed to the users on a pay-as-you-go model. SAP BusinessObjects solutions include SAP StreamWork and SAP BusinessObjects BI OnDemand, both SaaS.

Supply Chain   A supply chain is a system of organizations, people, technology, activities, information, and resources involved in moving a product or service from supplier to customer.

SWOT matrix   SWOT is as an acronym for Strengths, Weaknesses, Opportunities, and Threats. A SWOT matrix is a visual representation where elements are placed into quadrants along these mentioned categories. SAP StreamWork includes a SWOT matrix tool.

Universe   A universe is the materialization of the semantic layer. See *Semantic Layer*.

Universe Designer   Universe Designer is the tool used to design the classic SAP BusinessObjects semantic layer (.unv file extension). Starting with SAP

BusinessObjects 4.0, SAP introduced a new format called the dimensional semantic layer (.unx file extension), which is designed using the Information Design tool.

.UNV   File extension associated with the legacy universe files generated by the SAP BusinessObjects Universe Designer and consumed by Desktop Intelligence and SAP BusinessObjects Web Intelligence. This file format is still created and consumed in SAP BusinessObjects 4.0, although a new format was introduced in parallel, the .UNX format.

.UNX   File extension associated with the new version of the semantic layer introduced with SAP BusinessObjects 4.0. Such files can be created by the SAP BusinessObjects Information Design tool and consumed by the newer (4.0 and above) versions of the clients.

Update   In the SAP BusinessObjects solutions context, an update occurs when a newer release of the software gets applied to an existing system with no expected disruption. This is usually the case for service packs.

Upgrade   As opposed to an update, an upgrade brings significant enhancements and noticeable changes to the software. An upgrade does *not* involve architectural changes that require a migration to take place.

What-if analysis   A what-if analysis is a specific construction of a business intelligence report or dashboard that allows the user to modify some input parameters and immediately see the result in order to devise options and a strategy.

.WID   Extension of the files created and consumed by the SAP Business-

Objects Web Intelligence client. This file format can be opened by either the desktop version (also known as Rich Client) or directly within a web portal and the SAP BusinessObjects Web Intelligence applet.

XBRL   eXtensible Business Reporting Language. This is a standard for electronic communication of business and financial data, allowing them to be automatically processed by software and exchanged across heterogeneous systems. The SAP BusinessObjects Performance Management solutions offer XBRL publishing.

B   Technical Landscapes

 Caution

These Deployment Scenarios are not definitive and meant for initial planning purposes only.

Please refer to either *http://help.sap.com* or *http://service.sap.com/swdc* for more information.

SAP BusinessObjects Enterprise

Supported Operating Systems

> Windows Server 2003 SP2

> Windows Server 2003 R2 SP2

> Windows Server 2008

> AIX 5L 5.2

> AIX 5L 5.3

> AIX 6.1

> HP-UX 11.23 (PA-RISC)

> HP-UX 11.23 (IA-64)

> HP-UX 11.31 (IA-64)

> Red Hat Linux Enterprise Server 4

> Red Hat Linux Advanced Server 4

> Red Hat Linux Enterprise Advanced Platform Server 5

> SUSE Linux Enterprise Server 9 SP3

> SUSE Linux Enterprise Server 10

> SUSE Linux Enterprise Server 10 SP2

> Solaris 9 for SPARC

> Solaris 10 for SPARC

Supported Application Servers

> JBoss 4.0.4

> Microsoft IIS 7.0

> Microsoft IIS 6.0

> Oracle Application Server 10gR3

> SAP NetWeaver 7.0

> SAP NetWeaver 7.1

> Tomcat 5.5

> Tomcat 6.0.18

> WebLogic 9.2 MP2

> WebLogic 10

> WebLogic 10.3

> WebSphere Application Server 6.1.0.7

> WebSphere Application Server 7

> WebSphere Application Server Community Edition 2.0

Supported Browsers

> IE 6.0 SP2

> IE 7.0

> IE 8.0

> Firefox 2.0

> Firefox 3.0

> Safari 3.2.x

CMS and Audit Data Sources

> IBM DB2/UDB 8.2

> IBM DB2/UDB 9.1

> BIM DB2/UDB 9.5

> MS SQL Server 2000 SP4

> MS SQL Server 2005 SP2

> MS SQL Server 2008
> Oracle 9.2
> Oracle 10g R1
> Oracle 10g R2
> Oracle 11g R1
> Sybase Adaptive Server Enterprise 15

SAP Crystal Reports Reporting Data Sources

> Hyperion Essbase Server 7.1.x
> Hyperion System 9
> MS SQL Server Analysis Services 2000 SP4
> MS SQL Server Analysis Services 2005 SP1
> MS SQL Server Analysis Services 2008
> Generic JDBC Data Sources
> Generic ODBC Data Sources
> Generic OLEDB Data Sources
> Green Plum Database 3.2
> HP Neoview 2.3.1
> HP Neoview 2.4
> IBM DB2/UDB iSeries 5.3
> IBM DB2/UDB iSeries 5.4
> IBM DB2/UDB 8.2
> IBM DB2/UDB 9.1
> IBM DB2/UDB 9.5
> IBM DB2/UDB zSeries 8
> IBM DB2/UDB zSeries 9.1
> IBM Informix Dynamic Server 10.0
> IBM Informix Dynamic Server 11.1
> IBM Informix Dynamic Server 11.5
> Ingres 2006

> MS Access 2003
> MS Access 2007
> MS SQL Server 2000 SP4
> MS SQL Server 2005
> MS SQL Server 2008
> MySQL AB 5.0
> NCR Teradata V2R6.2
> Teradata V12.0
> Netezza NPS Server 3.1
> Netezza NPS Server 4.0
> Netezza NPS Server 4.5
> Oracle 9.2
> Oracle 10g R1
> Oracle 10g R2
> Oracle 11g R1
> Progress OpenEdge 10.0B
> PostgreSQL 8.2
> Sybase Adaptive Server Enterprise 12.5
> Sybase Adaptive Server Enterprise 15

Support for SAP Application Servers

> SAP R/3 4.6c
> SAP R/3 4.7
> mySAP ERP 2004
> mySAP ERP 2005
> SAP BW 3.5
> SAP NetWeaver BI 7.0
> SAP NetWeaver BI 7.02
> SAP Enterprise Portal 6 SP19
> SAP Enterprise Portal 7 SP10

Reverse Proxy Servers

> Apache HTTP Server 2.2
> WebSEAL 6.0
> Microsoft Internet Security and Acceleration Server 2006

LDAP Directory

> IBM Tivoli Directory Server 5.2
> IBM Tivoli Directory Server 6.0
> IBM Tivoli Directory Server 6.1
> Lotus Domino Directory 6.0.2
> Lotus Domino Directory 6.5.3
> MS Active Directory Application Mode 2003
> MS Active Directory Application Mode 2003 SP1
> MS Active Directory Application Mode 2008
> Novell eDirectory 8.7.3
> Novell eDirectory 8.8
> Oracle Internet Directory 10gR3
> Sun Java System Directory Server 5.2
> Sun Java System Directory Server Enterprise 6.0

Active Directory

> MS Active Directory 2000
> MS Active Directory 2003
> MS Active Directory 2008

Access Management

> eTrust (Netegrity) Siteminder 6.0
> eTrust (Computer Associates) Siteminder 12.0

Microsoft Office Support

> MS Office XP SP2

> MS Office XP SP3

> MS Office 2003 SP3

> MS Office 2007 SP1

.NET Framework

> .NET 1.1

> .NET 2.0

> .NET 3.0

> .NET 3.5

Deployment Scenarios for SAP BusinessObjects Enterprise Information Management

SAP BusinessObjects Data Services

Supported Operating Systems

> Windows Server 2003 (32 bit and 64 bit)

> AIX 5L 5.2 (64 bit)

> AIX 5L 5.3 (64 bit)

> HP-UX 11.23 (64 bit)

> HP-UX 11.31 (64 bit)

> Red Hat Linux Enterprise Server 4

> Red Hat Linux Advanced Server 4

> Red Hat Linux Enterprise Server 5

> Red Hat Linux Advanced Server 5

> SUSE Enterprise Server 9 SP3

> SUSE Enterprise Server 10

> Solaris SPARC 9 (64 bit)

> Solaris SPARC 10 (64 bit)

Supported Application Server

> Tomcat 5.5

> WebLogic 9.2

> WebLogic 10

> WebSphere Application Server 6.1.0.7

Supported Browsers

> IE 6.0 SP2

> IE 7.0

Application Connectivity

> JD Edwards B7.33

> JD Edwards World A7.1

> Oracle E-Business Suite 11i

> Oracle E-Business Suite 12

> PeopleTools 8.0

> PeopleTools 8.1

> PeopleTools 8.4

> Salesforce.com 12.0

> SAP BW 3.1c

> SAP BW 3.5

> SAP BW 7.0

> SAP R/3 3.1i via ABAP/BAPI/IDOC

> SAP R/3 4.6 via ABAP/BAPI/IDOC

> SAP R/3 4.7 via ABAP/BAPI/IDOC

> SAP ERP ECC 5.0 via ABAP/BAPI/IDOC

> SAP ERP ECC 6.0 via ABAP/BAPI/IDOC

> Siebel 7.5.2

> Siebel 7.7

> Siebel 8.0

Database Connectivity

> ODBC Generic Data Sources

> HP Neoview 2.2

> HP Neoview 2.3

> IBM DB2/UDB for iSeries 5.2

> IBM DB2/UDB for iSeries 5.3

> IBM DB2/UDB for iSeries 5.4

> IBM DB2/UDB 8.2

> IBM DB2/UDB 9.1

> IBM DB2/UDB 9.5

> IBM DB2/UDB for zSeries 7.1.1

> MS SQL Server 2000 SP4

> MS SQL Server 2005

> MySQL 4.1

> MySQL 5.0

> Netezza NPS 3.1.4

> Netezza NPS 4.0

> Netezza NPS 4.5

> Oracle 9.2

> Oracle 10gR1

> Oracle 10gR2

> Oracle 11g

> Sybase Adaptive Server Enterprise 12.5

> Sybase Adaptive Server Enterprise 15

> Sybase Adaptive Server IQ 12.6

> Sybase Adaptive Server IQ 12.7

> Teradata V2R6

> Teradata V2R6.1

> Teradata V2R6.2

> Teradata 12

Mainframe Connectivity

> Attunity 5.0

> Attunity 5.1

Technology Connectivity

> Data Federator XIR2 11.6.2

> Data Federator XIR2 11.7

> Data Federator XI 3.0 12.0

> HTTP/HTTPS 1.0

> HTTP/HTTPS 1.1

> JMS

> SOAP 1.1

> WSDL 1.1

File Connectivity

> Text Files (Delimited and fixed width)

> COBOL

> MS Excel

> XML 1.0

SAP BusinessObjects Data Insight

Supported Operating Systems

> Windows Server 2003

> Solaris SPARC 9 (32 bit)

> Solaris SPARC 10 (32 bit)

Supported Browsers

> IE 6.0 SP2

> IE 7.0

Database Connectivity

> ODBC to Generic Data Sources

> IBM DB2/UDB 7.2

> IBM DB2/UDB 8.1

> IBM DB2/UDB 8.2

> IBM DB2/UDB for iSeries 5.1

> IBM DB2/UDB for zSeries 7.1

> MS SQL Server 2000 SP4

> MS SQL Server 2005 SP1

> MS SQL Server 2005 SP2

> Oracle 9.2

> Oracle 10gR1

> Oracle 10gR2

> Teradata 2.0 R5

> MS Access 2000

> MS Access 2003

> Sybase ASE 12.5

SAP BusinessObjects Text Analysis 3.0

Supported Operating Systems

> Windows XP

> Windows Server 2003

> Red Hat Linux Enterprise Server 4.0 (32 bit)

> Red Hat Linux Advanced Server 4.0 (32 bit)

> Solaris SPARC 9 (32 bit)

> Solaris SPARC 10 (32 bit)

Deployment Scenarios for SAP BusinessObjects Enterprise Performance Management

SAP BusinessObjects Planning and Consolidation

Supported Operating Systems

> Windows Server 2003

> Windows Server 2008

Supported Database Platforms

> MS SQL Server 2005

> MS SQL Server 2008

Supported OLAP Platforms

> MS SQL Server Analysis Services 2005

> MS SQL Server Analysis Services 2008

Supported Application Servers

> IIS 6.0

> IIS 7.0

.NET Framework

> .NET 2.0

> .NET 3.5 SP1

Other Requirements

> MSXML 4.0 SP2 or later

> ADOMD.NET 9.0

> AmiUni PDF Creator

> MS Anti-Cross Site Scripting Library 3.0

> Xceed Zip Compression Library 6.0.7223.0 or later

> FarPoint 4.0

> Dundas Chart V7.0 for ASP.NET

SAP BusinessObjects Strategy Management

Supported Operating Systems

> Windows Server 2003 (64 bit)

> AIX 5.3 (64 bit)

> AIX 6.1 (64 bit)

> HP-UX 11.23 (64 bit)

> HP-UX 11.31 (64 bit)

> Solaris SPARC 10 (64 bit)

> Solaris SPARC X64 (64 bit)

> Red Hat Linux Enterprise Server 4 (64 bit)

> Red Hat Linux Enterprise Server 5 (64 bit)

> SUSE Enterprise Server 9 (64 bit)

> SUSE Enterprise Server 10 (64 bit)

Required SAP Application Component

> SAP NetWeaver CE 7.1 SP06

Supported Database Platforms

> Oracle

> SQL Server

> IBM DB2/UDB

Supported Browsers

> IE 6.0

> IE 7.0

> IE 8.0

SAP BusinessObjects Financial Consolidation

Supported Operating Systems

> Windows Server 2003 (32 bit or 64 bit)

> Windows Server 2008 (32 bit or 64 bit)

Supported Browser

> IE 7.0

Supported Database Platforms

> MS SQL Server 2005

> Oracle 10g

> Oracle 11g

Additional Required Components

> SAP BusinessObjects User Management Client

> Microsoft DHTML Editing Component
> MSXML 6.0 SP1
> Microsoft Component Category Manager Library
> MDAC 2.8
> Microsoft DCOM 95
> Visual C++ 8.0 ATL
> Visual C++ 8.0 CRT
> Visual C++ 8.0 MFC
> Visual C++ 8.0 MFCLOC
> Visual C++ 8.0 OpenMP
> MFCDLL 6
> MFCDLL 6 Unicode
> MFCDLL 7.1
> MFCDLL 7.1 Localized
> Microsoft C++ Runtime Library 6
> Microsoft C++ Runtime Library 7.1
> VC User ATL71 RTL X86
> VC User CRT71 RTL X86
> VC User MFC71 RTL
> VC User MFC71 Localized RTL
> Windows Scripting Host 5.6
> Microsoft .NET Framework 2.0
> Active PDF Server if printing in PDF is required

SAP BusinessObjects XBRL Publishing by UB Matrix

Supported Operating Systems
> Windows Server 2003
> Windows XP

Supported Browser
> IE 6.0 or later

Additional Required Applications
> MS Excel 2003 or later
> .NET Framework 2.0
> MS Primary Interop Assemblies
> MS Visual J# Redistributable Package 1.1

Supported Database Platforms
> SQL Server
> Oracle
> MySQL

SAP BusinessObjects Financial Information Management

Supported Operating Systems
> Windows Server 2003
> Windows Server 2008

Supported Database Platforms
> MS SQL Server 2005
> MS SQL Server 2008
> Oracle 10g
> Oracle 11g

Additional Required Applications
> SAP BusinessObjects Enterprise XI 3.1
> SAP BusinessObjects Data Services XI 3.1 or 3.2
> SAP BusinessObjects Financial Consolidation 7.5 or SAP Business-Objects Profitability and Cost Management 7.5

SAP BusinessObjects Intercompany

Supported Operating Systems
> Windows Server 2003
> Windows Server 2008

Supported Application Servers
> IIS 6.0
> IIS 7.0

Supported Database Platforms
> MS SQL Server 2005
> Oracle 10g
> Oracle 11g

Additional Required Applications
> SAP Crystal Reports 2008 Runtime SP1
> SAP Crystal Reports Server Embedded 2008
> SAP BusinessObjects User Management Client
> .NETFx3.5
> Microsoft WSE 3.0 Runtime

SAP BusinessObjects Profitability and Cost Management

Supported Operating Systems
> Windows Server 2003 (32 bit or 64 bit)
> Windows Server 2008 (32 bit or 64 bit)

Supported Application Servers
> IIS 6.0
> IIS 7.0

Supported Database Platforms
> MS SQL Server 2005
> MS SQL Server 2008
> Oracle 10g
> Oracle 11g

SAP BusinessObjects Spend Performance Management

Required SAP Application Components
> SAP NetWeaver Enterprise Portal 7.0 SP16

> SAP NetWeaver BW 7.0 SP18

> SAP NetWeaver BW Business Content 7.03 SP12

Deployment Scenarios for SAP BusinessObjects Governance, Risk, and Compliance

SAP BusinessObjects Risk Management

Required SAP Application Components
> Support Package Manager 32 or higher

> SAP EHP1 for SAP NetWeaver 7.0 SP 5 or higher

> SAP NetWeaver Application Server ABAP

> SAP NetWeaver Application Server Java

> TREX 7.10 Revision 27 or higher

> SAP Solution Manager 7.00 SP 19 or higher

> SAP NetWeaver Application Server Java for Adobe Forms

> Java Runtime 1.0 for Frontend Systems

Recommended SAP BusinessObjects Application Components
> SAP BusinessObjects Enterprise 3.1

> SAP BusinessObjects Enterprise SAP Integration Kit 3.1

SAP BusinessObjects Access Control

Required SAP Application Components
> SAP NetWeaver 7.0 SP 12

> SAP Internet Graphics Service

> SAP NetWeaver Enterprise Portal

> SAP GRC VIRCC00_0.sca – SAP GRC Risk Analysis and Remediation

> SAP GRC VIRAE00_0.sca – SAP GRC Compliant User Provisioning

364

> SAP GRC VIRRE00_0.sca – Enterprise Role Manager

> SAP GRC VIRFF00_0.sca – Superuser Privilege Management

> SAP GRC VIRSANH – SAP HR Run Time Agent

> SAP GRC VIRSAHR – SAP HR Run Time Agent

> SAP GRC VIREPRTA00_0.sca – SAP Enterprise Portal Run Time Agent

> SAP GRC VIRACLP00_0.sca – Single Launch Pad (Optional)

> SAP GRC VIRACCNTNT.SAR – SAP GRC Access Control Content File

SAP BusinessObjects Process Control

Required SAP Application Components
> Support Package Manager 32 or higher

> SAP EHP1 for SAP NetWeaver 7.0 SP 5 or higher

> SAP NetWeaver Application Server ABAP

> SAP NetWeaver Application Server Java

> TREX 7.10 Revision 27 or higher

> SAP Solution Manager 7.00 SP 19 or higher

> SAP NetWeaver Application Server Java for Adobe Forms

Recommended SAP BusinessObjects Application Components
> SAP BusinessObjects Enterprise 3.1

> SAP BusinessObjects Enterprise SAP Integration Kit 3.1

SAP BusinessObjects Global Trade Services

Required SAP Application Components
> SAP ERP 6.0

> SLL-LEG 800

> SAP_AP 700

> SAP NetWeaver Application Server ABAP

> SAP NetWeaver Application Server Java for Adobe Document Server

> TREX

> SAP NetWeaver BW 7.0

SAP BusinessObjects Sustainability Performance Management

Required SAP Application Components

> SAP NetWeaver BW EHP1 SP03 or higher

> SAP NetWeaver Application Server ABAP

> SAP NetWeaver Application Server Java

> OPMFNDUI.sca – Analytics OPM Foundation UI 3.0

> ANASUSTUI.sca – Analytics Sustainability UI 1.0

> SAP SUSTAINABILITY REPORTING (SR_CORE 100) latest SP

> ANALYTICS OPM FOUNDATION (OPMFND 200) SP03 or higher

C References

[Davenport07] Davenport, Thomas H., & Harris, Jeanne G. *Competing on analytics: The new science of winning*. Harvard Business School Press, 2007.

[Forrester09] Forrester Research, Inc. "BI Belt Tightening in a Tough Economic Climate," February 2009.

[Gartner09] Gartner EXP. CIO report, "Meeting the Challenge: The 2009 CIO Agenda," January 2009.

[Kaplan05] Kaplan, Robert S., and Norton, David P. *The office of strategy management*. Harvard Business Review, October 2005.

[Levy05] Levy, Frank, and Murnane, Richard J. "How computerized work and globalization shape human skill demands," September, 2005.

[McKinsey08] McKinsey & Company. "Managing IT in a downturn: Beyond cost cutting," Fall 2008.

[Quantcast09] Quantcast. "2009 Mobile Web Trends Report," January 2010.

[Sull07] Sull, Donald N. "Closing the gap between strategy and execution." *MIT Sloan Management Review*, Summer 2007.

Index

F

G

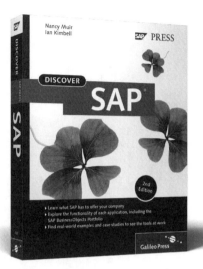

Learn what SAP has to offer
your company

Explore the functionality of each
application, including the SAP
BusinessObjects portfolio

Find real-world examples and case
studies to see the tools at work

Nancy Muir, Ian Kimbell

Discover SAP

Discover SAP, second edition will teach anyone new to SAP, decision
makers just considering SAP, and consultants getting started with SAP
the practical details you need to really understand what the SAP solution
is and how it can benefit your company. As part of the Discover series,
the book is written in practical language to clearly explain what SAP is in
layman's terms, while providing practical insights into the applications
that make up the SAP complete solution. The book is filled with
interesting examples, case studies, marginal notes, and tips for readers to
glean insights into how SAP can benefit their organization.

440 pp., 2. edition 2010, 39,95 Euro / US$ 39.95
ISBN 978-1-59229-320-9

>> www.sap-press.com

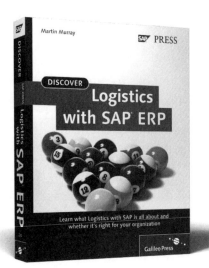

Discover what Logistics with SAP is all about and whether its right for your organization

Learn how this powerful, time-tested tool can improve your supply chain and transportation processes to save you money

Martin Murray

Discover Logistics with SAP ERP

With this reader-friendly book, anyone new to SAP or considering implementing it will discover the fundamental capabilities and uses of the Logistics components. You'll learn what's available, and how it works to help you determine if Logistics with SAP is the right tool for your organization. This book is written in a clear, practical style, and uses real-world examples, case studies, and insightful tips to give you a complete overview of the SAP logistics offerings.

385 pp., 2009, 39,95 Euro / US$ 39.95
ISBN 978-1-59229-230-1

>> www.sap-press.com